A Canoness of the order professed at Liège in 1768. It could be one of four – Clare Semmes, Martha Semmes, Ann Wright or Catherine Stourton, daughter of the great patron William, 16th Lord Stourton.

New Hall and its school

"A true school of virtuous demeanour"

Tony Tuckwell

Published 2006 by
Free Range Publishing

ISBN 1-872979-02-5

Printed in Great Britain by
Biddles Ltd, King's Lynn, Norfolk

Contents

Maps and Tables

Maps

Tables

𝔓ictures

Front cover – New Hall in 2000

Back cover – **New Hall in the 1790s** – watercolour by John Luttrell Olmius
Courtesy of the Canonesses of the Holy Sepulchre

Frontispiece – A canoness of the order professed in Liège in 1768.

Page 52-53

Henry VIII, portrait after the school of Holbein
Courtesy of Philip Mould, Historical Portraits Ltd

Mary I, portrait by Master John
Courtesy of the National Portrait Gallery

Thomas Radcliffe, 3rd Earl of Sussex, portrait attributed to Steven van de Muelen
Courtesy of Philip Mould, Historical Portraits Ltd

George Villiers, 1st Duke of Buckingham and his family, portrait after Gerrit van Honthorst   *Courtesy of the National Portrait Gallery*

Oliver Cromwell, portrait by Sir Peter Lely
Courtesy of the Museum of London

George Monck, 1st Earl of Albemarle, portrait by Sir Peter Lely
Courtesy of the National Maritime Museum

Benjamin Hoare, artist unknown
Courtesy of Hoare's Bank

Stone plaque of Henry VIII's arms, now in the Chapel

East Window of St. Margaret's Westminster, formerly in New Hall Royal Chapel
Courtesy of the Dean and Chapter of Westminster Abbey

Chapman and André Map 1777, showing New Hall's position

Earliest surviving plan of New Hall, c.1700

Page 116-117

Artist's impression of Beaulieu Palace   *Courtesy of I. Dunlop*

Front of Beaulieu, engraved by George Vertue

Engraving of Lord Waltham's New Hall from the south

Foreword

In 2001, the Canonesses of the Holy Sepulchre handed New Hall School over to Lay management. As a new chapter in its history began, those entrusted with the daunting responsibility for this great school going forward, were keen to ensure that its extraordinarily rich archive would be preserved. It was also important to us that the remarkable story of New Hall and its school was captured in a way that could be handed on for the benefit of future generations. In particular, this would enable pupils of the school to understand and to contribute to the living tradition of which they are part.

The search then began for someone who could help in this mammoth task, by writing a history of New Hall. Tony Tuckwell, with his local knowledge and interest in history and education was well placed to help. He had retired as Headmaster of King Edward VI Grammar School in Chelmsford and then researched and wrote that school's history.

We are grateful to Tony for allowing himself to be persuaded to spend the first years of his retirement immersed in the New Hall archives. This book is the fruit of three years of dedicated work.

Tony has been generous with his time, a generosity also expressed in his insistence that this book should be a truly charitable enterprise. The proceeds, therefore, of the book sales will be donated in support of Tony's local charities, particularly the Mid-Essex Alzheimer's Society and the Acorn Village Trust at Mistley, as well as the New Hall Voluntary Service.

Katherine Jeffrey

Principal, New Hall School.

ℭntroduction

In 2003 the Headmistress, Katherine Jeffrey, asked me if I might write the history of New Hall along the lines of *That Honourable and Gentlemanlike House; a History of King Edward VI Grammar School, Chelmsford, 1551-2001* which I had published in 2000. I agreed and have enjoyed every minute of the research.

This history comprises three fascinating stories – that of New Hall and its various owners up to 1799 when it frequently witnessed major dramas in this country's history; the emergence of the Canonesses of the Holy Sepulchre in Liège in 1642 up to their enforced migration to England in 1794; and the fusion of the two after 1799 as New Hall school developed. This is not a history of the Canonesses of the Holy Sepulchre though, given the centrality of their role in the whole story, they feature very large. However, there are many aspects of their liturgical and spiritual life that are not covered in this book. Nor is this a detailed architectural history of New Hall though there is some of that in it. Rather it is, I hope, the gripping story of the people and events associated with New Hall and the school that came to inhabit it.

To help sustain interest I have used modern spelling when quoting from documentary sources. When using financial figures I have indicated what the equivalent sums would have been in 2002 so that their value can be better appreciated. The authoritative sources for these figures are explained in Appendix B at the end of the book.

My thanks go to everyone at New Hall for making me feel so at home. The School and Community both have a very welcoming ethos truly in keeping with Augustinian principles of hospitality. Most particularly I would like to thank the Prioress, Sister Teresa Lenehan, for her interest and enthusiastic support, and all members of the Community now at Colchester, for delicious tea and cakes and fascinating conversation as they have kindly read through my text, correcting errors and suggesting useful additions. My thanks also go to Katherine Jeffrey for having the idea of the history in the first place and then for several fascinating chats about the past, present and future; Anne Sparrow, New Hall's Public Relations Co-ordinator up to the end of 2005, for many years of good friendship, suggesting my name to

Katherine in the first place and always being on the end of a telephone as an expert "fixer"; Jenny Bignold for continuing that task and sorting out copyright issues; Annabel Brown for help with photographs; New Hall's welcoming archivist, Sister Mary Magdalene Roskell, who saved me a lot of effort by making sure that relevant documents always appeared on my table at the most appropriate time; Sister Magdalen John Earle for her sharp memory of Community history and of the days at Goodings and Denford; Sister Angela Morris for helping me understand the role of the Pastoral Centre in modern times as well as facets of school life at Newnham Paddox and bomb-damaged New Hall; Sister Pauline Crowther, Moira Metcalfe and Elizabeth Townsend for talking to me about New Hall's more recent history; Eileen Lodge for letting us tape her reminiscences of pre-war New Hall; and John Furze of New Hall Farm for sharing his copious knowledge of life on the New Hall estate over the last fifty years. My thanks also go to Father Stewart Foster, the Brentwood Diocesan Archivist for putting some useful documents in my way; Anne Fitzgerald for sorting out some helpful *Essex Chronicle* cuttings; Angela Martin for pointing me to the 1805 Ordnance Survey map of New Hall; Dave Whitby of Free Range Publishing for practical advice and help on the layout and format of the book and Jon Vaughan for proof-reading the final draft. Above all, my thanks go to my wife, Kathleen, who, at the early stage of writing, read every chapter, corrected grammatical clumsiness, told me where it is not interesting enough and throughout has been a huge support.

There is one final thank you but I do not know to whom to address it. The anonymous nun who wrote the 1899 *History of the New Hall Community of the Canonesses of the Holy Sepulchre* is, I feel, a good ally. I have re-read her book many times. It is rather hagiographical for the modern palate but is full of good leads which spurred further research. Now I know the unsocial hours she kept while writing it without the benefit of a word processor I am even more of an admirer.

Tony Tuckwell

February 2006

Chapter 1

An Order out of Chaos

The Nuns and New Hall to 1516

In 135 A.D. Emperor Hadrian built a temple to Jupiter in Jerusalem to seal his victory over the Jews whose three year revolt he had bloodily extinguished. To symbolise Jewish servitude and their disbarment from Jerusalem, it was deliberately erected over the foundations of the Temple of Solomon which had been demolished sixty-five years before by Emperor Titus. It also, by chance, encompassed the area where Jesus was said to have been crucified but this was an unintended slight as Hadrian did not consider the small and passive Christian sect a serious concern. Not so some of his successors who were to find that the Christian message threatened a power structure based on a pantheon of gods which included the deified Emperor. Emperor Diocletian's violent persecution from 303 to 305 was the result

Yet in 312 the convert Emperor Constantine seized power and Christians were at last able to worship openly in the land of their Saviour. In 325 Constantine ordered the demolition of Jupiter's temple. According to tradition, one year later, amongst its ruins, Helena, the Emperor's mother, discovered a cavern which was Jesus' cave tomb and the three crosses of Golgotha of which Jesus' was identified through a healing miracle. Constantine venerated the site by building the Basilica of the Holy Sepulchre which was completed in 335. However the collapse of Roman authority in Western Europe a century later left the Holy Land vulnerable to Asian invaders.

In 614 the Basilica was devastated by Persian forces. It was rebuilt shortly after but a new religious movement immediately arose which proved a more permanent and potent rival. In 637 armies, inspired by the teachings of the Prophet Mohammed, who had died in 632, took control of Jerusalem, from whose Temple Mount the

Prophet had allegedly ascended to Heaven. There they built the Dome of the Rock as a Muslim holy shrine. For nearly four centuries there was some form of co-existence with Christians permitted access to their own Holy Places on payment of a tax until, in 969, Jerusalem fell under the control of the Fatimids, a radical and intolerant Shi'ite sect from Tunis, whose Caliph Al-Hakim in 1009 ordered the Basilica of the Holy Sepulchre and other churches to be destroyed and Jesus' tomb hacked down to the bedrock. From the Christian perspective things got even worse. In 1076 Turkish Saracen forces, who owed religious allegiance to the Caliphate of Baghdad, moved west out of central Asia and took Jerusalem, completely cut off access to Christian pilgrims and even threatened the eastern Christian church in Constantinople. The Fatimids, from their power base in Egypt, recaptured Jerusalem in 1098 but only in time to become the first victims of Crusader vengeance in the following year.

Since 1095, the year Pope Urban II had called for the First Crusade to repel Muslim forces, western rulers had been gathering their troops and moving south-east across Europe. This largely French expedition was led by Duke Robert of Normandy (William the Conqueror's brother), Count Robert of Flanders, Count Raymond of Toulouse, Hugh of Vermandois (brother of the King of France) and Godfrey, Baldwin and Eustace, Dukes of Boulogne. Their army triumphantly entered Jerusalem in the summer of 1099 having butchered about 70,000 defenders and civilians in the process and started to build a new, though smaller, Church of the Holy Sepulchre after which they elected one of their own to govern the city. According to William, Bishop of Tyre, the blond and pious Duke Godfrey of Boulogne was chosen. Godfrey died within a year[1] but not before tradition says he had established the order of the Canons of the Holy Sepulchre. In 1114 they adopted the Rule of St. Augustine.[2] Documentary evidence starts in 1143 when Pope Celestine III confirmed the Church and Canons of the Holy Sepulchre in all their possessions.[3]

In 1144 Muslim forces recaptured Edessa, an outlying area in modern Iraq where the land-greedy crusaders had extended their rule which sparked off the unsuccessful Second Crusade. In 1187 the Saracen leader, Saladin (a Kurdish Sunni who had overthrown the Fatimids in Egypt in 1169) re-conquered the Holy Land and banned all Christian pilgrimages. The resulting Third Crusade, led by Richard I of England, was another failure. At this point the Canons of the Holy Sepulchre let their heads rule their hearts and most of them took refuge in European monasteries in modern day Germany and Belgium.

For the Papacy there was no giving up on the quest to secure the Holy Places. "The recovery of the Holy Land, whether as an ideal, a symbol, or an immediate duty, pervaded the minds of men ... It was inseparable from the air they breathed".[4] A man who took the cross was a privileged person, protected by the courts. If he fulfilled his vow of fighting the Muslim he enjoyed plenary indulgence from suffering in purgatory for past sins. The financial requirements of the crusades were largely responsible for the development of the papal administration and a lucrative banking system in the industrial, commercial, and shipping houses of the north Italian cities. The Knights Templar, created in 1118, to protect pilgrims en route to the Holy Land, also developed huge land and trading interests with massive financial clout. Matilda of Boulogne, the wife of King Stephen of England (1135-1154) and niece of Godfrey of Boulogne, gave the Knights Templar their first English possessions, one of which was the manor of Cressing in Essex.[5] Other military orders dedicated to the crusades also arose, such as the Knights of the Holy Sepulchre, but they were a purely secular military fraternity, not to be confused with the Canons.

After nine crusades the Muslims in 1291 were still in firm control of the Holy Land. The fall of the fortress of Acre in that year marked their dominance. For the Canons of the Holy Sepulchre their title was now one of dedication rather than guardianship. That latter task had fallen to Greek Orthodox monks as the Muslims cleverly exploited the religious and territorial squabbles that had arisen between the crusaders of western Europe and their so-called co-religionists in the east. By giving special rights to the Orthodox Church the Muslim rulers hoped to aggravate the divisions within Christendom. Certainly no love was lost between Catholics and Orthodox. Over the centuries following the fall of Rome and the subsequent Dark Ages in western Europe, the eastern Church, based on Constantinople, continued to flourish in isolation, developing its own distinct liturgies and traditions which it saw as being an orthodox descent from the early church. Even in 1899 the *History of the New Hall Community* somewhat uncharitably refers to the Orthodox Church as a "schismatic rite".[6] Eventually in 1336 the Muslim authorities allowed a handful of impoverished Franciscan monks to dwell on the site of the Holy Sepulchre alongside the Orthodox monks and in 1342 Pope Clement VI officially committed the care of the Holy Places on behalf of the Catholic Church to the Franciscans.

The Holy Sepulchre remained an inspiration even though the Crusades had failed. In 1240 a crusader named Repen, founded a Priory of the Holy Sepulchre at Henengowe, near Hasselt, about twenty-four miles north-west of Liège in modern day Belgium, in thanksgiving for his safe return from the Holy Land. By the end of the fifteenth century it had just one monk but was given fresh life when it was joined by John à Broeck who, in 1474, founded another house at Kinroy, about twelve miles to the east. In 1480 he transformed it into a convent of Canonesses of the Holy Sepulchre which eventually became the mother house of thirty convents in the Low Countries, four in France and one in Germany, all dedicated to the teaching of children. Four of them were to develop in Liège and one at Tongres (the modern Tongeren),[7] just a few miles from Liège.

In a parallel universe in the County of Essex, the manor of New Hall, just north of Chelmsford, was circulating round various owners, whether by purchase, exchange, marriage or the vagaries of civil war. It was eventually to come into royal hands.

New Hall is first recorded as belonging to the Augustinian Canons of Waltham Abbey who acquired it from King Harold in 1062 as one of an endowment of seventeen manors, a pleasantly airy contrast to the monastery's position in marshy, ague-ridden land near the Thames. Half-way between London and Harwich it could also be used to entertain royalty as they travelled to and from the Continent.[8] Adelais of Louvain stayed at New Hall en route to her marriage to Henry I in 1121 and wrote about the Abbot's magnificent court. Going in the other direction Princess Maud, daughter of Henry II, stayed on her way to marry the Duke of Savoy and Bavaria. In 1301 the Abbot erected a large residence which became his summer home where, in 1347, John de Vere, who was the Lord Abbot of Waltham, entertained Queen Philippa, wife of Edward III. That sumptuous feast appears to have been the last. The Abbot's entertainments were becoming too princely in style and he was ordered to get rid of New Hall and concentrate on Waltham Abbey.

So in 1350 Sir John de Shardelowe and his wife and brother acquired New Hall from the Abbot in exchange for their family properties in Epping, a neat mutual territorial consolidation. In 1373 a similar swap took place. Sir Henry de Coggeshalle and his brother exchanged some properties in Shropshire and Norfolk for the Shardelowes' New Hall. The manor of New Hall remained in the Coggeshalle family for the next half century but, through lack of male heirs, passed to John de Boreham. He may have sold it to Queen Margaret of Anjou, wife of Henry VI who, downhearted by the loss of valued friends in the Wars of the Roses, passed it to Richard Alred, a favourite servant and husband of Elizabeth of Coggeshalle. Edward IV, having deposed Henry VI in 1461, seized it back as crown property and held his Whitsuntide court at New Hall in 1480.[9] New Hall stayed with the Yorkists until 1485 when it came into the hands of Henry VII as the victor's spoils at the end of the Wars of the Roses when Richard III was slain on Bosworth Field.

In 1491 Henry VII gave New Hall to Thomas Butler, Earl of Ormonde, together with the right to crenellate the walls and towers, probably for honorific and symbolic reasons rather than through military need. The gift was almost certainly a reward for the Ormonde family's sufferings during the recent civil strife.[10] One of Ormonde's brothers, a staunch Lancastrian, had fought for Henry VI at the battles of St. Albans, Wakefield and Mortimer's Cross in 1461, but was captured later that year at the battle of Towton and beheaded. We assume Ormonde's building was on or near the site of the present building. We know that it had walls and towers, that, in the absence of local stone, it must have been brick built, and that it was almost certainly surrounded by a moat. It probably resembled Oxburgh Hall in Norfolk.[11]

New Hall then passed to Ormonde's daughter, Margaret Butler, who married Sir William Boleyn. Their eldest son, Thomas, inherited the property and produced three children, the youngest of whom was Anne Boleyn. The young Henry VIII so liked the property and its position (though not at this stage Thomas' daughter) that in 1516 he bought it for £1,000 (£421,000 in today's money) plus an exchange of property. This deal also included the neighbouring manors of Culverts and Walkfares which had been owned by Lord Lovell, Richard III's Lord Chamberlain, who had lost them to John de Vere, 13th Earl of Oxford, after the Battle of Bosworth. De Vere then passed them on to the newly knighted Sir Thomas Boleyn.[12]

So, as the sixteenth century gets under way, the New Hall estate, comprising three large manors, is destined to become the site of a royal dwelling, one of the places where Henry VIII woos Ann Boleyn in a relationship which irrevocably splits Christendom, opens the door to the Protestant Reformation, and turns Catholicism in England into a persecuted and secretive faith. At the same time a religious order dedicated to the Holy Sepulchre has emerged out of the chaos of the Crusades and has established convents in some strength in the Low Countries.

Chapter 2

Of Palaces and Kings

New Hall 1516-1530

Henry VIII (1509-1547) was a prodigious builder and lived in great magnificence. He inherited about a dozen palaces and country houses from his frugal father, Henry VII (1485-1509), but left over sixty to his children,[1] a scale of property acquisition and new building unequalled by any monarch since.

The palace erected in the manor of New Hall was, at the time of its building, one of Henry's most lavish. The potential of the site must have caught his eye when he was a guest of the Earl of Ormonde in 1510 and 1515.[2] Henry began spending immediately he acquired the estate in 1516. Over £17,000 was dispensed. With the purchase price this made a total outlay of about £7,000,000 in today's money. Sufficient progress had been made for him to be able to stay there in 1519 when a masque was staged but the building was not completed until 1521. Building work was managed by William Bolton, Prior of St. Bartholomew's in Smithfield, Cardinal Wolsey's most favoured buildings adviser.[3] Indeed in the first half of his reign Henry left all the buildings details to Wolsey and there is no record of his taking a personal interest in architectural projects until after Wolsey fell from power in 1529. [4]

New Hall was one of four major construction projects in the 1515-1529 period. The other three were Bridewell Palace built just to the west of the city of London on the western bank of the confluence of the Rivers Fleet and Thames between 1515 and 1523 to replace Westminster Palace which had burned down in 1512; Eltham Palace which was modernised between 1519 and 1522; and an expensive updating of Henry VII's Greenwich Palace in the 1520s. At the time New Hall cost only slightly less than Bridewell's £22,000 (about £9,000,000 in today's money) but was dwarfed in the

1530s and 1540s by the costs of the palaces at Hampton Court (£62,000 or nearly £20,000,000 in today's money), and Whitehall, where there is no figure for the immediate costs after acquisition, but an additional £28,676 was spent on it in the 1540s, making a probable overall cost of at least £50,000 (a modern equivalent of at least £17,000,000). Nonsuch, a hunting annex to Hampton Court, built in the 1540s cost a mere £24,000 (£7,600,000 in today's money). [5]

Henry was so pleased with his new palace at New Hall that he renamed it Beaulieu. It may, indeed, have been a beautiful place but, as with Nonsuch Palace, he also had a liking for fancy descriptions.[6] When Beaulieu was finished a contemporary account[7] says that it had eight courtyards, a five hundred feet entrance façade adorned with the royal coat of arms, a great hall, a tennis court, a vast kitchen and a gallery, and the royal apartments were in a wing three storeys high. This wing would have had service quarters at the bottom, the Queen's lodgings on the first floor, and the King's, with much larger windows and the most elevated position, as was appropriate to his status, on the top floor, with a grand staircase connecting the two royal suites. The interiors of the royal apartments and other public chambers would have been replete with gold and silver decoration, murals portraying regal glories, very expensive wall tapestries from the Netherlands shot with gold and silver thread, maps and plans, paintings and much linenfold wooden panelling carved with grotesques. Paintings would have stayed in situ while the King was away but, in his absence, the huge wall tapestries would have been stored in large wardrobe presses off one of the outer courtyards. Responsibility for Beaulieu when the King was elsewhere lay with the Keeper. The Keepers of Beaulieu were consecutively Nicholas Carew, William Carey, George Boleyn, Robert 1st Earl of Sussex and the Marquis of Northampton.[8] The Keeper had permission to use the house when the King was not there. He alone had the keys and would also have had a house in the grounds in which he would live when the King was in residence.

There was also a splendid chapel at Beaulieu with an east window of superb quality, showing the Crucifixion and a commemoration of the marriage in 1506 of the young Prince Henry and Catherine of Aragon who are depicted kneeling on either side. It was originally a gift from a Dutch town to Henry VII who gave it, most aptly, to Waltham Abbey, the first recorded owners of the manor of New Hall, but it was then taken back by Henry VIII at the dissolution of the monasteries in the 1530s and installed in Beaulieu. It was sold in the eighteenth century for £50 (about £5,500 today) to John Conyers of Copped Hall, Epping. He sold it in 1758 to St. Margaret's Church, Westminster for 400 guineas (£55,000 today), so he had the best of the deal. It can still be seen there today.[9] The royal chapel at Beaulieu would also have been richly gilded and lavishly decorated and would probably have contained an organ, an instrument on which Henry VIII placed great value, though not as an accompaniment for voices. We definitely know that the King had separate royal pews elevated above the entrance and screened off from the rest of the Chapel. However he would have heard Mass in his private closet off his own privy chambers and would only have attended the Chapel, which was intended for household worship, at Christmas and Easter, if he was ever in residence at Beaulieu at these times, after a procession which enabled a display of royal magnificence along a route lined with supplicants seeking his favour.[10]

On a more mundane level Beaulieu also had the latest in royal mod cons with a lead-lined water conduit system installed in 1522[11] to provide service needs in general and, not least, to aid ablutions in the royal bathroom with its rectangular bath sunk into a wooden floor.[12] The many courtyards would have been necessary to accommodate the vast numbers of courtiers' horses and horse-drawn carts that brought all the luggage as the court went on its progress. For example, Princess Mary alone needed twenty-six carts when she travelled.[13]

Beaulieu was one of only six Henrician properties where Hall could be kept;[14] in other words it could accommodate the full six hundred lower members of the court who were entitled to dine communally at the set times of 12.00 p.m. and 4.00 p.m..[15] Food was served in "messes", an allocation for four people. The "mess" was then divided up by the most senior officer at the table and proved more economic than a free-for-all self-service approach.[16] In addition, when the Court was in residence, about 230 domestic servants would have eaten elsewhere, mostly at their place of work. Senior members of the court would have dined with the King, probably in the Presence Chamber.

Beaulieu was not used by the King after 1530 when it became a home for Princess Mary instead. Henry and his new Queen, Anne Boleyn, disliked Wolsey's stacked multi-storey royal lodgings, preferring King's and Queen's suites on the same level linked by galleries. Beaulieu and Bridewell were left as they were and disappeared from the royal itinerary with Bridewell finding alternative use as an ambassadors' residence.[17] Beaulieu also had other disadvantages which meant that no money was likely to be spent on adapting it. It was somewhat out on a limb compared with the Thames Valley trio of Richmond, Eltham and Greenwich which Henry augmented to a quintet, in the 1530s, by seizing and modernising Hampton Court and Whitehall, properties that had formerly belonged to the disgraced Cardinal Wolsey. Richmond, as a medieval-style castle, rapidly passed out of favour. Eltham was five miles from the Thames, a sufficient disadvantage to diminish its usefulness in days when land transport was so cumbersome. This meant that Greenwich, Whitehall and Hampton Court, each fronting onto the Thames, became the favoured three. Whitehall was officially designated as the centre of royal government and assumed state functions, Greenwich became the most used palace as a home and Hampton

Court as a much-loved leisure retreat. All three had large areas of land emparked to provide royal hunting facilities, indeed Hampton Court Chase was the first new royal forest for over 200 years. Tilt yards guaranteed entertainment through the popular spectator sport of jousting in which Henry VIII probably ceased to be an active competitor after being knocked unconscious in 1536.[18]   Each of the favoured palaces also had the King's and Queen's quarters horizontally arranged. Access by river transport in the winter months was easy (except, in this mini ice age, when the river sometimes froze over) and became essential in the 1540s when Henry's obesity, ulcerated legs and generally poor health made road transport an agony. If five miles overland was an inconvenience at Eltham, Beaulieu, nigh on forty miles from London, at least a full day's journey even in good weather, posed a daunting challenge when winter rains turned roads into quagmires. So it faded into relative obscurity.

The earliest surviving plan of New Hall (the name to which it seemed soon to revert) dates from about 1700 and shows a slightly smaller layout than Henry VIII would have recognised from his Beaulieu days. It had seven courts, only one of which was large, the others being stable yards.[19] Other details show the chapel and the great hall facing each other on a north/south axis on either side of the great courtyard. In the west wing there were lodgings and apartments well lit by large bay windows. On the east side there was an extensive complex of service buildings devoted to food preparation. On the south side were stables and other outbuildings. The house would probably have been surrounded by walled gardens and may well have been moated. Its reduced size was probably the result of a fire that occurred in Henry VIII's time.[20] Once it had gone out of favour as a royal residence there was no compelling need to restore it. With naked flames as the only sources of heating and light, fires were not that rare. Whitehall, Westminster and Richmond had all had major conflagrations in the twenty years before Beaulieu was built.

There is some archaeological evidence for the palace's original extent. Some additional foundations were found in 1968 during building work[21] and, in the very dry summer months of the 1975-1976 drought, the shape of the old palace foundations could be picked out on the stretch of lawn to the south in front of the present building.[22] Even if it had lost some of its original magnificence the seventeenth century New Hall was certainly not seen as a modest residence when visited by the Duke of Tuscany in 1669. He described it as "surpassing in extent and bearing, almost every other in the kingdom".[23]

Of Henry's palace all that remains today is the short east wing and the cellars. The windows in this wing are Elizabethan and have been cut into the Tudor brickwork. At the back of this wing there are late Perpendicular windows with their typical low arched heads giving some light into the cellars which are on a grand scale and are, more accurately, a semi-basement or undercroft, as on one side they are not entirely below the ground. There are similar arcades in the cellars at Hampton Court.[24]

No sooner had Beaulieu Palace been completed than, in 1525, Henry VIII began to hatch plans to divorce Catherine of Aragon, his wife since 1506, and before that of his dead brother Arthur. She had provided one daughter for the king, Mary, but no son. Anne Boleyn, whose father had previously owned New Hall, became the new attraction. When she became irresistible is hard to fathom but she may have enhanced her attractions by playing hard to get:

> "What had hitherto been light dalliance with an eighteen or nineteen year old girl had begun to grow into something deeper and more dangerous. In the normal course of events, Anne ... would have been used and discarded – along with those others whom Henry had taken and who are now forgotten. But, either because of virtue or ambition, Anne refused to become his mistress ... and the more she resisted, the more, apparently, did Henry prize her".[25]

Maybe Anne had seen how Henry had cast off her sister, Mary, after a sexual liaison and wanted greater security. No matter, the dissolution of the marriage had to be done by due process of law sanctified by the Pope otherwise children by a future marriage would be bastards and lack clear rights of succession. On the same basis Princess Mary would be bastardised if the marriage with Catherine was shown to have been based on a false theological argument. Cardinal Wolsey and Henry agreed that the Pope's original dispensation that had enabled Henry to marry his dead brother's wife should be challenged. Deuteronomy xxv 5 said that "if brethren dwell together, and one of them die, and have no child ... her husband's brother shall go in unto her and take her to him to wife..." By contrast Leviticus xx 21 would legitimise the divorce of Catherine and re-marriage – "... If a man shall take his brother's wife, it is an unclean thing ..." Which of the conflicting texts the Pope selected would depend on the diplomatic and military pressure that could be brought to bear.

Twisting the papal arm soon became a tricky proposition for Henry when Emperor Charles V, Catherine of Aragon's nephew, crushed the French troops at the Battle of Pavia, invaded Italy, captured Rome and held Pope Clement VII prisoner. Henry now had no chance of receiving a favourable papal decision. Cardinal Wolsey was therefore despatched to France to meet with the other cardinals at Avignon, take over the Papacy himself, settle peace in Europe and bring Henry's search for a divorce to a satisfactory conclusion. But the Pope would not let the cardinals leave Rome and Francis I of France and Emperor Charles V began to move closer together in opposition to English presumption.

As Wolsey crossed the Channel on July 22nd 1527, Anne Boleyn was conspiring with Henry, convincing him that the Cardinal had never wanted the King to marry her. This was a little harsh. Wolsey was unaware of Henry's well-hidden intention. He believed he was looking for a way out of the King's first marriage so that his second wife could be a diplomatically credible spouse, like Renée the sister-in-law of Francis I of France.[26] Wolsey had never believed Anne to be a serious prospect for marriage. She was just another pretty young woman whom the King would take into his bed and then cast aside.

On the very next day, July 23rd, Henry and Catherine with the queen's ladies-in-waiting, amongst them Anne, left one of the King's many other houses, at Hunsdon, near Ware in Hertfordshire, for Beaulieu. By this time the King's decision to marry Anne was irrevocable. He just needed to sort out the means. Richard Sampson, Dean to the Chapel Royal, secretly wrote to the horrified Wolsey to keep him abreast of the situation. Wolsey was to discover that Henry, who usually spent only a few days at a time at a series of manors on his summer tour, this time stayed for over a month at Beaulieu, from July 23rd to August 27th, hatching the plot to marry Anne.[27]

For a month Beaulieu was the centre of intrigue. Henry was surrounded there by his most trusted friends and relations, notably Thomas Howard, 3rd Duke of Norfolk who was his cousin by marriage and Anne's uncle, Charles Brandon, 1st Duke of Suffolk, who was his brother-in-law and Henry Courtenay, 1st Marquis of Exeter, who was his first cousin. The 1st Viscount Rochford, the former Sir Thomas Boleyn, now with a new title, was also invited back to his former residence. "The house party at Beaulieu turned into an extended think tank on the Great Matter ... like a modern company away-day at a country hotel"[28] with incidental hunting at the 16th Earl of Oxford's fortress a few miles north at Castle Hedingham. The decision was taken that Henry would by-pass Wolsey and make a direct appeal to the Pope. To that end Henry sent a deceitful letter from Beaulieu to Wolsey praising his diligence while at the same time sending his own secretary, William Knight, to Rome to gain access to the Pope with a document for him to sign agreeing a dispensation for the King to marry again.

The failure of this mission and subsequent attempts to secure the Pope's co-operation led ultimately to the break with Rome. Beaulieu had been the centre of conspiracy. Anne Boleyn was also there during that fateful month supping daily, and possibly more, in the King's Chamber. Having worked so hard to snare him she lived less than three years as Queen. Married in January 1533 and crowned in June, she gave birth to an heir (albeit yet another unsatisfactory female, Elizabeth) in September, but died on the executioner's block in May 1536.

It is pleasantly ironic that nearly three centuries later Catholic nuns should come to occupy the place where that ill-fated marriage was hatched and teach their girls the godly virtues that were so lacking in pursuit of the King's Great Matter.

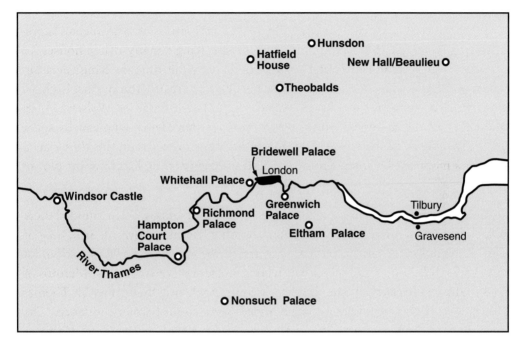

MAP 1:
Tudor palaces and royal houses

Chapter 3

The Great Escape

New Hall 1530-1553

Henry VIII may have made himself supreme head of the Church in England but Princess Mary remained true to the Catholic religion based on papal authority that her mother, Catherine of Aragon, had taught her. She continued to observe the Catholic rites at New Hall and Hunsdon, her two favourite properties in which she had lived since her enforced separation from Catherine in 1532, at the age of seventeen, when the King's first marriage had so conveniently been found to have been illegal. The birth of Princess Elizabeth in September 1533 ensured that the succession was secure. In October it was announced that Mary's large household of 160 would be severely reduced to a size more appropriate for a royal bastard, a downsizing that she managed to delay until 1534[1] when her own badge was eventually cut off her servants' liveries to be replaced by the King's. She was now barred from the succession and reduced in status from Princess to Lady Mary.

Mary was not prepared to concede quietly. She wrote to Henry VIII from New Hall asserting that she was the lawful heir – "If I agreed to the contrary I should offend God". The King sent the Earls of Oxford, Essex and Sussex with Dr. Sampson, the Dean of the Chapel Royal, to lay down the law. The Dean warned Mary that "she had worthily deserved the King's high displeasure and punishment by law but that, conforming to his will, he might incline, of his fatherly pity, to promote her welfare".[2] Mary was forced to concede and left New Hall a few days later for a smaller house more fitting to her lowered status. To rub salt into the wound New Hall was to be taken from her to give to Anne Boleyn's brother, George, 2nd Viscount Rochford, one of Beaulieu's former Keepers. In December 1533 Mary was forced to attend at Hatfield, the house assigned to Elizabeth and Queen Anne, and in 1536 gave way to pressure to take the oath of succession, accepting the so-called illegality of her mother's marriage and thereby her own illegitimacy, and abjuring the pope's authority in England.

Contrast the pressure on Mary with the relative comfort of Reginald Pole, a dire opponent of Henry VIII. He lived abroad, accepted a cardinal's hat in 1536 and conspired to organise an invasion of England to restore papal authority. His mother, Margaret Pole, Countess of Salisbury, was Mary's childhood governess and had stayed loyal to her as a confidante throughout her travails at New Hall and elsewhere. Margaret's direct descent from the Yorkist Edward IV, was, in its own right, a dangerously symbolic threat to Tudor authority. Her son's enthusiasm to destroy Tudor rule literally put the last nail in her coffin. A Catholic uprising in the north of England in 1538 saw Margaret arrested and eventually executed in 1541. Guilt by association was sufficient. It must have been some consolation that Jane Seymour, now Henry's third queen, was well-disposed to the Lady Mary whom she treated with kindness so that in 1538 Mary was allowed to return to New Hall. Jane had been a former maid of Mary's mother so perhaps they had a common bond. We do not know whether Mary was at New Hall in 1540 when yet another royal consort, this time Anne of Cleves, stopped off on the way to London for Henry VIII's fourth marriage, Jane Seymour having tragically died in 1538 ten days after giving birth to Henry's longed-for male heir.

In 1547 the nine year old Edward VI succeeded his father. Edward was not a pleasant prospect for Catholics for "like all his family he had a marked intellectual ability which an appalling schooling had turned into a passion for Protestant theology".[3] Real power lay not with the boy but with the Privy Council under his uncle, Edward Seymour, the Duke of Somerset, who assumed the title of Protector. Over the next six years the Protestant Reformation took a strong grip on the country starting in December 1548 when Archbishop Cranmer publicly announced the rejection of the doctrine of transubstantiation and the Catholic Mass was banned.

On his accession Edward VI had granted New Hall and Hunsdon to Mary for life. She was once again the heir apparent to Edward, a position re-established by the ailing Henry VIII three years before in 1544 as he sought to leave his affairs in order. She and Elizabeth were both daughters of marriages which it had pleased Henry, earlier in his reign, to declare invalid, so that they were on an equal footing with Mary claiming prior rights as the elder child. Her adherence to the Old Faith was potentially a problem for Edward VI's ministers as they sought to consolidate the Protestant Reformation, but they seemed content not to interfere with her Catholic religious observances as long as they were low key and private. Mary, who could be as combative over religion as she was indecisive in other matters, always took pleasure in pointing out that her form of worship was exactly that observed by Henry VIII who never himself heard Mass in English.

When the Catholic Mass was banned Mary was asked to exercise discretion in the practice of her faith. Somerset was afraid of Mary's potential popularity and, for international diplomatic reasons, did not want to offend her cousin, Emperor Charles V who had warned the King's Privy Council not to put pressure on her. Somerset was therefore prepared to allow Mary and two or three serving women to worship in the privacy of her private chamber but she refused to comply and insisted on worshipping in the Chapel with her whole household. Who would blink first?

In November 1549 further legislation removed idolatrous images and "superstitious books" from churches and an Act of Uniformity enforced the new Book of Common Prayer. Edward invited his two half-sisters, Elizabeth and Mary, to join him at court for Christmas but Mary declined, pleading illness, and remained at New Hall with her friends and servants. "They wish me to be at court so that I could not get the Mass celebrated for me and that the King might take me with him to hear their sermons and masses".[4] During 1550 Mary's chaplains continued to celebrate Mass at her various houses. Nobility and gentry who clung to the Old Faith sent their daughters to serve her at New Hall. Jane Dormer, one of her ladies-in-waiting, recollected that "in those days this house of the princess was the only harbour for honourable young women given any way to piety and devotion. It was a true school of virtuous demeanour..."[5]

Mary felt she needed to make contingency plans for escape as she dreaded an enforced marriage and submission to Protestant theology. In April 1550 she summoned Emperor Charles V's ambassador, Van der Delft, to a smaller house she owned at Woodham Walter, two miles from Maldon, and only four miles from New Hall. This house, owned by the Earls of Sussex, was probably associated with their manor at Woodham Walter, today a ruin of dramatic earthworks.[6]

Van der Delft tried to urge caution on Mary. This was an unpropitious time for an escape. In 1549 Ket's Rebellion in Norfolk had taken control of Norwich. Although we now know that the rebellion was the result of agricultural depression the Council feared that it might have been inspired by Catholics eager to put Mary on the throne. This was understandable as it followed hot on the heels of an insurgency in Cornwall which had definitely been provoked by hostility to the new Prayer Book. In these volatile circumstances, if Mary were caught trying to escape to the clutches of Charles V, the greatest Catholic monarch in Europe, she would inevitably be branded a traitor with awful consequences.

Nonetheless, she was adamant - "I will rather suffer death than stain my conscience".[7] It was agreed that a trading boat would be sent to Maldon, ostensibly to sell corn, in reality to rescue Mary. However, the recent uprisings elsewhere meant that rumours were rife, including one that a local revolt was about to erupt.

Essex coastal villages and towns were placed on a state of alert. Householders were ordered to challenge anyone found on quiet back roads, especially at night. It was also feared that Charles V was about to invade England to restore papal authority. In such circumstances all foreign ships would be suspect. Mary knew that to escape detection she would have to walk to Maldon with just one or two companions.

At the end of June 1550 a small fleet of four great Imperial warships and four smaller boats sailed from the Netherlands for Harwich under the pretext of looking for Scottish pirates in the North Sea. On the evening of June 30th the smaller vessels dropped anchor off Maldon whilst the larger ships lay off Harwich.

Dubois, secretary to Van der Delft, was the main protagonist in this escape plot. He had disguised himself as the master of a merchant ship bringing corn from the Netherlands to Maldon and sailing under the protection of the men-of-war. The plan called for Dubois to be rowed in one of the smaller corn ships up the River Blackwater into Maldon where he would sell his cargo. His brother-in-law, Peter Marchant, was to travel ahead to Woodham Walter and inform Mary that rescue was at hand. He would smuggle Mary on board and they would return to the waiting fleet. Mary would then be conveyed to Antwerp or Brussels.

It soon became clear that Sir Robert Rochester, Mary's Household Controller, was opposed to the escape plan, pointing out the dangers from the increased watch and his belief that there were spies in Mary's household. He also felt that escape was unnecessary as Mary was not in imminent danger. He argued that she would lose her place in the succession if she left England. So when Dubois arrived at Maldon on July 2nd and made secret contact with Woodham Walter, he found Mary to be surprisingly hesitant but would not abandon the plan until instructed by her to do so.

Dubois suspected that Rochester had put Mary off the idea. He therefore went himself to see her at Woodham Walter. Mary said she definitely wished to escape but she was not yet ready. Could Dubois wait another two days until July 4th when she would be with her ladies on the beach at 4.00 a.m. after the watch went off duty? Knowing that this would be courting extreme danger, Dubois urged her to leave everything and come at once. He had sold his corn and had no excuse for staying longer at Maldon. At that point Rochester came into the room to say that the people of Maldon had rumbled Dubois and knew that he had some illegal purpose connected with a warship which was then off nearby Stansgate. He said the watch at Maldon was going to be doubled with men posted in the church tower and possibly a warning beacon lit.

Mary tried to delay Dubois saying that another escape attempt should take place after she had left for New Hall in a few days' time and promising that she would send a messenger to him with instructions to rendezvous with her at Stansgate. However Dubois could risk his life no further. The escape plan was abandoned but, after a secret journey back through the woods to Maldon, Dubois found that Rochester's panicky account of heightened surveillance was untrue. It had been a ruse to make his mistress abandon her madcap plan.

The Emperor's fleet was immobilised by storms for five days. By the time they sailed on July 7th the King's Privy Council had received reports of foreign visitors to Maldon and guessed that an abortive escape attempt had taken place. The Council ordered that precautions should be taken to ensure that Mary never left England. When he learned what had happened Charles V also vetoed any future escape plan as too fraught with danger. He had cause for concern. Rumours of Mary's intended flight spread in this adamantly Protestant corner of England. To calm the people, the Council issued a statement saying that the Emperor, wishing to marry Mary to his son Philip, and so claim England for the Hapsburgs, had tried to kidnap her but that the attempt had failed.

This is an extraordinary story which captures the intense fears of the time. But Mary had half declared her hand and the pressures on her were now going to mount. On July 17th Sir John Gates rode into Essex with a band of armed horsemen "to stop the going away of the Lady Mary"[8] but she was free to leave Woodham Walter for New Hall, and sent her chaplain ahead of her to prepare a celebration of Mass on her arrival. By now the King's Privy Council had managed to place spies in her household. They noted that the Chaplain, Francis Mallett, celebrated Mass at New Hall before Mary arrived back home, thus breaking the agreement that private Mass could be held for her but no one else. The Council ordered her chaplains to cease holding illegal Catholic services and sought Mallett's arrest but he disappeared to the Catholic stronghold of Yorkshire. The military presence in the vicinity of New Hall was intensified. There was an increased watch on the East Anglian ports.

Pressure was put on Mary to come to court where she would be under effective palace arrest and far from the sea. She again pleaded ill health. Eventually she met at Leigh-on-Sea with two Essex noblemen and King's ministers, Lord Chancellor Richard Rich of Great Leighs Priory and Secretary Sir William Petre of Ingatestone Hall. They gave her letters from the King guaranteeing her safety at court. Rich tried to turn the ill-health excuse back on Mary – "The truth is that neither the house [New Hall] nor the air is herein to be suspected, but the time of the year being the fall of the leaf, at the which time I have seldom escaped the disease these many years".[9] Therefore to leave New Hall for a change of air would do her good. Rich visited her at New Hall with his wife and took her hunting. Still Mary would not budge.

The Council and King had had enough. On December 1st 1550 altars were removed from all churches in the land and the death penalty was restored for heresy. Mary's two chaplains were summoned to appear before the Council. She refused to let them go saying that the Council had previously promised that she could hear Mass with her servants. She was again formally summoned to court and this time knew she had to obey. Her half-sister Elizabeth, not wishing to get involved in this dispute, wisely left the court.

On March 15th 1551 Mary arrived in London and two days later processed to Whitehall where Edward VI berated her for hearing Mass. Charles V privately told Mary to comply with the Council's wishes while putting on a public show of protest. The Council could not work out what to do with Mary. Some wanted her sent to the Tower but feared the King's reaction. Others felt it would be simpler to turn a blind eye. The King went along with the latter view despite the fact that he had been brought up to believe that it was a sin to ignore a sin. Mary was allowed to leave court and return to New Hall though not before protesting to Sir William Petre that "my soul is God's; my body is the King's".[10]

Mary was now exempt from prosecution but her Masses would henceforth not be open to outsiders. She could not be allowed, wittingly or unwittingly, to become a focus for discontented Catholic nobility. Her priest, Francis Mallett, who had now been located, was arrested for celebrating Mass in her absence. In August 1551 the Council became more emboldened, perhaps influenced by the King who, at thirteen, was now attending their meetings and asserting himself. He decided to prohibit Mary from attending even a private Mass. She accepted the inevitability of her situation but protested that "none of your new service shall be said in any house of mine".[11] Mary dismissed her chaplains so that they would not be put in a compromising position. Her trusty household staff, including Rochester, were arrested and put in the Tower for a year.

One story suggests that Mary may have continued her private Masses despite royal prohibition though, as the source is the propagandist Foxe's *Book of Martyrs*, it needs to be treated with caution. The story alleges that in the summer of 1552 Mary had to put up with snide religious mockery from the staunchly Protestant Lady Jane Grey on a visit to New Hall. When Lady Ann Wharton, the wife of one of Mary's household officers, curtsied to the exposed Host at the Chapel altar, Jane asked facetiously if the Lady Mary had come in. When Lady Ann replied that she had curtsied "to Him that made us all", Jane came up with the punch-line, "Why, how can that be when the baker made him",[12] a piece of wordplay that would have had Protestants who rejected transubstantiation rolling in the aisles but was a painful blow to Catholics, many of whom died as martyrs on this point of theological principle. A year later Mary and Jane would vie for the throne on this very issue.

In 1553 Edward VI became seriously ill with consumption. John Dudley, Duke of Northumberland, who had replaced and executed Somerset in 1550, rushed to marry his son, Guildford, to Lady Jane Grey who was the granddaughter of Henry VIII's sister, another Mary. Northumberland persuaded the dying Edward to alter his will in favour of Jane's succession on the grounds that Mary and Elizabeth were illegitimate children of illegal marriages. The Council went along with it. This would secure the Protestant Reformation and Northumberland's fortune but it required Mary to be captured first. She was forewarned and fled New Hall for Norfolk.

Edward died on July 6th 1553. Lady Jane Grey was proclaimed Queen in London and similarly Mary in Norfolk. Northumberland set out to seize Mary by armed force but the country was in her favour because she was Henry VIII's daughter. Northumberland's troops deserted and the Council turned on him. He got no further than Cambridge. After nine days Lady Jane Grey's reign came to an end. Mary moved by daily stages from Framlingham via Ipswich and Colchester to New Hall where she was greeted by representatives from the City of London with £500 in sovereigns[13], over £117,000 in today's money. On July 26th the Duchess of Northumberland rode to New Hall to beg mercy for her husband and son. Mary refused to receive her. The Duchess of Suffolk, Lady Jane Grey's mother, was granted an interview at New Hall and received assurance that neither her husband nor her daughter would be harmed, a promise that was kept for seven months until a Protestant uprising sealed their fate. On July 29th the new Imperial Ambassador, Simon Renard, arrived at New Hall with a message for Mary from Charles V "not to be led by her zeal to be too hasty in reforming, but to show herself to be accommodating"[14] and to marry as soon as possible, planting the idea that a suitable groom might be Philip of Spain. On July 30th Mary left for London. She stayed en route with Sir William Petre at Ingatestone and then moved on to Havering-atte-Bower, the former home of her mother, Catherine of Aragon. She met her half-sister Elizabeth at Wanstead on August 2nd and received her embrace. On August 3rd she entered London through Aldgate. Mary would not return to her beloved New Hall again.

Queen Mary I reigned for five years. She accepted one piece of Charles V's advice and ignored the other. Sadly she got them the wrong way round. She married Philip of Spain, perhaps the most unpopular royal marriage in English history, which only served to strengthen the Protestant character of English nationalism. But she did not go slowly in her religious reforms. Her religious zeal created 273 Protestant martyrs. Their fate, commemorated in the famous Foxe's *Book of Martyrs*, would, for many generations, be an invaluable Puritan propaganda tool with which to beat the Catholics.

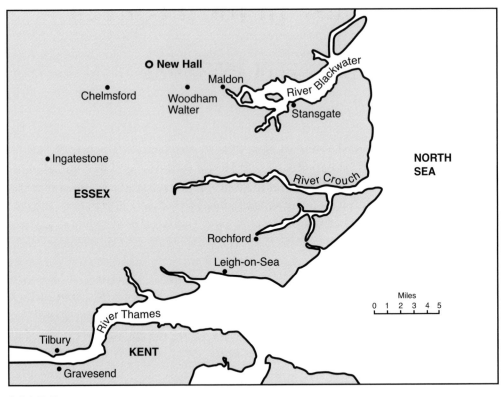

MAP 2:
Mary Tudor's planned escape

Chapter 4

A House fit for a Queen

New Hall 1553-1622

From 1553 Queen Mary leased New Hall to Sir Thomas Wharton, the son-in-law of Robert Radcliffe, 1st Earl of Sussex. Wharton had entered Mary's household in 1552 and accompanied her from Framlingham on her triumphant procession the following year. He then became a member of her Privy Council. He and his family were now able to celebrate Mass freely in the house where his former mistress had been so harassed.

The house was in poor condition. A letter from Sir Thomas to a Mr Yaxby notes that "the house is in great ruin, being burned in Henry VIII's time and not repaired since. It is falling down, so that the Queen will not sell it unless she sell it in time for repair. If I had it I would make a little corner for me and my wife to dwell in, and put away the rest".[1]

But dilapidations were not Wharton's only problem. The accession of Elizabeth I on Mary's death in 1558 led to a new Protestant Act of Uniformity in 1559. The Marian bishops were removed but treated quite leniently, living out their lives under a mild surveillance. The lesser clergy gave little trouble. Most bent with the wind. Evasion of the new rules was winked at and no action taken against the Mass in remoter districts.[2]   However Essex was not remote. Elizabeth did not want to make a "window into men's souls" but she had to work with a parliament increasingly dominated by Puritans who wanted any expression of Catholicism repressed. Within Essex New Hall had been a symbol of Catholic obduracy in Edward VI's reign and since then Mary Tudor had been demonised by the Puritans as a Catholic tyrant.

Sir Thomas Wharton therefore became an early victim of this retaliatory intolerance when in 1561 John Coxe was seized at Gravesend en route to the continent with a message for a well-known Catholic exile. Coxe was travelling under an alias and was proved to be a Catholic priest whose real name was John Devon. The Justice of the Peace who questioned him wrote that:

> "first the said John Devon did come to Sir Thomas Wharton's house ... at New Hall in Essex in Candlemas even[ing] last ... with two other gentlemen and also the said John Devon being required to hear Mass at a back door by one Jollye, a priest, who said Mass in Latin in a chamber next within my lady's chamber. At which Mass time they did bear candles in their hands. And there was also ministered that day a holy water and holy bread".

It happened again the next week "in the said chamber and two pictures of Mary and John standing in a window; and a board with certain painted images upon the altar". Perhaps the priests also used the hidden secret room, twelve feet square, reached by going up a sham chimney which had never had a fire lit, that was discovered in 1725.3

The Earl of Oxford, who was Lord Lieutenant of Essex, had to search the houses of Wharton and another suspect, Sir Edward Waldegrave, at Borley (significantly Frances Carey, one of the founding nuns of the Canonesses' house in Liège in 1642 will come from Borley). Oxford wrote to the Privy Council about Wharton:

> "only touching the Masses was he an offender ... I could neither in caskets, chests or other places find any cause or presumption whereby his faith and allegiance to the state was any what impaired .... And not knowing him culpable but in this only offence ... I do right earnestly pray your good lordships ... to show him your lawful favour ... I will stand bound to the Queen's majesty for him in whatsoever your lordships shall think mete".

The two priests, Jollye and Coxe (alias Devon) were imprisoned. So was Sir Thomas Wharton who was convicted at Brentwood on June 3rd 1561 and sent to the Tower where he lived in relative comfort. He was set free shortly after in return for paying a fine of 100 marks which suggests that the Earl of Oxford's plea for mercy was noted. Lady Ann Wharton was a dying woman when the search of the house was made. She passed away at New Hall four days later on June 7th and was buried in Boreham Church.4

Under Elizabeth I there was no chance that New Hall would revert to being a royal palace. She was as financially careful as her father had been profligate and, because Mary Tudor had added to the monarchy's financial problems with her expensive wars that a hostile Protestant Parliament was reluctant to finance, she inherited an empty treasury. She was therefore content to go on summer progress from the house of one great noble to another, keeping away from the heat of plague-ridden London and leaving her great men to finance three months' court expenses, a sort of taxation in kind. The royal progress may have been very costly for the nobility but many of them were prepared to invest in stylish properties to ingratiate themselves with the Queen and offset their debts against hoped-for profits from future royal appointments. New Hall received a four or five day visit in Wharton's time, starting on July 22nd 1561, as Elizabeth made her way to Colchester[5] just after Sir Thomas came out of the Tower. Perhaps the Queen was trying to soften the blow, showing that she recognised his loyalty even if he had infringed the laws on religion.

To reduce her overheads further Elizabeth also disposed of many of the royal properties, using them as gifts and rewards. Thus New Hall was given to Thomas Radcliffe, 3rd Earl of Sussex. The Radcliffes were relative newcomers to the peerage. The earldom had been settled in 1542 on Robert who had been Henry VIII's Steward to the Household and, for a time, Keeper at Beaulieu, where he would therefore have lived. This was quite a comeback for the family as Robert's father, Richard, had been executed for participating in the Perkin Warbeck conspiracy against Henry VII and had lost his lands which were, however, returned to the family in 1505. As 1st Earl of Sussex, Robert was one of the enforcers who came to New Hall in 1533 to make Mary Tudor accept her demotion in the succession. In 1540 he was made Great Chamberlain of England. His children perversely proved to be great supporters of Mary, Anne marrying Sir Thomas Wharton, one of Mary's household and Henry, the 2nd Earl of Sussex, giving Mary the house at Woodham Walter[6] from which she plotted her abortive escape.

Thomas, 3rd Earl of Sussex, was a political ally of William Cecil (who became 1st Lord Burghley in 1571), and, as nephew to Lady Ann Wharton, managed to keep New Hall in the family. Thomas was one of those statesmen who had successfully negotiated the change in the creeds of successive monarchs. He had been instrumental in negotiating Queen Mary's marriage to Philip of Spain to help restore the Catholic religion but was now steadfastly loyal to the Protestant Elizabeth and served many years on her Privy Council. His early career had been principally as a soldier. He was Lord Lieutenant of Ireland from 1556 to 1564 where he had repelled invasions from Scotland and rebellions by Irish nobles. On his return to England in 1569 he was made President of the Council of the North and was responsible for trying to keep the peace when Thomas Percy, 7th Earl of Northumberland, and Charles Neville, 6th Earl of Westmorland, in reality almost autonomous magnates in those distant border territories, had declared for the Catholic faith and Mary, Queen of Scots. The rebellion failed although Sussex played only a small military role. His major task was that of sorting out the culprits so that those with property might buy reprieves to replenish the royal coffers. Elizabeth executed 750 of the rest.[7] So in May 1573 New Hall was probably a gift for services rendered while, at the same time, recognising that the Radcliffes already had strong family connections there and at nearby Woodham Walter. However New Hall's poor state made it a financial liability. As a job lot it may have reflected Elizabeth's impatience with Sussex's preference for subtler diplomacy and lighter sentences during the northern rebellion when she demanded tough action.

New Hall was not only in desperate need of repair but was also out of fashion. It could not bear comparison with the other great houses being built by men of the court, such as William Cecil's Burghley House at Stamford in Lincolnshire, Sir Christopher Hatton's Kirby Hall in Leicestershire and Sir John Thynne's Longleat in Wiltshire. In an effort to keep up with his contemporaries, Sussex completely rebuilt New Hall's residential north wing to produce the splendid Elizabethan frontage with its unique and dramatic use of closely set, strongly projecting bays that still today enchants the eye from the approach up the long avenue although, in those days, that view would have been masked by the Henrician gatehouse. He also wisely inscribed Viva Elizabetta over the front door.[8] Like Longleat, New Hall's windows are smaller on the ground floor than the first floor, as the Great Chamber and other principal rooms were upstairs. On the other hand three favourite Tudor architectural devices are missing. There is no elaborate external decoration such as is found at Burghley, probably because New Hall is built in brick, no pilaster classical columns to divide up the façade, except round the modest entrance doorway, and no massed gables. Possibly Sussex was trying to make sure that his additions blended in with other existing buildings. Or maybe he did not have the money for grander designs. After all he had already refurbished the King's Manor at York, which was the monarch's residence in that city, and had rebuilt Woodham Walter church on a new site, probably because the existing one impeded the view from his former family home. [9]

The rest of the buildings round the courtyard in front of the refurbished part of the house were retained. Evidence for this comes from the 1671 hearth tax returns which show that there were only two Essex houses with over 100 hearths, Audley End and New Hall. The north wing of New Hall had only about twenty-five chimneys. The other seventy-five must have represented the buildings ranged round the courtyard. Sussex may also have had grander plans for the area north of the house. The north wing is wider than the space behind it and has great bays at each end looking out onto apparently dead areas, which suggests that Sussex possibly planned to create a more splendid vista to the north and side of the buildings, even though this was probably not carried out.[10] Again this might suggest shortage of funds.

The Sussex badge, an estoile or wavy-rayed star, can be found on the pinnacles on the parapet of the renovated north wing and on the architrave over the main door where it is combined with a porcupine, the badge of Sussex's second wife, Frances

Sidney, who survived her husband and endowed Sidney Sussex College, Cambridge, thus memorialising both families.

The scale and sumptuousness of the furnishings inside may be gauged from Sussex's will. This was clearly a house worthy of receiving the Sovereign, her favourites and retinue:

> "My meaning hath been to have New Hall to remain honourably furnished as well for receiving the Queen's Majesty when it shall please her to come hither ... I shall therefore bequeath to Sir Henry [his brother and heir] the suit of hangings which did hang in Her Majesty's Bedchamber at New Hall at Her Majesty's last being there and the suit of hangings which did hang in Her Majesty's Inner Chamber Lodging, the hangings which I bought of Horatio Palavicino to hang in the Withdrawing Chamber and the Privy Chamber for Her Majesty, the hangings of gilt leather which did hang in the chambers where Mistress Frances Howard did lie, the hangings of the Dance of Death, which did hang in the Presence Chamber, the suit of hangings which did hang in my lord of Leicester's bedchamber, and the bed of lozenges of cloth of gold and silver and gold embroidered on crimson satin which my lord of Leicester lay in ..."[11]

We do not know when the royal visit mentioned in the will was made in the decade between Sussex's acquisition of New Hall and his death. Although the Queen traversed Essex in July and September 1578 on her way to and from Norwich the latest research suggests that New Hall was not on the itinerary.[12] Whenever it was, we do know that two people mentioned in the will, the Earl of Leicester, the Queen's favourite whom she loved but dared not marry, and Lady Frances Howard, a maid of honour to Elizabeth I, made a complicated web in which Sussex became involved.

Back in 1573 Lady Frances Howard and her married sister, Lady Douglas Sheffield, were both having an affair with Leicester. Gilbert Talbot, Lord Shrewsbury's son, observed that they were "very far in love with him. They, of like striving who shall love him better, are at great wars together and the Queen thinketh not well of them, and not the better of him".[13] The Queen was always likely to be jealous of Leicester's other women and was related to the sisters whose father, the 1st Baron of Effingham, was the uncle of Anne Boleyn, the Queen's mother. It is not surprising therefore that when, later in 1573, Leicester cohabited with the by then widowed Lady Sheffield, the whole matter was kept secret. In September 1578 Leicester did contract a secret marriage, but this time to Lettice Knollys, Countess of Essex, the Queen's cousin. Elizabeth found out in 1579 and would have nothing to do with Leicester for the next year. Although Sussex had had bitter rows with Leicester, usually over plans for the Queen's marriage, he also had a keen eye for her reputation and dissuaded her from sending Leicester to the Tower for not having told her about his marriage which, as Sussex pointed out, was lawful and "a thing always counted honourable".[14] Nonetheless, suspecting bigamy, the Queen determined to find out whether Leicester had actually married Lady Sheffield, who was still alive (although herself now remarried), and gave Sussex the task of interrogation. She chose well. If anyone would have liked to sink Leicester it would have been Sussex. But he was a fair man. He could find no evidence that the Earl had married the lady although her tearful confession that "she had trusted the Earl too much", [15] reinforced his loathing of Leicester. Indeed the Queen had often had her work cut out to make the two men behave decently to each other in her presence and another massive row between them broke out in 1581 in the Privy Council with each calling the other traitor.[16] Elizabeth had to confine them to their rooms in Greenwich Palace and lay down the law about seemly conduct.

In November 1582 Sussex fell seriously ill with what may have been consumption.[17] On his death bed he warned Sir Christopher Hatton to "beware of the gipsy [Leicester]. He will be too hard for you all. You do not know the beast as well as I do".[18] That was a bit harsh on Leicester whose loyalty to the Queen was not in doubt. But his morals did not appeal to Sussex and he had, on several occasions, taken a different line from Sussex in advising the Queen on affairs of state.

Sussex died on June 9th 1583. He is buried in Boreham Church in a splendid marble and alabaster tomb adorned with the effigies of himself and his two noble predecessors. It took twelve wagons to bring it from London. Elizabeth I also visited New Hall in that same year[19] as part of her summer progress which did not start until the middle of July. The new Earl of Sussex would therefore have had an early opportunity to appreciate the expense of entertaining royalty.

Henry and Robert, the 4th and 5th Earls of Sussex , were not such prominent figures and were encumbered by debt. A house of this size was too much for them. Robert sold it in 1622 to George Villiers for £22,000 (over £3,000,000 in today's money).

Chapter 5

An English Country Garden

New Hall 1622-1660

George Villiers' rise to prominence under James I (1603-1625) was meteoric. The King first set eyes on him in 1614 and was infatuated with him emotionally and physically as was his wont with delicately handsome young men. Within a year they were sharing a bed.[1] James nicknamed him Steenie, short for Stephen whom the Bible records had the face of an angel.

In 1616 Villiers was made Master of the Horse, an exceptionally influential household position, and received the Lord Lieutenancy of Buckinghamshire, the Order of the Garter and a Viscountcy. In 1617 he became Earl of Buckingham and a Privy Councillor. To those who raised an eyebrow James declared, "I love the Earl of Buckingham more than any other men ... Christ had his John, I have my George".[2] In 1618 he added the Marquisate of Buckingham to his earldom and patched up a quarrel between James I and Prince Charles, thereby becoming indispensable to both. Later that year he became joint Lord Admiral. By 1620, when the King arranged a marriage between Buckingham and Catherine (Kate) Manners, the only daughter of the Earl of Rutland, Buckingham owned Whaddon and other properties in Buckinghamshire, lands in Yorkshire and Leicestershire (the county of his birth), a great estate in Rutland and lands in Wanstead in Essex. In 1621 he came into possession of Wallingford House in London next to St. James' Palace and purchased York House between the Thames and Charing Cross.

The two properties in London provided his political base in the capital. But he needed a country property nearer town which he could use to escape the press of suitors and for entertaining. In June 1622 Buckingham and his mother went to look at

New Hall. He was obviously taken with it and bought it in July of that year. Inigo Jones, the King's Surveyor, was ordered to alter it "according to the modern fashion" and in September 1622 Buckingham showed it off to the King and Prince Charles who spent two days there as his guests though, because building work was in progress, they limited their retinue to fifty courtiers.[3] It is also probable that New Hall still had its two great Tudor courtyards. Buckingham's ambition would not have settled for anything ordinary.

Buckingham was an inveterate spender who could also raise significant loans, as he did to purchase and modernise New Hall while turning York House into an artistic treasure trove. He would always get his loans. Potential creditors dare not offend the King's favourite. In any case Buckingham controlled so much patronage that he might do considerable favours for the families of those who helped him.

So New Hall was once again at the hub of national affairs. In 1525 it had been the centre of intrigue in planning Henry VIII's marriage to Anne Boleyn. In 1623 royal marriage was again in the air. Prince Charles needed to beget heirs to secure the Stuart dynasty. He also had the appetites of a young man and was only too aware of what James I euphemistically called "the cod piece point". A Spanish marriage might be the answer. James liked the idea. An alliance with Spain would split them from the Hapsburg Austrian Empire. This division in the Catholic bloc would ensure a favourable balance of power for England's interests in Europe and give some possible leverage over the Protestant Palatinate, where James' daughter, Elizabeth, had married the Elector, Frederick. The Palatinate had recently been invaded by the Catholic League backed by Austria, an early event in the religious conflict of the Thirty Years' War (1618-1648) that was convulsing central Europe. On a simpler level Charles had seen a picture of Maria, the Spanish Infanta, was completely taken by her and had started taking Spanish lessons.

In February 1623 Buckingham and Charles were hunting with James I at Theobalds near Cheshunt in Hertfordshire. The King left for his palace at Royston on Monday, February 17th. Buckingham and Charles gained permission from the King to go instead to New Hall for a few days on the understanding that they would join him again on the Friday, February 20th, though this appears to have been a ruse for the benefit of onlookers as the King was aware of their plans. On the Tuesday morning they put on hoods and false beards and rode off from New Hall down the Great Essex Road towards Tilbury and Spain under the aliases of Thomas and John Smith, accompanied only by Sir Richard Graham, Buckingham's Gentleman of the Horse.[4] Whose idea was it? Buckingham's general unpopularity meant that he later got the blame. But it was clear that Prince Charles was an enthusiastic proponent and Buckingham knew when to concede to a royal urge.

This episode had all the farcical flavour of the Keystone Cops. The intrepid horsemen took the Tilbury ferry to Gravesend, one of them losing a beard which fell off during the crossing. This inability to control stage props and a sovereign tip from Buckingham, over-extravagant for a man in such downmarket costume, made the ferry-men suspicious. They let the authorities know that they suspected two men were going to France to fight a duel. On the far side of Rochester the "Smiths" spotted the Imperial Ambassador on his way to London and, having little confidence in their disguises, hastily leapt over a hedge into the adjacent fields to avert discovery. They were observed by one of the English escort who sent a horseman to Canterbury urging that they should be intercepted. The messenger overtook Charles and Buckingham at Sittingbourne and the Mayor of Canterbury was duly ready to stop them when they changed horses in his city. They were allowed to proceed only when Buckingham took off his false beard and disclosed his identity, fabricating a story that he was making a secret visit to the fleet. Even at Dover they were stopped again and not allowed to continue until they had given satisfaction as to their true identity. They reached Montreuil on February 21st, the day after they were supposed to have rejoined the King at Royston.

Back in England the King, who had given his sanction, if not his blessing, to this naïve venture, hoped to give the young men a good start by holding up the news of their departure as long as possible. But he could not prevent sensational rumours spreading. Privy Councillors rode to Newmarket, where James was in residence, to ask if the rumours were true.

On March 7th, sixteen days after leaving New Hall, Buckingham and the Prince arrived in Madrid, having travelled at an average of sixty miles a day. The Spaniards were relentless in reminding Charles that his grandmother, Mary, Queen of Scots, had been a Catholic martyr. They insisted that an English marriage must be conditional on an end to recusancy laws and freedom of Catholic worship. On the other hand Spain wanted good relations with England so that they could concentrate on war with the United Provinces (modern day Netherlands). None of these conditions would be acceptable to a Puritan Parliament which believed that Spain was Britain's natural enemy, her coastal shipping a legitimate target and the Protestants of the United Provinces co-religionists.

Charles promised the suspension of the recusancy laws within three years but refused to accept the right of English Catholics to have access to the Infanta's chapel (shades of Mary Tudor's problem with Edward VI here) adding, as an aside, that if they went secretly he would take no action. Charles insisted that the improvement in the Catholic position would have to be gradual to avoid risk of civil disturbance. On the other side it was clear that Spain would not take any action over the Palatinate and that the Infanta, immersed in her religion, would never marry a Protestant. After six months of socializing and unsuccessful wooing, Buckingham and Charles returned to England.

During his absence Buckingham wrote letters to James I addressed to "Dear Dad and Gossip" (Godfather) and signed "your humble slave and dog" and James I replied to "my sweet boys and dear venturous knights". Buckingham was a royal hero and James' reward in May 1623, while his "boys" were away, was to make him the 1st Duke of Buckingham. The last commoner to have become a Duke was John Dudley, Duke of Northumberland, way back in 1551, the man who lost his head after trying to put Lady Jane Grey on the throne in 1558. Buckingham was now the most powerful occupant of New Hall since Henry VIII.

On his return to England, by boat this time from Santander, Buckingham set about beautifying New Hall's gardens. For this task he had already employed John Tradescant as gardener. Tradescant broke away from the herbal gardens of old. Size, colour and new plants were what he sought. Because he lacked all sense of smell the traditional herb garden probably meant little to him and this may have stimulated him to seek flowers that were new and colourful.[5] Tradescant had first made his name at Cobham Hall in Kent, considered one of the four great gardens in England. He next worked for Robert Cecil at Hatfield. Cecil, son of the 1st Lord Burghley who had been the 3rd Earl of Sussex's contemporary, had been forced to accept Hatfield in a swap for Theobalds which James I desperately wanted. Nor was Tradescant afraid of an adventure, sailing in 1618 with Sir Dudley Digges on the search for the north-west passage so that he could go plant hunting[6] and from 1619 to 1621 accompanying a piracy expedition against Algiers with the same quest for plants in mind.[7]

In 1623 Kate, the Duchess of Buckingham, wrote to her husband in Spain on the progress at New Hall reporting that "the walk to the house is done, and the tennis court, but the garden is not done, nor nothing to the bowling green ... my lady [Mary, Buckingham's mother] ... is about making a little river to run through the park. It will be about sixteen feet broad". In 1624 Cornelius Drebbel, an engineer, was paid for works at New Hall and in 1626 for "divers models" which he delivered there. This refers to elaborate waterworks, probably with fountains and hydraulic automata. A gift of one thousand oak trees from James I from the royal woods in Kent and five hundred oaks from Charles I, who succeeded his father in 1625, suggests that the parks were also improved.[8]

The effect Tradescant had on New Hall can be partly gauged from the diary entry of John Evelyn who visited on July 10th 1656, albeit thirty years after Tradescant left the area:

"I returned homeward, passing again through Colchester; and by the way, near the ancient town of Chelmsford, saw New Hall ... It is a fair old house, built with brick, low, being only of two storeys, as the manner then was; the gatehouse better; the court large and pretty; the staircase, of extraordinary wideness, with a piece representing Sir Francis Drake's action in the year 1580, an excellent sea-piece; the galleries are trifling; the hall is noble; the garden is a fair plot, and the whole seat well accommodated with water; but above all, I admired the fair avenue planted with stately lime trees, in four rows, for nearly a mile in length. It has three descents, which is the only fault, and may be reformed. There is another fair walk of the same at the mall and wilderness, with a tennis-court, and pleasant terrace towards the park, which was well stored with deer and ponds".[9]

The gallery was so "trifling" because of the need to enlarge the grand staircase to a width of fourteen feet[10] and by that stage only one courtyard remained, probably a result of the general decay in the property under the 2nd Duke of Buckingham and during the Civil War.

New Hall's must have been one of the very earliest lime avenues in England, for the custom of making these scented alleyways was not widely adopted until the time of Louis XIV of France later in the seventeenth century, and was then copied in England. Tradescant may have got the idea much earlier from Holland where he did a lot of plant purchasing, especially bulbs. He had bought two hundred limes for Hatfield in 1611 from Cornelius Helin in Holland where they already had the habit of planting lime avenues along their widest streets and by the sides of their canals. Other evidence that Tradescant may have planted the lime avenues comes from an entry in the Duke of Buckingham's accounts in 1623; "Paid to John Tradescant by his L'ship's order for his journey into the Low Countries, for his charges, and Trees bought for his L'ship there etc. £124 14s 0d" (over £15,000 in today's money).

John Evelyn somewhat understates the splendours of New Hall, for until the building of such great houses as Hatfield, it was one of the largest mansions in England. Part of the glories of Tradescant's gardens elsewhere were the arbours and avenues, and the woven tapestries of "knot" borders which were box hedged geometrical shapes in-planted with flowers. Embroiderers came to the gardens to copy the actual designs and transferred them to material for dress-making. It would be reasonable to assume that Tradescant's skill and Buckingham's love for the best would have ensured similar gardens at New Hall.[11]

Buckingham wanted to make New Hall another York House which he had already richly furnished with treasures of every kind − paintings by Michelangelo,

Leonardo da Vinci, Holbein, Raphael, Rubens, marble and bronze statues, figures in ivory and alabaster, tapestries, plate and furniture upholstered with Persian cloth of gold. But although New Hall gardens were finished in 1625 the estate proved to be too far from London for Buckingham to make it a real home so these bold artistic plans for the interior never materialised. With gardens in three of Buckingham's London houses to look after (the Duke had added a house in Chelsea to Wallingford and York Houses), Tradescant and his family moved to Lambeth in 1626 though he kept a property in Woodham Walter which he had acquired from Buckingham.[12]

Buckingham himself did not live much longer. He was very unpopular in the country and bore the brunt of criticism for Charles I's Catholic marriage to the French princess, Henrietta Maria, and unsuccessful foreign policy, in particular failed attacks on Cadiz and the Spanish fleet and his inability to relieve the Catholic French siege of Huguenot La Rochelle, yet another example of enmity between Catholic and Protestant working itself out in war. La Rochelle was to prove his undoing. Buckingham was personally a brave man but, as in his private life, he conceived magnificent plans with no idea how they would be financed. A hostile Parliament would not grant taxes so that the fleet sent to relieve the Protestants in La Rochelle was badly equipped. Buckingham, as the Admiral, compounded the problem by showing a poor sense of military strategy. The losses of men were huge, the humiliation complete and the sailors remained unpaid. Pilfering goods from their ships and selling them on the black market was their only source of cash.[13] Buckingham returned to England towards the end of 1627 to equip yet another relief fleet, at Portsmouth. On August 23rd 1628 he was knifed by a sailor, John Felton, in the Greyhound Inn in High Street, Portsmouth and died on the spot. His friends had been urging him for some time to wear a protective coat of mail but he had casually responded, "It needs not: there are no Roman spirits left".[14] His words showed both arrogance and courage but proved to be a fatal last misjudgement. His wife was with him when he was assassinated, pregnant with their second son Francis. His sister, wife of the 1st Lord Denbigh, whose descendants were to play a part in the history of New Hall School 312 years later, was also there and the monument she dedicated to her thirty-five year old brother can still be seen in Portsmouth Anglican Cathedral,[15] just up the street from the scene of the crime. Charles I had come to inspect his troops and was staying in the village of Southwick just three miles north so he was in immediate receipt of the news. His misery was not widely shared. As one courtier, Sir Francis Nethersole, said, "the base multitudes ... drink healths to Fenton and there are infinitely more cheerful than sad faces of better people".[16]

Within a few months the new child owner of New Hall, George, 2nd Duke of Buckingham, and his infant brother, Francis, who was born in 1629, were taken into royal care by Charles I and grew up with the royal princes. The Duchess was a

34

Catholic and considered unsuitable to bring up the boys given their close relationship with the royal family.[17] Seven years later she married Randal McDonnell, the 2nd Earl of Antrim, and lived out the rest of her life in Ireland.

George inherited huge debts from his father and added to them as a hopeless adult spendthrift and debauchee. When Parliament and King faced each other on the battlefield in 1642 he sided with the King. Yet again an owner of New Hall chose the losing side in a civil war. He was declared a traitor by Parliament after the Battle of Kingston in 1648 where his brother, Francis, was killed. Later that year he fled to the Netherlands. He returned to fight for Charles II at the Battle of Worcester in 1651 after which he again fled across the North Sea. In the meantime New Hall had been confiscated by Parliament and sold to Oliver Cromwell for five shillings (£23 today) although its yearly value was calculated at £1,340 (£201,000 in modern values). Cromwell never lived at New Hall though his wife, Elizabeth, the daughter of Sir James Bourchier of Little Stambridge in Essex, entertained her family there in April 1652. When Cromwell became Lord Protector in 1653 he exchanged New Hall for Hampton Court, which was much more convenient for London, and paid the difference. New Hall was then sold to three wealthy London citizens, names unknown, for £18,000,[18] (about £2,250,000 in modern values).

Chapter 6

The Nuns' Story

Liège 1642-1657

As the English Civil War approached the lot of English Catholics remained parlous. Their position had been undermined by the Pope's Bull of Excommunication in 1570 which legitimised the assassination of Elizabeth, Mary, Queen of Scots' treasonable dealings with Catholic foreign powers leading to her execution in 1587 and Philip II of Spain's attempt to invade England with his Armada in 1588, all of which gave credence to the idea of a Catholic international conspiracy. The attempted terrorist outrage of the Gunpowder Plotters in 1605 provided evidence of an enemy within. As always in such situations the moderate majority, who wished to be loyal to the monarch, were compromised by the fundamentalist extremism of the few.

Catholics therefore became a criminalised minority. Under Henry VIII they had been required to take the oath of supremacy. Thomas More famously would not place his King above his God. Edward VI required the licensing of all teachers by their local Anglican bishops and the teaching of the Anglican catechism and Articles of Church governance and belief. This effectively eliminated Catholic schools. Strict control over all publications through the Crown also ensured that Catholic religious literature was driven underground. Under Elizabeth I the heads of Oxford and Cambridge colleges were purged and entry to university required a religious test. In 1563 schoolmasters and "public and private teachers of children" were required to take an oath denying the authority of the Pope and the teachings of the Catholic Church. The third time of refusal would rank as treason. The rising of the Northern Earls in 1569 and the Pope's excommunication of Elizabeth in 1570 led to a sharper implementation of this law. Twenty-two illicit schoolmasters were executed for treason between 1570 and 1610 though the offences for which they were condemned, such as harbouring priests, were not directly connected with teaching.[1]

For Catholic men, the only educational alternative was to go abroad, first to Louvain in the Low Countries and later to English Colleges that were established at Douay and St. Omer in France, Valladolid and Seville in Spain and Rome. For Catholic women the way ahead had been shown early on when Elizabeth Woodford, of the Canonesses of St. Augustine, opened St. Ursula's School for girls in Louvain in 1548. An act of 1571 tried to seal the exit. No one could leave the country without licence and those who did were liable to lose their property.[2] That would have hit Catholic men more than Catholic women whose lack of legal property rights revealed an unexpected advantage.

As time passed the penal laws were enforced with greater or lesser zeal depending partly on the potential victim's social status and the urgency of the times. For example, in Essex, between 1625 and 1639, over a thousand Catholics were presented for recusancy offences but less than half were indicted[3] and, in general, Catholic aristocrats and gentry were rarely summoned before their peers in the courts for non-attendance at the local Anglican Church. In the 1620s and 1630s Catholics lived in greater hope when Charles I's French Queen, Henrietta Maria, was allowed to have her own Catholic Chapel and priests. All this merely infuriated the Puritans.

As Parliament and King came into headlong conflict in the 1640s many of the Catholic gentry sided with the King. This reinforced the Puritan view that Catholics were a sinister threat. Catholic noble households and their retainers tended to be centred on large, relatively isolated rural estates and were all connected by intermarriage. They appeared to constitute a dangerous fifth column within England. If they secured arms to defend themselves it only confirmed their opponents' worst suspicions. Church Papists i.e. those Catholics who made the statutory attendance at the Anglican Church while continuing to practise Catholicism privately at home, led frightened Protestants to assume that they were the tip of an iceberg with thousands more lurking undetected waiting to strike.

In 1642 in Colchester and south Suffolk attacks on Catholic estates began in earnest. The Rivers family at Melford Hall , who had made many homeless by enclosing land in an extended private park, and had been political allies of the loathed Duke of Buckingham, were one such vulnerable family.[4] Borley, the birthplace of Frances Cary, was just a few miles away. In the same year the Civil War began with set battles at Powicke Bridge in September and Edgehill in October.

In such violent conditions the Low Countries may have appeared to be a safer place for Catholic women. In July 1641 nineteen year old Susan Hawley presented herself at the house of the Canonesses of the Holy Sepulchre at Tongres, not far north of Liège. She had been born in Brentford, a leafy village west of London, but was probably living in the Low Countries with her parents as they sought the freedom of worship that was denied them in England.[5] Frances Cary, born in Borley on the Essex/Suffolk border, joined Susan just before Christmas. The two women wanted to found an English community in the neighbourhood and decided to do so at Liège where there was a Jesuit College whose priests could provide spiritual direction. Several of the founding nuns had relatives at the College. The Prince-Bishop of Liège, Ferdinand of Bavaria, gave his consent. That they were also given permission by the nuns at Tongres shows what strength of character and conviction Susan and Frances displayed. Normally newcomers to a convent would have not have been expected to be so forcefully independent.

On October 8th 1642 the two young English women, a Belgian lay sister and Mother Margaret of the Tongres Community left for Liège. Mother Margaret was the Mistress of Novices at Tongres and was to act as Superior to Susan and Frances until they were sufficiently experienced for one of them to take charge. The house at Tongres, newly established with only five nuns, could not really spare Mother Margaret so when the English nuns became settled at Liège, they were expected to make financial compensation.

On November 9th Frances' sister, Jane, joined them. A Liège widow lent this fledgling Community three rooms for six weeks. They used a silver bell from one of the widow's children to call them to Office. They soon hired part of a house opposite St. Hubert's Church. Four more nuns were professed there. After another two years they finally bought a large house and garden on Pierreuse Hill overlooking the town and moved in at Christmas 1644. The house had formerly been the home of another English woman, Mary Ward and her teaching order, but their desire to be rather like friars, as free-moving, unenclosed nuns, living amongst the people they served and wearing the clothes of the time, offended papal sensibilities and was doomed to failure. By contrast the Canonesses were a conventional enclosed order, albeit observing enclosure with difficulty in these temporary premises. In 1651 Mother Margaret returned to Tongres by which time the Liège Community had expanded to twenty-two nuns.

In 1652 Susan Hawley published her *Brief Relation of the Order and Institute of the English Women at Liège* which detailed the schedule of prayer, meditation, meals, work and worship for the Canonesses from rising at 4.00 a.m. to bed at 8.30 p.m.. A few lines are given about the school – "this Order admitteth Convictrices, or Pensioners, who be yet children or young gentlewomen, desirous of good breeding.

These they bring up until they be ripe enough to choose some state of life. They teach them all qualities befitting their sex, as writing, needlework, French, music ...” Practical details are not overlooked. On the inside cover Susan Hawley has written “the best and shortest way from England to Liège is by Holland and Rotterdam, thence to Bois-le-Duc, then to Maastricht, so to Liège”.

The Pierreuse Hill did not prove ideal. The Prince-Bishop built a fort nearby. There had been violence on the streets because he had taken away the right of electing the Burgomasters. Authority needed to be reasserted with military reinforcements commanding the high ground. The soldiers proved undesirable neighbours so the Prince-Bishop gave the nuns another house in downtown Liège, in the Faubourg d’Avroy, which formerly belonged to a monastic community of Coquins. These monks had been suppressed by the Pope for being too liberal, idle and prone to discord but refused to leave their premises until, eventually, they were expelled by the Prince-Bishop’s troops. The dilapidated state of their building reflected their lazy ill-temper, so the nuns stayed at the Pierreuse Hill while, from May 1655 to Easter 1656, their new Church was built, allowing them to take up residence in May 1656.

Unfortunately, displacement of the Coquins came at a price. The Prince-Bishop decided that each of the nine monks, now without a home, should be paid £23 quarterly (nearly £3,000 in modern values) by the nuns, presumably so that they would not become vagrants at a cost to the city. The nuns also agreed to keep open the hospital for the poor which the Prince-Bishops had expected of the Coquins in return for their rights of residence. This hospital was a place of hospitality rather than of medical care and had, at some undetermined recent time, replaced the redundant requirement to provide food and hospitality for pilgrims en route to the Holy Land. The former pilgrims had been restricted to a maximum three nights’ stay and this limit also applied to any paupers who now presented themselves at the nuns’ door. However, the hospital needed to be repaired and that was completed in 1657. In 1711 the nuns, probably keen to preserve their enclosure, made a fresh agreement with the Prince-Bishop commuting their obligation to one of baking twenty-seven loaves a week for the local poor.[6]

In 1656 there were sufficient nuns to enable the Community to hold its own Chapter. Mother Mary of the Conception (Susan Hawley) was chosen as the first Prioress and Mother Francis of St. Ignatius (Frances Cary) as Sub-Prioress. The nuns also bought up several small houses close to the convent to form a quadrangle to provide proper enclosure.[7]

So Liège was now the Community’s home. At first glance it was a good choice. The Prince-Bishopric of Liège was an independent Catholic principality about 3,650 square miles in size (about the size of Devon and Cornwall) bordered by the Catholic Spanish Netherlands to the west (which became the Austrian Netherlands in 1713), the Protestant United Provinces to the north (who secured their freedom from Spanish rule in 1648), France to the south and the hundreds of medium and pocket sized German kingdoms, electorates, bishoprics and city states to the east that were part of the Holy Roman Empire. The Empire was an inoffensive anachronism by the seventeenth century. Its Emperor was customarily the Hapsburg ruler of Austria who did not govern directly over this largely German patchwork but saw them as being within his sphere of diplomatic influence. Although the Prince-Bishopric of Liège was part of the Empire its effects were benign. When religious splits resulted in the bloody Thirty Years' War, the Principality was far to the west out of harm's way and managed to stay neutral. Liège itself was also a wealthy city with an advanced coal mining industry, metal and glass works and gun factories. The position of the city on the River Meuse provided good water communications via the United Provinces (where it was re-named the River Maas) to the Rhine delta and across the North Sea to England. The Jesuits were already in Liège and the local population was supportive. In the new convent there was scarcely a gallery or window that did not display the arms of a local donor – the families of Plenevaux, Vanbuel (both of whom provided daughters amongst the first nuns in the Community) and Randach were particularly prominent.

However Liège was also dangerously close to France to the south. The growth of French military power under Louis XIV (1642-1715) led to a series of wars in the late seventeenth and early eighteenth centuries between France and England with the Low Countries as a frequent battleground, so that the convent and its school were constantly at the mercy of events beyond their control. Eventually this French menace was to lead to their forced migration to England.

MAP 3:
The Low Countries in 1648 including the migration route of 1794

Chapter 7

Nuns' Business

Liège 1642-1670

"In this book is begun to be written in English the counts of all the Reparations of this House and the workmens' wages etc as it shall appear by figures". So begins this account book which runs from 1642 to 1770.[1]

The economic necessities of making ends meet necessarily kept religious orders attached at arm's length to the outside world. The enclosed spiritual life of a convent may have required isolation, obedient dedication to prayer and the forms of worship laid down in its papal approved constitutions, yet farms still had to be run and buildings maintained, gardens needed tending to supply vegetables, fruits and medicinal herbs, and communal or individual efforts needed to be devoted to other money-making schemes such as needlework, lace, spices and medicines.[2] At Liège the Procuratrix was the main business link with the secular world and was responsible to the Community for the proper use of its financial resources. The first Procuratrix, Ann Barbara Plenevaux, was well-chosen. She was the daughter of the Burgomaster of Liège,[3] whose mercantile contacts must have been a great help to the convent.

Whatever the rigours of Prioress Susan Hawley's 1652 schedule that governed the nuns' spiritual lives, achieving a sufficient form of income was a major challenge. There was a convent to be built, a school to be run and a whole community of nuns, pupils, servants and visitors to be sustained. There was also the costly business of paying off the Coquins. To meet all these ends the nuns relied on nine sources of income. The three largest were the dowries given by their families, benefactions from well-wishers and rents from lands with which supporters had endowed them. Then came income from pensions paid for the keep and expenses of the children at the school or novice nuns in training, bed and board paid by visitors or those on long-stay residence, profits from a variety of in-house businesses, profits from converting sterling via Antwerp florins in the Spanish Netherlands into King's florins in Liège, and money given for saying prayers or masses for the departed. Finally small occasional injections of income came from the sale of unwanted clothes, furniture or other convent possessions that had served their purpose. Towards the middle of the eighteenth century these sources would be supplemented by a tenth income stream, investments.

Early entries in Susan Hawley's own hand show the settling of accounts with Tongres for the services of Mother Margaret. Even for nuns time can mean money. However, once the convent was established, the Prioress at Tongres reciprocated with a generous gift of 400 florins, equivalent to £60 then or £7,800 today.

For financial stability the immediate receipt of nuns' dowries was crucial. These were large lump sums paid up front by their families in a contractual arrangement similar to that of a marriage dowry, and backed up by appropriate legal documents. In October 1642 the convent would have been pleased that Mr Chichester of Arlington in Devon not only sent 3,000 florins (£450 or £58,600 today) as a dowry for his daughter Elizabeth, the first choir nun novice in Liège, but also gave 1,666 florins (£250 then, £37,500 today) to the Chapel on the Pierreuse Hill. The size of this dowry was not untypical.

It was also the custom in those early days to attribute the dowry income to specific projects. So Susan Hawley was at pains to establish that from 1642 to 1650 none of the dowries were applied to the Community's general running expenses, except in 1649 for a sum of 770 florins (£115 then, £10,000 today) when corn was very expensive and they had to bake bread both for the convent and the hospital. The implication is that all the rest was applied as capital expenditure to setting up costs.

From 1651, while they were still on the Pierreuse Hill, the nuns' accounts took a more regular form with annual lists of pensions paid by parents for their children or visiting adults on bed and board separated out as a distinct income source. From this we can work out that in 1651 there were eight children at the school. One of them was the daughter of a local timber merchant who was able to pay 40% of school fees in kind with timber given to the nuns for building purposes. His daughter's four months at the school cost him 50 florins in cash and wood (£7.50 then, £770 today).

Profits from the "garden and other such like things" were also, from 1651, kept in separate accounts. Taking 1652 as an example, the garden provided over 51 florins in income (£7.65 then, £855 today) from health flowers, salad crops, herbs and general garden produce. The nuns also kept farm animals for meat and milk. Presumably they also bred them, for the sale of a cow fetched 25 florins (£3.75 then, £420 today) and a sheep 1½ florins (22p then, £25 today). The sale of clothes, probably secular clothes that were no longer needed by the nuns or their visitors, was an irregular source of income and, in that year, realised about 84 florins (£12.60 then, £1,400 today). Rents were a very significant source of income and brought in a handsome 1,146 florins (£172 then, £19,250 today). This large sum is not explained at this stage but six years later there is a reference to "eight life rents of Brussels paid by the States" which suggests that someone had given land in Brussels, the capital of the Spanish Netherlands, from which rent income provided pensions for some of the nuns, in this case possibly lay sisters who were mostly local women. Some of them may not have been as wealthy as the Catholic English gentry and aristocrats and this may have been a substitute for a one-off dowry.

By 1656 the nuns had made the transition to the Faubourg d'Avroy and were branching out into new businesses. An immediate heavy cost was the upfront capital required to build the church and hospital. In 1655-1656 the buildings costs were 14,461 florins (£2,170 then, nearly £300,000 today). Extra income urgently needed to be generated and so, in the same year, the nuns made and sold 129 pairs of socks and eighteen caps. Now living in the town centre, the nuns were nearer the Jesuit fathers and this may explain the first entry for making and washing the priests' clothes and for pleating their surplices, bringing in 57 florins (£8.55 then, £1,170 today). Brewing and selling yeast was also a small business and realised nearly 14 florins (£2.10 then, £287 today).

By 1659 profits from the "garden and other like things" had more than doubled to over 530 florins (£79.50 then, £8,240 today). This again included work on the Jesuit Fathers' surplices where income had also more than doubled, to 140 florins (£21 then, £2,175 today). The sale of milk brought in nearly the same amount, so clearly the dairy was working well. Sales of hops, beer and other brewing profits brought in 57 florins (£8.55 then, £885 today) and the sale of bran, wheat, rye, corn and seeds 51 florins (£7.65, then, nearly £800 today). Selling surplus goods was also quite profitable. Silverware brought in over 21 florins (£3.15 then, £325 today) and a red petticoat 30 florins (£4.50 then, £470 today). These may well have been gifts from wealthy patrons as there is evidence elsewhere in the accounts of gifts in kind, for example from the ever generous Mr Chichester, whose silver candlesticks brought in 181 florins (£27.15 then, £2,600 today). Medical skills could also bring in a little cash. Sister Frances Nandyke, one of the lay sisters, treated a local who made a small payment equivalent to a couple of pence, just over £2 in modern values.

In 1660 loans were taken out. They were all raised locally – from the Celestines who were another religious order in Liège, a widow called Mrs Stephanie, and Mr Godfroid, a Liège lawyer – and amounted to 5,500 florins (£825 then, £87,500 today).

We assume these loans were for buildings and possibly the buying up of neighbouring properties in the Faubourg d'Avroy. Mr Wascart, another local lawyer, gave 2,000 florins (£300 then, £31,800 today) so that the nuns could commute one of the Coquins' pensions to a lump sum one-off payment. With interest varying between 4% and 6% the nuns would have had very large annual debt charges. In 1660 the accounts say they paid 350 florins in interest (£53 then, £5,600 today) so they would have been grateful for a "loan in friendship" from Mr Herlan, which probably means that it was interest free.

It may have been the large interest payments that led the nuns to tap the possibilities of making profits on the exchange of money paid by their English patrons as it was changed first of all into Antwerp florins and then Liège florins. In 1660 a £200 payment (£21,200 today) on behalf of Sister Elizabeth (probably Chichester) gained nearly 257 florins profit through the exchanges (£38.55 then, £4,100 today). This is the first such mention of this new venture. One can only assume that the practice before had been for the donor to effect the exchange and keep the extra for himself.

Moving on to 1661 we find that the drinks business was doing well. Drying and making malt are two new entries in the accounts and some red wine was sold for 78 florins (£11.70 then, £1,300 today). Business with the Jesuit Fathers was becoming reciprocal. The priests were charging for the cost of letters they were writing for the nuns, so perhaps they were acting as legal and business advisers as well as spiritual pastors. This may have been necessary if the nuns' concept of enclosure was to keep business contacts with outsiders to a minimum.

By 1662 a pattern has definitely emerged. Dowries, pensions, profits from sterling exchanges, garden produce, selling animals, washing for the Jesuit fathers and pleating their surplices, brewing and milk sales have become the staple income sources. Land rents too must be added to this list. They evened out annually in the 1660s at between 2,100 florins (£315 then, £30,000 today) and 2,500 florins (£375 then, £35,400 today). But of all sources of income the greatest advance was in the money market where profits doubled over the space of a few years.

By 1665 two rather contrasting sources of regular income begin to make a significant impact in the accounts, pensions paid by adult guests and kitchen fat sales. There had always been adult guests but not in the numbers that were now appearing. Perhaps it had taken time to develop their quarters. Some of them were charged 400 florins p.a. (£60 then, £6,600 today) so this was a lucrative business. Occasionally guests were related to pupils but some women, possibly widows, were quite long-term boarders, suggesting that they chose to spend significant periods within the convent on a personal religious retreat. Kitchen fat sales brought in 61 florins (£9.15 then,

£1,000 today). For poorer people a piece of tallow dipped in kitchen fat made a reasonable candle. This was to become a permanent and growing money spinner.

In 1670 saying masses for the dead assumed greater financial significance. The Book of Benefactors records two gifts aggregating 40 florins (£6 then, £755 today) from Mary the Washerwoman to "have her Service made when she die with a dirge, a high mass and a Communion by all the Community". Not a wealthy woman, she may well have washed for the Community and the Jesuits and was giving this huge amount to speed her soul through Purgatory to Heaven.

Throughout these early decades the nuns received gifts and legacies that were exceptionally important in permitting major capital expenditure to be undertaken. The accounting process is somewhat complicated. The accounts book lists "charities to the Community" as generic sums, only occasionally giving details of the source. The separate Book of Benefactors[4] deals with larger donations and is explicit about donors, amounts and projects on which the money was to be spent, with nearly all gifts supporting a major building and furnishing programme as the secular property acquired in Liège was converted to religious use. The two are probably complementary records, the "charities to the Community" recording more casual donations, maybe from people of less social consequence, and possibly used for general living costs, the Book of Benefactors recording donors' names, the majority high-born, many related to members of the Community, whose help may have been directly solicited. In the 1660s "charities to the Community" brought in 6,567 florins (£985 then, £111,350 today) of which almost a quarter came in 1669 with a legacy of 1,333 florins (£200 then, £25,000 today) from William Cary (a brother of co-foundress Frances Cary), a priest who died in Spain. The accounts book says that the legacy was used for building the convent and the cloisters. The Benefactors' Book, which starts in 1662, and its predecessor volume, Receptions made by Charities[5], show that in the 1660s benefactors gave 7,721 florins (£1,158 then, £131,000 today). Adding the two together all gifts brought in £242,350 in modern values. Without them the nuns would have had difficulty in building a convent from scratch.

Building progress can be traced in the Benefactors' Book. The Church was already built and in use by 1656 but it would need to be beautified and land bought to extend the convent and provide enclosed cloisters. These needs may have been financed by the loans raised in 1660. From 1660 to 1662 the benefactions are unspecific, merely being listed as "an item" though Mr Macraell was grateful that his daughter had learned the lute and gave a large sum worth about £750 in today's money. In 1663 the benefactions mostly went towards the ceiling of the Church and in 1664 to the ceiling and windows while the legacy from William Cary enabled a start to be made on building the convent. In 1665 the emphasis was on Church hangings, carpets, pictures and communion cloths plus some coats of arms for the cloisters which, therefore, must have been well under way. In 1666 windows for the cloisters predominated and a very expensive silver lamp, costing about £3,000 in today's money, was given by the Plenevaux family, whose daughter was one of the nuns. But there is a clear distinction between the mighty and the humble. The glazier, tiler and butcher each gave a window in the "lavatory" (probably the laundry rather than the toilet), but the amount was unspecified. In 1667 and 1668 the emphasis turned to the nuns' new chambers and dormitories with a very large gift in 1668 of £3,600 in today's money from a father for prayers for his son. In 1669 money was given for the organ and viols.

So by 1670, after fifteen years' hard work, building the convent seemed to be complete.

Chapter 8

Moncks at New Hall

New Hall 1660-1713

While the nuns were establishing themselves in their new convent in Liège, New Hall came into the hands of its last great owner, General George Monck.

As a young soldier the Devonian Monck had fought alongside the 1st Duke of Buckingham and John Tradescant in the ill-fated La Rochelle expedition of 1627. From 1627 to 1638 he fought under Robert Sidney, 2nd Earl of Leicester for William of Orange and the Protestant cause of the United Provinces against the Spanish in the Netherlands. In 1639 he followed Leicester to fight for the King in Ireland. He was imprisoned because he refused to take an oath of allegiance to Charles I but only because his troops had not been paid. He reckoned that loyalty should work both ways. Charles I seemed to admire this principled stance and put him back in command but in 1644 Monck was taken prisoner by Parliament at Nantwich. By this time he felt that Charles I had strained the loyalty of reasonable men too far and decided to fight for Parliament instead.

Cromwell took Monck to the north of England to raise an army and hoped to use his skills in siege warfare that he had perfected earlier in the United Provinces. Monck fought in Scotland and was then appointed General-at-Sea because of his knowledge of artillery (the same cannon were used on sea as on land). In a conflict with the Dutch in 1652 he destroyed twenty enemy ships off Southwold. He then returned to achieve further military success in Scotland.

On Oliver Cromwell's death in 1658 it soon became apparent to Monck that Richard Cromwell was an inadequate substitute. He was becoming increasingly subject to extreme Puritan advisers and the English army was losing its discipline as religious factionalism spread. Monck publicly maintained a pro-Parliament stance but was rapidly coming to the view that the country needed stability and was only likely to get it from the restoration of the monarchy. Charles Stuart made secret contacts and offered Monck £100,000 p.a for life (an incredible £10,300,000 in modern values) for his military support.

The Scottish army's personal loyalty to Monck made him the essential power-broker in an increasingly anarchic situation. He knew that there must be a royal restoration but he had to play a canny game to achieve it. He marched on London supposedly to back the authority of Parliament against the fractious English Army. He quietly purged his own army of any possible opposition ringleaders and secured free elections for a new Parliament, knowing that it would probably produce a significant Royalist element. The army went along with Monck as he promised that the new Parliament would pay their arrears. At this point, with his troops in the capital, Monck went public and declared for the King.

On May 25th 1660 Monck knelt before Charles II at Dover. He was immediately knighted and received the Order of the Garter. Six weeks later he was created 1st Duke of Albemarle, Privy Councillor and Lord-Lieutenant of Ireland. There is no doubt that, although there would have been a restoration of the monarchy, Monck used his military position to ensure that it was bloodless.

Monck was now a wealthy man. The Lord-Lieutenancy of Ireland, a private pension paid by a grateful Parliament, income from lands he owned in Scotland and Ireland and his other manors in England, all brought in about £20,000 p.a. (over £2,100,000 in modern values). He was therefore able to buy New Hall and its estate which was not too far from Theobalds, formerly beloved by Robert Cecil and James I, which had also been included in his package of rewards. His London base was The Cockpit in Whitehall. His loyalty to the new regime was amply demonstrated in 1661 with a magnificent display of fireworks at New Hall to celebrate the marriage of Charles II and Catherine of Braganza. Charles II was subsequently a fairly frequent visitor and, it is alleged, Nell Gwynne performed in *The Merry Wives of Windsor* in the Great Hall (now the Chapel).[1] In 1662 Thomas Baskerville passed New Hall and described "a stately walk on riding to the house, set on both sides in exact order double rows of limes and hornbeam trees set at such distance that at the end of this flourishing walk you may discover the front of the Duke's magnificent palace". [2]

It may have been magnificent but Monck's tastes were modest. His one amusement was breeding horses. His frugality and lack of conversation made him a poor host in the eyes of London bon viveurs like Samuel Pepys. When at New Hall he never drank to excess and was tough with visiting officers who became drunk. With a life-time of hard military experience behind him, he could manage with one good meal a day and four hours sleep. He never swore, and was a devout Protestant but did not like religious enthusiasm in others which, in his experience, generally led to extremism. Anne Monck, his wife, may have been disappointed with New Hall as in 1659 Hampton Court seemed to be on offer. For a short while she had actually lived in St. James' Palace and had made herself unpopular by her sycophancy to royalty. 3

Monck saw further military service at sea in the wars against the Dutch in the mid 1660s. Then in 1667 his health broke down. He had to leave London and spend all his time at New Hall. He suffered from water retention and shortage of breath, which points to heart trouble. He occupied himself by building a stone wall round New Hall and by entertaining visitors including the diarist John Evelyn (see Chapter 5) who was commissioner for sick and wounded seamen and had therefore come to know his former General-at-Sea quite well.[4]

In the summer of 1669 Monck received a visit from Cosmo III, Grand Duke of Tuscany, who recorded his impressions. Having stopped with the 6th Lord Petre at Thorndon, where "dinner was served with as much elegance and skill as is usually met with at tables of English noblemen, who do not in general keep French cooks", he moved to Chelmsford, stopping overnight at the Black Boy Inn. The next day:

> "... the son of General Monck came to Chelmsford from his villa to pay his respects to his Highness in the name of the Duke, his father, and to give him an invitation. The General was prevented by his illness from doing it in person ... Travelling the greatest part of the way through woods and meadows [the Grand Duke] descended into a valley which serves as a sort of receptacle to the streams of water that flow from the surrounding hills, forming a lake, that approaches nearly to New Hall. His Highness was received by General Monck in his dressing gown, he being obliged by his complaint, which was a confirmed dropsy, to keep to the house and to return from court to the quiet of the country. His Highness was ushered by the General, as well as his infirmity would permit, into the room where refreshments were prepared which had, however, more the appearance of a parsimonious collation than of a handsome dinner. Afterwards His Highness went to see the grounds which are surrounded by a wall, and extended round the whole of the large mansion, being regularly divided into spacious walks, parterres and hedgerows of fruit trees, and having surveyed the whole of the premises, returned to the house where the carriage was ready for his departure ...
>
> General Monck, Earl of Albemarle ... is of the middle size, of a stout and square-built make, of a complexion partly sanguine and partly phlegmatic, as indeed is generally the case with the English; his face is

fair, but somewhat wrinkled from age, he being upward of sixty years old; his hair is grey and his features not particularly fine or noble ... Monck is married to a lady of low origin ... Her former situation shows itself in her meanness and her dress, she being in no way remarkable for elegance and gentility. Her son, however, makes up for his mother's deficiency.

New Hall is a spacious and magnificent edifice, not only equalling, but surpassing in extent and bearing, almost every other in the kingdom ... The tout ensemble of the structure is of a high character and, although the architecture is not in that perfect style which is observable in modern buildings, yet it is by no means destitute of grandeur, owing to the size and elegance of the apartments, more especially the principal ones. The splendour of this royal habitation is augmented by several sheets of water and delightful gardens which the General has of late greatly improved, and surrounded the whole with a wall ... He lives in a style equal to that of other noblemen in the kingdom ..."[5]

Poor Lady Anne Monck! She was a milliner's daughter who had formerly looked after the linen of the well-to-do prisoners in the Tower where she had met her future husband back in the 1640s.[6] She failed to cut the mustard with those who considered themselves born to gentility and greatness. But Monck was content with her and unfailingly loyal.

Monck ended his days in The Cockpit in London but not before he had arranged the marriage of his seventeen year old son, Christopher, with the fifteen year old Elizabeth Cavendish. Monck died on January 1st 1670. His widow Anne did not live to see his State Funeral, dying on January 29th. She had lost all taste for living when he went.

Christopher became the 2nd Duke of Albemarle and entered into the profligate spirit of Charles II's court, gambling, giving parties and patronising plays. In 1686 he entertained James II at New Hall where he and the King killed stags together. In that same year he was made Governor of Jamaica where a tropical disease killed him at the age of thirty-five. His wife went insane and lived to be eighty. She died in 1734 having earlier, in 1713, sold the reversion of New Hall to Benjamin Hoare, youngest son of Sir Richard Hoare, a rich banker of Fleet Street and Lord Mayor of London. She carried on living at New Hall and, by the time he acquired it, it had nearly gone to ruin.

Henry VIII in the 1530s when he was still youthful and enamoured of Anne Boleyn. It is very much the Henry whose face would have been familiar at New Hall.

Princess Mary in 1544, the year she was restored to the royal succession. Of her many portraits it gets closest to capturing the young woman for whom New Hall had been home.

Thomas Radcliffe, 3rd Earl of Sussex, dressed as a Knight of the Garter, towards the end of his career when he lived at New Hall and remodelled the north wing, now the frontage of the modern school, with its glorious Elizabethan bays.

George Villiers, 1st Duke of Buckingham with his wife Kate Manners, eldest child Mary and heir George who became 2nd Duke and lost New Hall to Parliament in the Civil War. The picture was painted in 1628. Within a few months Buckingham was assassinated.

Courtesy of the Museum of London

Courtesy of the National maritime Museum

Oliver Cromwell in 1653, the year he sold New Hall.
He told the portraitist to paint a true likeness 'warts
and everything, otherwise I will never pay a farthing
for it." He always drove hard bargains, having
bought New Hall for only five shillings.

George Monck in 1665 or 1666, just before his
sudden decline in health and retirement to New Hall.
He wears the Ribbon of the Garter, one of the many
decorations and rewards he received for engineering
the restoration of Charles II.

Courtesy of Hoare's Bank

Benjamin Hoare inherited a dilapidated New Hall from the aged and insane daughter-in-law of George Monck,
stripped it of its best possessions to furnish his newly built Boreham House and sold New Hall to John Olmius.

Photograph by Annabel Brown

Stone plaque of Henry VIII's arms in Chapel

East window of St. Margaret's Westminster once adorned the royal Chapel at New Hall. It commemmorates the marriage of Prince Henry (bottom left) and Catherine of Aragon (bottom right).

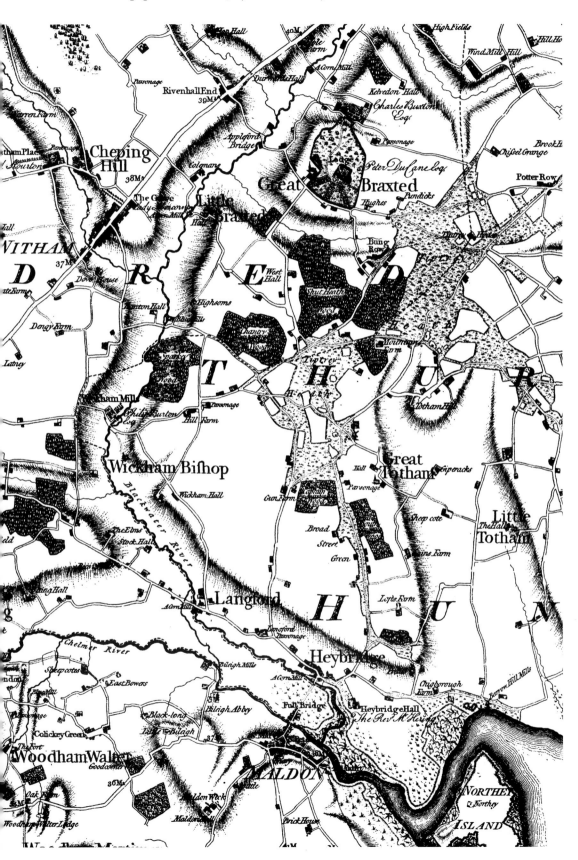

1777 Chapman André map of New Hall and its surrounding area, showing Boreham House, then belonging to Richard Hoare, to furnish which Benjamin Hoare cannibalised New Hall in 1737

A plan of the house dating from
the early eighteenth century,
slightly reduced in extent from
Henry VIII's time.

A – Great Hall (now the Chapel
     and Refectory)
B – Great Kitchen
C – great stair
D – tennis court
E – north range rebuilt by Sussex

Courtesy of Simon Thurley

Chapter 9

War and Peace

Liège 1670-1712

Susan Hawley was the Canonesses' first Prioress until her resignation in 1698 through ill-health although she continued to serve the Community until her death in 1706, sixty-four years after she first set foot in Liège. She was replaced as Prioress by Mother Marina Dolman of whom very little is known.[1]

Susan Hawley was not only a distinguished spiritual leader but also a generous woman in financial terms. The Book of Benefactors[2] shows that, between 1662, when it starts, and 1706 she personally gave nearly 10% of the total value of gifts with the rest of the Community collectively giving about 11%. So, although the nuns, many of them from genteel backgrounds, were, until 1770, allowed to retain comfortable sums from their pensions, they did not necessarily keep them for excessive personal use. £10 p.a. (about £1,300 today) was not uncommon "pocket money" required by a nun's family to be kept aside for her. In forty-four years between 1662 and 1706 the nuns gave about 7,000 florins (£1,050 then, £155,000 today) of their own personal money to the convent.

The benefactions were by and large for the sorts of purposes one might expect – one-off gifts and legacies to beautify the buildings and for Masses to be said for the departed now or in the future. In 1689 the Prioress and her Chapter laid down rules as to what benefactors should receive for their money by way of masses. Those who left £20 (£2,750 in today's money) received a plainsong mass sung and an office of the dead with three lessons said in the Choir. Additionally all the nuns would communicate for them and everyone in the Community would hear five Masses and say five pairs of beads. £10 would secure half of this package (although the arithmetic does not quite work out in whole numbers) and a said Mass in place of a sung Mass. At one end of the scale, £5 and £1 gifts, and at the other £30 or £40 gifts, would receive the appropriate fractions or multiples of the £20 package. It sounds somewhat calculating but logic required that all was seen to be fair and, following the parable of the widow's mite, God would judge according to the degree of sacrifice not on the raw amount.

In 1691 a supportive priest, Canon Hennin, had a more down-to-earth aim. He gave a large quantity of wheat from which he required a major portion to be added to the brewing of beer to make it better. Presumably he sought to make it more commercially attractive in the market-place as well as, perhaps, more tasty to his own palate.

Three gifts were very significant in amount and provenance. In 1673 Louis XIV of France gave 1,442 florins (£214 then, £24,400 today) which the nuns used to pay off debts, particularly money owed to the Brothers Coquin. In 1679 Pope Innocent XI gave 846 florins (£127 then, £16,250 today) and in 1681 800 florins (£120 then, £15,100 today). As the King and Pope were at loggerheads over Louis' determination to create a Gallican church in France where he controlled appointments, there may be an element of neither being seen to be outdone by the other, to the nuns' financial advantage.

However, Louis XIV's generosity to the Canonesses was soon cancelled out by the disastrous effects of his wars of expansion on the economy of the Low Countries. In 1689 the French army invaded the Palatinate in southern Germany and a Grand Alliance, including England, was formed to force him back across the Rhine into France. This was a war of attrition with few set piece battles but several exhausting sieges which mostly occurred in the Low Countries – Walcourt 1689, Fleurus 1690, Mons 1691, Namur 1692 and 1695 and Charleroi 1693, all in or close to the Meuse valley not far to the west of the Canonesses. Famine became endemic for those who could not afford the sky-high corn prices as agricultural production was devastated by besieging armies which either lived off the land or bought up most of the available produce. In 1691 Margaret Goffin, a servant for twenty-three years, left the convent 80 florins (£12 then, £1,680 today) in her will and one of the nuns gave 35 florins (£5.25 then, £690 today). In both cases the money was earmarked by the donors to buy corn. In 1694 and 1695 the nuns' records show that "the House is wholly unprovided with corn and other provisions ..."[3] In 1697 "Mr Fetizon gave us in Charity by reason of our being impoverished by the wars, 158 florins" (£23.70 then, £2,370 today). He sent another 166 florins in 1698 (£24.90 then, £2,490 today). Similarly Susan Hawley gave the Community two cows in 1697 valued expensively at 50 florins (£7.50 then, £750 today) and, at about the same time, the Community received another cow as a gift valued at a vast 72 florins (£10.80 then, £1,080 today).

In 1700 we see the last of the brewery. It does not appear again in the accounts. Was it too a victim of war? Or had Canon Hennin been right about the quality of the product so that the business became untenable?

As if war were not a sufficient problem harsh winters also made life difficult. One nun records that "in the year of Our Lord 1687 the 24th of November begun a frost which never ceased until the 12th week after but only 2 days, and it began to thaw upon the 14th day of February and it was so terrible hard frost that people fell short of their provisions offering. The rivers were so frozen this time that the carters brought coals in carts ... [The ice] splitted many ships and carried away a flying bridge ... and some horses upon the riverside. It was said such a long sharp frost had not been since the memory of man."[4]

There was an interlude of four years' strained peace from 1698 and then in 1702 another eleven years of war started with armies trudging and fighting across the Low Countries in or near Liège. The childless Spanish King, Charles II, had died and bequeathed his throne and territories to Louis XIV's grandson. A European coalition formed to prevent this unwanted aggrandisement of France which had already demonstrated its over-acquisitive tendencies. The War of the Spanish Succession resulted though the major battles were in northern Europe, not Spain. Liège itself was besieged in 1702 and Tongres in 1703 with the former occupied by the forces of John Churchill, the 1st Duke of Marlborough. There were battles at Huy, the next town west on the Meuse and the huge Battle of Ramillies in 1706 just twenty miles west of Liège. Tongres and Mons were scenes of further sieges in 1709.

With all this turbulence benefactions dipped alarmingly. In 1712 at the end of the war's ravages the convent's income from gifts was less than half the level of the 1670s.

Table 1:
Income from benefactions 1670-1712

Years	Florins	Sterling	Modern equivalent	Modern equivalent averaged per year
1670-79	8,007	£1,213	£149,500	£14,950
1680-89	5,047	£757	£100,500	£10,050
1690-99	4,539	£681	£78,000	£7,800
1700-12	3,887	£583	£75,850	£5,835

The school also suffered although, it has to be said, it seemed never to have been more than a marginal activity of the convent. As there are no separate lists of pupils their identity has to be sorted out from the accounts which are kept in a rather confusing way.[5] Although there is a Book of Pensioners and Boarders, school children are mixed up with other paying guests, novices and nuns. With some care, the school pupils are reasonably identifiable as "little", "children of ..." or "daughters of ..." whereas other categories have more adult titles.

In 1651 we have already seen that there were eight children in the school. Subsequently it struggled to approach even that level. In 1655 there were five. By 1658 the school seems to have reduced to two, and by 1659 to three. In 1660 there were five pupils each paying 225 florins p.a. (£33.75 then,£3,580 today), in 1663 two, but then there appear to be no more pupils until 1670 when there are two sisters, at £20 p.a. each (£2,150 in modern values), a much smaller school fee than ten years' previously. These two stay until 1673 when they are joined by another pair of sisters to make four. The number rises to five in 1676 and appears to sink to one in 1677. There may have been none at all in 1678. There is no further evidence of a child in the school until the war with the French temporarily ceases in 1698 when five or six children came to the school.

The numbers take less of a dip during the War of Spanish Succession. There are possibly two pupils from 1700 to 1705, in 1706 four, in 1707 five, between two and seven in 1708 (the ages and status of those paying fees are not clear), eight in 1709, seven in 1710, one in 1711 and four in 1712. In 1706 Lady Tyrconnell gave 40 florins (£6 then, £885 today) towards "fitting up the school" but that would have been for basic facilities not expansion through pressure of numbers.

The 1899 *History of the New Hall Community* says that "during all this time the school was very small, seldom numbering more than six or seven children"[6], but this is, if anything, an overstatement. For about twenty-five years there were no pupils at all.

Chapter 10

Lords and Ladies

Liège 1713-1777

In the period 1713-1777 the Book of Benefactors[1] shows that 94% of the convent's income from benefactions came from English connections, thirteen English aristocrats giving 46%, fifty other English donors 35% and the nuns, who were predominantly English, 13% from their private allowances. The rest came from eleven local Liège donors and four priests. This is in contrast to the fifty years up to 1712 when only 68% of the income from benefactions was of English origin, twenty of the English aristocracy giving 26%, thirty-six other English donors of lesser birth 21% and the nuns 21%. Of the rest Pope Innocent XI, four other religious orders and six priests gave 18%, forty-nine small local Liège donors 10% and Louis XIV of France 4%. So from 1713 the convent was becoming almost exclusively an English affair within which the contributions of the English Catholic aristocracy were very significant. Three donors stand out, Lady Goring in the period up to 1737 and, from 1741 to 1777, Charles, 15th Lord Stourton , his wife, the former Lady Petre, and William, 16th Lord Stourton.

Lady Goring was the wife of Sir William Goring, the 3rd Baronet of Burton in Sussex who lived at Lancing House.[2] He had visited the school in 1698 and 1699.[3] At about the same time there were two Plowden girls at the school, perhaps his relatives by marriage, for a genealogical search[4] shows that Lady Goring was born as Dorothy Plowden of the Shropshire Plowdens, a staunch Catholic family who provided ten Jesuit priests in their time.[5] Sir William died in 1724, the very year that Lady Goring took up residence at Liège. Amongst the pupils she sponsored was a Dorothy (or Dolly) Plowden. An Elizabeth Plowden was also professed as a nun in 1748.[6]

After Sir William's death Lady Goring was a wealthy women with a jointure of £1,000 p.a. (over £130,000 in today's money). She gave very generously to the Canonesses, the Jesuits in Liège and the poor, "scarcely allowing herself the necessaries of life". [7] Between 1724 and 1737 she donated 8,888 florins to the convent (£1,333 then, £176,000 in modern values).[8] Her gifts over thirteen years accounted for nearly 40% of the total given to the convent in the quarter century between the end of the war in 1713 and January 8th 1737 when she died. She was also a source of revenue to the convent in other ways. From the Boarders' Accounts we can see that she lived at the convent with her servants from 1724 until her death paying 13,435 florins rent in the process (£2,025 then, £267,000 today). In addition she sponsored five pupils at a personal cost of 5,609 florins (£841 then, £111,000 today).[9] So in total she enriched the convent by £554,000 in modern values including the repair of the school in 1726 and of the old house that had been damaged by a fire in 1736. In this same period the convent businesses made only about one tenth of the amount raised by benefactions. This does not so much belittle the importance of the businesses as emphasise the crucial significance of the benefactors.

The Stourtons carried on where Lady Goring left off. Charles, 15th Lord Stourton, had married Catherine Petre, whose first husband, the 7th Lord Petre, had died when she was expecting their first child. It was not until the boy had reached his majority that she contracted the marriage to Stourton. As the only surviving child of the Walmesleys of Lancashire, Catherine had always been exceptionally wealthy with a fortune of £50,000 (about £6,000,000 in today's money) and an annual income of £5,000 (about £600,000 today), irrespective of the Stourton money.[10] She gave generously to convents in Europe, including the Canonesses at Liège. Charles Stourton died in 1753 and Catherine made her last gift, for Masses for his soul, in 1755 by which time her total gifts amounted to £770 (£97,350 in modern terms).[11] She lived for another thirty years and turned her charitable work elsewhere during that time.

Charles and Catherine did not have any of their own children so the title passed to Charles' brother, William, 16th Lord Stourton who was married to Winifred Howard, thus continuing his brother's strategy of making an alliance with a major influential English Catholic family. William stayed at the convent for lengthy periods starting in 1763 prior to the entry to the school of his daughters Catherine and Charlotte who were professed as nuns in 1767 and 1768 respectively. Over eleven years he and his servants stayed annually at the convent, aggregating in total three and half years. For three consecutive winters, from 1767 to 1769, he kept the convent warm with gifts of coal and he twice gave barrels of salt fish. He provided water cisterns and pipes which may have meant less dependence on wells and would certainly have eased the task of carrying water for servants and lay sisters. He financed a new school building in 1771-1772, possibly because he saw the school's shortcomings while his daughters were being educated. For a short time he sponsored four nuns in addition to his own daughters. In total he spent 12,906 florins (£1,936 then, £202,000 today) paying for pupils and nuns, in addition to his gifts which totalled £1,975 (£215,410 in today's money). If one totals the contributions made by Catherine Stourton, William Stourton, and his sisters, Mother Angela Stourton, who was professed in 1726 and gave £42 (£4,540 today), and Mrs Jane Kemp,[12] who, on her death, left all her money to the convent (£2,280 then, £183,000 today), the Stourton connection provided well over half the convent's gifts in the thirty years up to 1777 at a modern value of just over £700,000

The Accounts Book shows that the convent's business side had also picked up in the 1760s and 1770s, with an average income of about £10,000 p.a. in modern values of which two-thirds or more came from profits on money exchange, with the bulk of the rest from kitchen fat sales. In other word the convent seemed to have rationalised its business to concentrate on those few activities that made a significant financial difference. In addition, after the end of the Seven Years' War in 1763, there is growing evidence of the nuns investing in Consolidated Bank Annuities, East India Company stock and other English stocks, with annual returns of 3% - 4%. This may be connected with an entry in the Book of Benefactions showing that the nuns were taking a more professional approach to their business life. In 1748-1749 Lady Peterborough gave 200 florins (£30 then, £4,000 today) "to pay the Lawyer for coming to teach us our business".[13] Lady Peterborough herself is a fascinating character. She was originally a professional singer, Anastasia Robinson, well-known in London for creating new roles in operas by Handel and Bononconi. She became the mistress of the widowed Charles Mordaunt, 3rd Earl of Peterborough, who was twice her age but he made an honest woman of her just before his death in 1735. From 1745 to 1750 she lived with the Canonesses in Liège.[14]

With such financial growth the sixty-five years after the end of Louis XIV's wars saw much greater stability though it was slow to start with. By 1730 benefactions had recovered only to the level of 1670 and as late as 1740 the nuns were recording significant hardships. In that year the Meuse flooded the cellars and Church and there were food shortages.[15] However after that low point benefactions grew hugely over the next half century (see Table 2), even during the War of Austrian Succession 1740-1748 and the Seven Years' War 1756-1763. The former saw the Low Countries once more become a cockpit of battle but only from 1744 and less intensively so than in former wars. In the latter European battles were fought much further east with France and Britain also scrapping in India, North America and on the sea rather than in the Low Countries.

Table 2:

Income from benefactions 1713-1777

Years	Florins	Sterling	Modern equivalent	Modern equivalent averaged per year
1713-19	4,287	£113	£14,500	£2,071
1720-29	6,633	£995	£126,000	£12,600
1730-39	9,239	£1,386	£192,250	£19,225
1740-49	15,644	£2,346	£323,000	£32,300
1750-59	23,861	£3,579	£461,500	£46,150
1760-69	15,223	£2,328	£267,600	£26,760
1770-77	14,188	£2,128	£212,000	£21,200

So the Gorings, Stourtons and Petres showed that, despite the penal laws, Catholic landowners certainly had disposable wealth. Debarred from public occupations and places at court they stayed profitable by concentrating on their estates. Although Catholics were subject to a double land tax it was generally absorbed by their growing affluence, shared generally by eighteenth century landowners. Income tax and inheritance tax were nineteenth and twentieth century inventions and had not yet come to haunt the rich.

Inbreeding also had the unintended effect of making the Catholic aristocracy richer. Constant intermarriage made them less prolific child-bearers. The increasing frequency with which the male line died out led to an accumulation of property amongst fewer families, inherited through distant relatives or marriage. The Stourtons were one such family. In 1700 they possessed a poverty-stricken peerage and a small estate, Stourton House, in Wiltshire, which they sold to the Hoare banking family,[16] but then progressed to affluence through marriages and chance inheritance that gave them the Walmesley estate in Lancashire and those of the last Lord Lonsdale in Yorkshire and Staffordshire. They also owned Witham Place in Essex. In 1700 there had been about four hundred Catholic heads of landowning families. This had halved by 1770[17] so that, in 1778, at the time of the first Catholic Relief Act, there were only eight Catholic peers, nineteen baronets and 150 "gentlemen of substantial property".[18]

Although the convent's income grew the numbers in the school stayed low until the 1760s.[19] From 1713 to 1717 there were no more than one or two girls each year, with none in 1718-1719. In the 1720s numbers averaged about four each year.

Most unusually, we actually know something about one of the families that attended the school in the 1720s. Two girls called Miss Carol [sic] appear in the accounts book, the sisters of Charles Carroll of Baltimore in the American colonies. He was a wealthy land speculator who later became a significant patriot politician and was the only Catholic to sign the American Declaration of Independence in 1776. His 1723 account book records that he paid for his two younger sisters to go to the Canonesses' school in Liège. They were accompanied by their uncle Henry Darnall and his two daughters joined their cousins for a short time at school.[20] Another member of the family, John Carroll became the first Bishop of Baltimore immediately after independence which gave him oversight of Catholics in all thirteen American states. He was consecrated in England at the Welds' home at Lulworth Castle. He had also taught for a while in the early eighteenth century at the Jesuits' college in Liège. It may have been through these Carroll connections that the three Semmes sisters, Mary Ann, Martha and Teresa, came to Liège from Maryland to be professed as nuns between 1766 and 1768 though, tragically, each died within a year of profession.[21]

Pupil numbers stayed much the same in the 1730s when three or four girls were at the school each year. In the 1740s numbers fell to just under two and in the 1750s reverted to between three and four. The big difference came in the 1760s with an average of seven, topping out in 1766-1767 with thirteen. In the years between 1770 and 1777 numbers still averaged thirteen. The reasons for this sudden blossoming are not explicit. The Seven Years War had ended in 1763 but wars had ended before without such large increases in pupil numbers. However this time the return of peace coincided with new leadership within the Chapter supported by an unusually high involvement in the convent by several of England's leading Catholic families and, within a few years, a new enlightened Prince-Bishop of Liège.

The driving force within the convent was Mother Christina Dennett. She was appointed second mistress of the school in 1761, Sub-Prioress in 1769 and Prioress in 1770. She seems to have reinvigorated the Community. In 1770 she ended the practice whereby nuns could keep some of their pensions for private use. As prioress she would control the pot thereby reinforcing the vows of poverty and obedience.

But although Christina Dennett may have had the vision she did not have the means or the confidence. She needed the support of moneyed families. She was in the right place at the right time for the devotion of the major Catholic aristocratic families to the convent was at its height in the mid eighteenth century with a major spiritual commitment from their women. Not only had the daughters of the Stourton, Petre, Arundell, Berington, Weld, Dormer, Talbot and Haggerston families, all major Catholic titled families, come to the school but several were professed as nuns – from the Petre family, Bridget in 1711, Penelope in 1713, Mary in 1726 and Winifred in 1728; Ann Dormer in 1715; from the Stourton family Elizabeth in 1730, two Catherines, one in 1726 and the other in 1767, and Charlotte in 1768; from the Berington family Catherine in 1763, Bridget in 1767, Frances in 1772; and from the Talbots, who were also Earls of Shrewsbury and historically major sponsors of the Jesuits, Elizabeth in 1756.[22] This solid core of professed aristocratic women may have been influential in the convent's decision to make the school more central in its life with Lord William Stourton as the prime lay mover, supported by the Howards, namely William Stourton's wife, Winifred, and Christina Dennett's confessor, Father John Howard, who was also President of the Jesuit Academy in Liège . He was very instrumental in persuading the Prioress to commit to educational expansion when she began to worry that it would detract from the spiritual and devotional duties of the Community.[23]

While the drive to expand the school may have come from within, it also needed the approval of the secular ruler. In 1772 a new Prince-Bishop came to power, Francois-Charles de Velbrück. He was inspired by the liberal ideas of the late eighteenth century enlightenment and introduced schools which offered free education for the poor. He may have wanted the nuns to show equal enthusiasm. For one cannot escape the fact that their educational activity was slight compared with the scholastic work of the Jesuits in Liège where they had been since 1614, having transferred from Louvain. When, in 1773, their Order was suppressed worldwide by Pope Clement XIV, de Velbrück allowed them to reopen their college as the Anglo-Bavarian Liège Academy. Joined by their colleagues from the disbanded English College at St. Omer, training for the priesthood continued surreptitiously alongside the more open business of teaching schoolboys.

Similar heroic efforts were being made in England by Catholic convent schools that were defying the penal laws. Frances Bedingfield's Bar Convent School in York, founded in 1686, had survived nearly a century of penal laws in response to the wishes of the Catholic north country gentry to have their children educated in the Catholic faith.[24] There was a similar school for girls at Hammersmith. In 1694 the Mother Superior at York had been arrested and imprisoned. She was released but in 1696 a mob threatened to attack the convent. Letters between York and Hammersmith used codes – nuns were "shepherdesses", the chaplain was "a smith", a bishop was "a myth". There were other Catholic girls' schools in and round London – Mr and Mrs Hughes ran one at Hackney which moved to Greenwich in 1769.[25]

One feels that these invidious comparisons may have acted as a spur in the Prioress' decision to expand. The wording of the 1899 history supports this view when the writer says that Christina Dennett "set her heart on giving Catholic girls the same advantages which they would have in the great schools in England".[26] If those schools could achieve what they had done under the penal laws what might the nuns not achieve in the comfort of Liège? This is not to underestimate the importance of

Christina Dennett. Indeed, the 1899 history quite properly describes her as the second foundress.[27]   But there certainly seem to have been external forces at work as well.

In its first 135 years only 156 girls had passed through the school. With a new school building in 1772 and a second building added from 1776 it would take only nine years for the next 156 to pass through the front door.

Chapter 11

School of Virtuous Demeanour

Ladies' Education in the 1770s

The legacy of Eve conditioned women's lives in an age when the literal truth of the Old Testament was unquestioned. "And the Lord God said, It is not good that the man should be alone: I will make an help meet for him".[1] So woman was created to aid and support man, not to rival him. As the story of the Garden of Eden unfolds it is Eve who disobeys God's instruction concerning the tree of knowledge for which her punishment was to be the pain of childbirth and subjection – "I will greatly multiply thy sorrow ... in sorrow thou shalt bring forth children and thy desire shall be thy husband, and he shall rule over thee".[2] Thus woman is the temptress, man the victim and henceforth her master. Indeed in the seventeenth and eighteenth centuries woman, the original biblical seductress, was seen as more sexually predatory than man with an appetite that must be confined within the strictures of marriage.

In reality, the high-born took a less harsh view. A Renaissance sense of chivalric honour and confidence in the effects of good breeding and a proper religious and moral upbringing gave them a purer view of their women. Only the coarser woman of the lower orders would continue to be morally suspect. However, all other aspects of a genteel woman's subordinate position remained. The reality of continuous pregnancy and its effects tended to reinforce the biblical warning as 45% of aristocratic women in the seventeenth century died before the age of fifty, one quarter from the complications of child-birth, many others from illnesses resulting from their general debilitation caused by constant pregnancy.[3] Even in the eighteenth century married women rarely lived beyond the menopause.[4] From this developed the concept of woman as the weaker sex, subject to nerves and likely to collapse under strain. For the more calculating woman this could be a way of avoiding intimacy and further pregnancies. A woman, being smaller and less strong than a man, was also thought to have less intellectual ability.

Woman's role as helpmate was the bedrock of marriage. The Book of Proverbs reinforced this view – "a virtuous woman is a crown to her husband".5 Her religious piety and social conformity were essential buttresses to her husband's position. She would exercise these virtues as the nurturer of children, manager of an extended household and trainer of servants and thereby add lustre to her husband's social position. Education, insofar as it was felt that a young woman needed it, would enhance her piety and charitableness and add social skills and graces that would make her a demurely supportive wife.

For a Protestant woman her religious role could be realised only through marriage. A Catholic woman had the alternative of life in a convent in Europe. Two Protestant women did not share the conventional scorn for Catholic practices nor accept the inevitability of their subordinate role. Margaret, Duchess of Newcastle complained:

> "We are become like worms, that only live in the dull earth of ignorance, winding ourselves sometimes out by the help of some refreshing rain of good education, which seldom is given us, for we are kept like birds in cages, to hop up and down in our houses, not suffered to fly abroad ... We are shut out of all power and authority, by reason we are never employed either in civil or martial affairs, our counsels are despised, and laughed at, the best of our actions are trodden down with scorn".6

She thought it better for a girl to be "walled up" in "a monastery" than be unhappily married. Margaret Godolphin, who was to die in childbirth, was impressed in the mid seventeenth century by the convents she visited in France. "Their Nunneries seem to be holy Institutions ..."7

The Liège school reflected these assumptions about women. A bill poster published by the Canonesses in French in the 1790s, intended to attract local custom in Liège, demonstrated the point. The school's aims were:

> "to form the hearts of young girls to virtue; to teach them to love the practices of religion and to instruct in them thoroughly; to inspire them with a taste for application and for work, order and domestic economy; to adorn their minds and accustom them to act from sentiments of honour; to bring them up in the ways of the polite and Christian world; such is the aim of all the exercises of this house. Christian doctrine is explained by Holy Scripture in points which are controverted for the sake of those to whom such knowledge may become necessary".8

We have already seen how Jane Dormer had described Mary Tudor's household at New Hall in the 1540s as a "true school of virtuous demeanour".[9] It would have been a description of the school in Liège which was embellished by the attendance of two more Miss Dormers, one from 1774 to 1783 and the second from 1779 to 1781.

In addition to the spiritual aims of the school we know that the curriculum included reading, writing, English, French and Italian grammar, biblical and classical history, arithmetic, book-keeping, letter-writing, heraldry, the use of the globes, geography, the principles of natural history "so far as may be found useful for girls", embroidery and all sorts of needlework, and the art of drawing and painting flowers. Dancing, music and portrait painting were all extras, as was making miniatures in ivory. The basic school fee was 22 guineas (£2,100 in modern values) which was subdivided into seventeen guineas for table, bedroom linen, fire and light, two guineas a year for washing, two for writing materials and one for an entrance fee. The extra subjects cost three guineas a year each[10] (£315 in modern values).

The girls were also to be taught to do the "honours of the table" and to be very attentive to one another. Demeanour and manners were a very important part of a genteel girls' formal or informal education, whatever her religion. As one historian of eighteenth century manners observed:

> "the élite hostess might wield considerable power from the head of her dining table ... good breeding was intimately linked with education and nurture, conveying a sense of a rounded personality, a cultivated understanding and a thorough knowledge of ceremony ... Outer manners were the reflection of an inner civility ... distinguished by an air of dignified ease and graceful control ... In addition she was encouraged to be clean, to adopt nice table manners and foster the art of diverting conversation. Above all she was to be modest and chaste".[11]

Modest and chaste behaviour would probably have been second nature to Catholic girls. One historian of Catholic England noted that "tolerance of English people depended upon the modesty and unthreatening demeanour of Roman Catholics, especially the absence of an energetic schooling to raise new generations of 'papists.'"[12] Pious and private behaviour had long been the hallmark of many a Catholic family. The Petre household at Ingatestone was described as "a small, quiet, well-established, inoffensive and non-proselytising Catholic community with a discreet chaplain who wore no robes so that his real role could only be supposed". Catholic households had survived for over two centuries by being contained and unostentatious.[13]

Did the girls at Liège fare better or worse than Protestant children of English genteel families?

In broad terms the nuns' academic and social education could have served the needs of any high-born young woman. For Protestants the slant on history and doctrine would have been different but all else in the classroom would have been the same. Since there was no requirement for academic education for women, and very little opportunity for women to use such knowledge, female academic learning was solely for general improvement of the mind and to be able to make intelligent conversation in social situations. Jane Austen in *Emma* described a school that may have resembled the one she attended in 1785:

> "... a ... real, honest, old-fashioned boarding school, where a reasonable quantity of accomplishments were sold at a reasonable price, and where girls might be sent to be out of the way, and scramble themselves into a little education, without any danger of coming back prodigies".

A prodigy would have been too distinct a rival to men. Demure acquiescence was expected so that self-censorship became second nature. Lady Mary Wortley Montagu advised her daughter to "conceal whatever learning she attains, with as much solicitude as she would hide crookedness or lameness".[14] Hence ladies withdrew after dinner for tittle-tattle gossip while men smoked cigars, drank port and discussed business and affairs of state. Ladies were not expected to bother their pretty little heads with these matters but to confine themselves to their four cardinal virtues – obedience, producing heirs, running the household and being ladylike adornments of their husbands.

Therefore a girl's education and general accomplishments were geared to these ends, to make her an attractive marriage prospect, though her general accomplishments were also important in their own right in an age when all entertainments were home-made and households were mostly economically self-sufficient. This led Hannah Moore at the end of the eighteenth century to make the sardonic comment that "the life of a young lady now too much resembles that of an actress ... the morning is all rehearsal and the evening is all performance".[15] But their lives were not entirely passive. Even in wealthier households with a significant infrastructure of servants, a woman would need to be adept in her skills and accomplishments to evaluate others' standards of work and to manage servants and a household budget. This was the woman's province with which the master of the household did not expect to be bothered and the one area of genuine female power. One lady who used this position with great energy was the Catholic Mary Blount. She married the 9th Duke of Norfolk and became one of the foremost female builders and decorators of her day.[16]

But in some respects the education received by girls at Liège was not typical and had many advantages. Their curriculum was certainly broader than that enjoyed by boys at the English endowed grammar schools which were tied by their founders' statutes to an antiquated curriculum of Latin, Greek and Anglican religious instruction that was subject to much criticism but was fiercely defended by the Court of Chancery as representing the founders' wishes. Although the boys' clerical teachers, all graduates, would, have been better qualified, as women were debarred from higher education, they were often compelled to work into infirm old age with dire consequences for standards. By contrast the Liège girls had the advantage of continuity. As a Community the nuns recruited and trained their novices in the accepted ways and practices of the convent. Although only a small number of nuns at any one time would have been involved in teaching the capacity for replacement was there, especially when a teacher became infirm.

Girls' boarding schools in England had similar continuity problems. They were often privately owned and tended to expire with the owner or whenever she became tired of the job. Nor were they very widespread for the education of Protestant women in England was not greatly valued. A Protestant girl of the upper classes was more fortunate if she came from a large family of brothers spread out over a number of years. She might then enjoy the services of their tutor. When the last brother departed then the girls would probably be given over to the dancing master, music teacher and French master.[17] While there was a great expansion of schools for ladies in the late eighteenth century (Chelmsford and Colchester had several each and all major towns and small villages in Essex had one),[18] these were for the aspiring middle classes and would have been inappropriate on social and religious grounds for the families of the local Catholic gentry and aristocracy.

Most importantly Liège permitted the girls to be totally immersed all year, without holidays, in the spiritual life of an enclosed convent in a way that was totally alien to the Anglican world. In terms of moral and spiritual training there was nothing in England which could compare. Indeed, there lies the difference between comfortably established Georgian Anglicanism and still illegal and clandestine Catholicism. For a Catholic girl in a moneyed household there was a huge importance attached to education. The wife and mother in a marriage would play a vital role in sustaining the Old Faith. It was essential that Catholic daughters should be imbued with the beliefs, practices and history of their faith so that the corporate worship of extended Catholic households and moral leadership of the servants was in safe hands. The existence of convents just across the Channel provided an opportunity that did not exist for their Protestant counterparts.

Chapter 12

The Young Ladies

Liège 1770-1794

From 1770 the nuns kept careful notes on each "young lady" in a new pupil register.[1] The register contained not just each girl's name and entry date but some details on what she was taught, whether she had been confirmed and taken first communion, her exposure to infectious diseases, personal requests (if any) from her parents, sometimes her place of residence, and, for a few, confirmation of taking the Canonesses' habit or, sadly, dying while at school. Complementing these records the account book details fees paid and sometimes indicates the presence of girls at the school, usually for very short stays, who were never recorded in the pupil register. The account book is also the more reliable source for first names and leaving dates, although, following the conventions of the time, first names are only given for younger sisters.

From these sources we can see that the new school really began to blossom from 1777 (see Table 3).

Table 3:

Average monthly pupil numbers 1770-1794

1770	6	1775	16	1780	43	1785	42	1790	44
1771	10	1776	15	1781	49	1786	39	1791	50
1772	14	1777	23	1782	45	1787	36	1792	65
1773	11	1778	30	1783	42	1788	42	1793	58
1774	11	1779	44	1784	43	1789	44	1794	28

We have places of origin for 44% of the 309 girls who entered the school between 1770 and 1794. Nearly all the rest can be allocated either a specific place of origin because they were sisters of existing pupils or, by the nature of their surname, they can be allocated with reasonable confidence to particular countries. We know that marrying a Catholic or foreigner was anathema to Protestant England[2] and even Catholic families were concerned that education abroad should not lead to their children coming home as foreigners.[3] Therefore mainland British and Irish Catholic girls tended not to have continental fathers and surnames.

On this basis we can establish reasonably well that between 1770 and 1794 44% of the young ladies came from mainland Britain and Ireland, 36% from the Low Countries, 8% from the German states, 6% from France, 3% from the West Indies (probably merchants or plantation owners), 1% from Spain (an English family resident in the Canary Islands) with 2% undetermined. So, although the school was established to educate the daughters of English Catholic families, its net was cast much wider. At least 56% of the girls came from Europe, predominantly from the Prince-Bishopric of Liège and other Catholic communities in nearby countries. Specific place-names that can be identified are Aix-la-Chapelle, Angers, Antwerp, Artroy, Bonn, Brussels, Coblenz, Düsseldorf, Lorraine, Maastricht, Namur, Spa, Vervier and Vervix.

We also know how long the girls stayed at school. The mean length of stay was just under two years. 24% stayed for less than a year, 45% between one and three years, 21% between three and five years, 8% between five and seven years, and 3% over seven years. Only a few girls have details of their ages recorded. However we can assume that most of the long-stayers over three years (just under one-third of the total) started at a young age of six to eight, and that most of the shorter stayers (forming just over two-thirds of the total) were starting in their mid to late teens having probably had some previous form of private tuition at home.

Of those whose stay at the school was less than a year just over half had typically Flemish names with only about one-third from mainland Britain and Ireland. This suggests that many more families in the Low Countries may have used the convent as a handily placed finishing school that happened to be in the Catholic tradition.

If one looks just at the mainland British and Irish girls their commitment was greater. Their mean length of stay was three years. This makes sense. As a persecuted minority they were more committed to Catholic education for its moral and spiritual training. What better way than to have one's daughter taught in an enclosed convent where the beliefs and rites of the faith suffused every activity of the day to ensure that she emerged into society in her mid to late teens as an assured and devout

Catholic woman? For generations Catholic families had been used to leading a secluded existence. A convent education would be only a variation on that theme.

There was a significant European aristocratic connection from 1782 on. Baroness d'Engantin de Grips came from Germany 1782-1788, Baroness de Mettercoren from France 1783-1786, two Comtesses de Marveldts from Germany, one from 1782-1787 and the other 1789-1790. The Baronne of Arnoldine and the Baronne of Tornaco both came from Vervix in 1784-1785. The Baroness de Furth of Aix-la-Chapelle and five Düsseldorf nobility comprising two sisters, the Baronesses de Ritz, and three sisters, the Baronesses Gangrebens, all attended variously between 1786 and 1788. Baroness Vannerfels of Bonn was there from 1786 to 1789, La Comtesse de Kesselstadt from Coblenz in 1788, two Comtesses de Looz in 1793-1794, La Comtesse Hompesch from 1788-1790 and La Comtesse de Goldstein from 1793-1794. From France, the Countess Maximilienne de Brie and Louise de Choiseul came in 1794. By contrast the representatives from the great English Catholic aristocratic families fell away in this period.

The records confirm that all the girls followed the common curriculum. From 1778 to 1785 there are only sporadic references to girls paying extra for dancing, music and portrait painting. Probably the school took time to build up contacts of suitable buy-in teachers. From 1785 nearly all are paying for extra lessons in some or all of these subjects although singing (with one French aristocrat learning to sing in English and Italian) joined dancing, music and portraiture, as the most sought after attributes plus, for a few, Italian (so perhaps it did not last long as part of the common curriculum), harpsichord and embroidery.

Disease was always a major threat. Smallpox was the most feared, followed by whooping cough and measles. According to the records 61% of girls had had smallpox before they entered the school. The other 39% either definitely had not or there was no statement one way or the other.

Sisters often came in batches of two or more. Between 1770 and 1794 thirty-seven pairs of sisters, seven trios, one quartet, the Mercers in 1776, and one quintet, the Cliffords in 1777, came to the school. Each group of sisters started on the same day. In three-quarters of these cases they all left on the same day as well. In total they account for nearly one-third of the total entry. Sisters would have been good company for each other in a strange land. Education was not linear leading to qualifications. The precise length of time that should be spent at the school was not written in stone. Nor should one forget the difficulty of the journey when storm force winds and high seas could oblige sailing ships to lay to for lengthy periods because of the impossibility of getting out of or into port safely. In such cases a crossing might experience long delays waiting for the wind to shift to the right quarter. In those unpredictable circumstances it would be easier, and cheaper, for adults to accompany a group of children rather than to take each one separately.

However, by the 1790s a stormy channel crossing was to be the least of the parents' worries as political events began to impinge on the school.

Chapter 13

Revolution

Liège 1789-1794

In 1789 the moderate reformers in France who were calling for a constitutional monarchy were sitting on a powder keg. The weather problems that had caused three consecutive failed harvests in France had created an underlying well of popular unrest aggravated by the rural poor flocking to Paris and other cities. These circumstances would soon be exploited by republican extremists resulting in the destruction of the French monarchy and an aggressive French revolutionary militarism that would engulf Europe.

In Liège the liberal Prince-Bishop Velbrück had been succeeded in 1784 by the reactionary Caesar Constantin de Hoensbroeck. He introduced press censorship and proscribed books that he regarded as pernicious. The enlightened Liègeois middle classes were furious but, like their French counterparts, were about to be overwhelmed by a rising of the impoverished and starving lower orders. Not long after the Parisian mob stormed the Bastille on July 14th 1789 to arm themselves, street revolution also broke out in Liège. On August 17th the Liègeois mob took over the Citadel, which commanded the town, in a bloodless coup and Hoensbroeck was confined to a palace arrest. He persuaded his captors that his health was poor and was allowed to move to his country residence whence he petitioned the Hapsburg Emperor for support, leaving Liège with a restless and hungry populace and the prospect of probable military intervention not just by Austria but also Prussia. Both monarchies had a vested interest in stemming the tide of republicanism.

Military patrols were established in Liège by the rebels and the convent was obliged to give one such band food and drink for a couple of months at a cost of £30 (£2,800 in modern values). As in France the wealth of the church was held up to question and targeted as wasted assets. In June 1790 the locals demanded a patriotic gift from all convents, no doubt linked to the financial need to pay troops to repel the Prussians who were threatening the city. In response the nuns declared that they had an annual revenue of 4,700 florins (£470[1] or £43,560 in modern values) and agreed to pay a bill for 1,000 florins (£100 then, £9,270 today) on the understanding that no further demands would be made.

However fears remained that hungry mobs would attack the convent for bread. In September 1790 the twenty-seven loaves baked weekly for the poor under the 1711 agreement with the Prince-Bishop were claimed specifically by the poor of the Parish of St. Christopher in which the convent lay. The nuns claimed that they were not a local bakery and had the right to distribute the bread to those in the city whom they judged to be the most needy. They appear to have persuaded the magistrates of their rights in principle but were then somewhat embarrassed to find that the 1711 agreement made no specific mention of the amount of bread that they should produce, though they could demonstrate that their loaves were larger in size than those from secular bakeries. The nuns' lawyer may have helped them create a persuasive case but counselled caution and advised that they should concede to the local parishioners' demands.[2]

Although the Liègeois had managed to see off Prussian troops in 1790, Austrian troops retook the city in January 1791 on behalf of the Prince-Bishop. Despite much damage incurred by looting, the convent escaped unscathed, probably because of the nuns' sensible compromise with the local poor over provision of bread. The nuns had twenty Austrian soldiers billeted on them but managed to secure their removal after a day and were allowed to return to their former practice of distributing bread to the poor of their choosing. They also set about trying to collect rent from their tenants who had reneged on payment during the recent revolution.

Ominously a glimpse across the border into France would have shown that there may be worse to come. In 1791 the French revolutionaries had required an oath denying the authority of the church from every teacher in French public education, many of them priests. The majority refused and dissidents were imprisoned. In June 1791 Louis XVIII fled Paris to seek refuge in the Austrian Netherlands but was halted on the frontier at Varennes, returned abjectly to Paris and placed under palace arrest. Parisian Republicanism came into the ascendant. In April 1792 French revolutionary troops invaded the Low Countries. In September 1792 in Paris, many imprisoned priests were slaughtered as potential fifth columnists as the revolutionaries anticipated an Austrian invasion. Fired by Republican zeal, the French armies fought back. In November 1792 the Austrian forces were heavily defeated at Jemappes, and Mons and Brussels fell into French hands. On November 28th 1792 the French entered Liège. The Prince-Bishop fled for a second time.

England had not yet declared war on France but this provided no protection for the nuns. The French occupying forces ordered the convent to provide a thousand loaves which could only be done by employing bakers in the town at cost to make up the batch. Four days later two thousand loaves were demanded. Bedding and mattresses were taken for a hospital the French army had set up in a local Benedictine monastery. Sixty soldiers were immediately billeted on the convent on the first day of occupation. After three days' negotiations they were removed in exchange for four men and a corporal who would act as a protective guard. The make-up of this group constantly varied and after a month the nuns managed to get five regulars allocated on a permanent basis.

This guard kept further billeting at bay but the atmosphere was tense. On Christmas Day 1792 the nuns quietly said rather than joyously sang High Mass to avoid provocation. The faithless French Revolutionary Army used a statue of the Virgin Mary in the Convent of the Poor Clares for target practice. On January 21st 1793 Louis XVIII was executed in Paris. In February England declared war on France. The French troops in Liège moved out to take Maastricht but were then defeated by the Austrians at Aix-la-Chappelle. On March 5th Austrian troops re-entered Liège. They, however, needed their army to be financed. Convents were expected to lend 1,000 florins at 5% interest, which the nuns did, but managed to get someone else to buy them out of the loan just before they left Liège in 1794.

Yet, during all these troubles the school roll continued to rise, from forty-four in 1790 to sixty-five in 1792 and fifty-eight in 1793. Nearly half of the total entrants during this three year period of tension had Low Countries' surnames. Twelve French girls also came in during this threatening period, and the last two, in 1794, were aristocrats, Countess Maximilienne de Brie and Louise de Choiseul. In Paris aristocratic heads were falling to the guillotine and the Duc de Choiseul had been one of the conspirators behind the royal flight to Varennes.[3] Those who bore his name would have been in peril when guilt by association was sufficient cause to earn the death penalty. Louise would have been safer in Liège. Despite its difficulties the convent was clearly seen as a relative oasis in a turbulent political landscape for the worried parents of local girls.

By January 1794 the French Reign of Terror was in full swing under Maximilien Robespierre's direction. French economic circumstances were dire. The republican motto "Vivre libre ou mourir" (Loot or starve) was adopted.[4] The French Revolutionary Army had suffered setbacks in 1793 but was re-grouping.

The nuns needed to get ready to leave. But what sort of welcome would they get in England?

Chapter 14

Grudging Acceptance

Catholic Relief 1778-1791

In 1642 Susan Hawley had to leave England to escape the penal laws that made Catholic education a criminal offence. Just over 150 years later her spiritual successors were hoping to return to these same English shores. What had changed?

With the end of Cromwell's Puritan Protectorate and the restoration of Charles II in 1660, Catholics had breathed a sigh of relief. Charles had a Portuguese Catholic wife and converted to Catholicism on his deathbed.[1] However he had to make concessions to Protestant pressure so the 1673 Test Act required all public office holders to be Anglican communicants. This meant that Catholics were barred from the army and navy, membership of parliament, and from entry to Oxford and Cambridge Universities. In effect this meant that they were unable to qualify to practice as doctors, barristers or teachers, although they could act as conveyancers of property. Within a few years the Popish Plot of 1678 showed the ease with which anti-Catholic fever could be whipped up. Innocent men were smeared with the taint of being treasonable Catholics. Many died or were imprisoned for their faith, and the ensuing unsuccessful attempts to exclude the Catholic James, Duke of York, from succeeding his brother, showed that there was an underlying Protestant hostility that would not be appeased.

James II's short-lived attempt to restore Catholicism between 1685 and 1688, and the birth of a son to sustain this threatened counter-reformation, merely consolidated the Protestant opposition. James fled and a bloodless revolution led to the joint monarchy of the Dutch Protestant champion of Europe, William of Orange, as William III and his wife Mary II, the daughter of the recently departed James II.

Parliament passed a fresh raft of penal laws including the 1702 Act of Succession which eventually bequeathed the throne to the Protestant Hanoverians and effectively prevented any future monarch or heir to the throne from being a Catholic or marrying one. In addition the old penal laws still applied. Catholics could not keep arms, could be fined if they sent their children abroad for education or did not attend the local Anglican Church, were subject to a double land tax, could have any property confiscated that was dedicated to the support of illegal Catholic priests, could not inherit property which must pass to the next Protestant in line (a law that was never taken advantage of by any potential Protestant beneficiary), and a horse worth more than £5 might be confiscated, presumably as a potential cavalry weapon (in 1700 £5 was worth about £650 in today's money). Despite all these difficulties Catholics still found ways to earn a good living as landowners and farmers, bankers and merchants or as diplomats and army officers in the service of Catholic monarchs abroad or, from 1714, in the army of George I's Hanover where English anti-Catholic laws held no sway.

Catholicism lived on in many noble and gentry households in England. For two hundred years these estates had provided an isolated and protective cloak under which Catholic worship could continue, though many families experienced breaks in the tradition when a patriarchal leader decided to conform (or turn heretic, depending on one's viewpoint), and this happened with greater frequency in the eighteenth century. Former Catholic lords such as Sefton, Molyneux, Gascoigne and Montagu became impatient with being on the social margins and chose Anglicanism (it would be too strong a statement to say that they converted) taking with them their dependent local communities. Thus the number of Catholics shrank by nearly a third in the eighteenth century. The number of Protestant Dissenters shrank by an even larger percentage, 40%, as many of them too found it more socially and financially comfortable to adopt the trappings of Anglicanism.[2]

Such inconsistencies, though, do not detract from the huge contribution made by the many recusant Catholic families to the survival of the Old Religion, especially in the north where they were to be found in a band of hills and dales on the eastern side of the Pennines from York to the Scottish border, in Cleveland and around the moorlands of North Yorkshire.[3] It was on the Yorkshire moors that the Canonesses would make their first English home in 1794. Catholic families felt a lot safer with a good stretch of moorland coming down to the back of the house and, if they had property so situated, they would often choose to live here rather than in comfortable houses elsewhere. This was cattle country where the eye that was kept open for rustlers could also encompass Protestant snoopers. There were pockets of Catholic gentry in Lancashire (but not in Cumbria) and the working-class Catholic numbers in Preston, Wigan and Liverpool were increasing in the middle of the century.

From the West Midlands to the Thames Valley there was a chain of evenly-spaced Catholic estates. There were fairly strong Catholic families in Shropshire, Staffordshire, Warwickshire and Worcestershire, areas associated with the Gunpowder conspirators and the escape of Charles II in 1651, but none in the East Midlands. In the Thames Valley, the Talbots, Webbs, Fermors and Stonors were to be found north of the river in Oxfordshire. The Englefields, Blounts and others were to the south in Berkshire.

Catholic gentry were fairly numerous in West Sussex, Hampshire and the Dorset/Wiltshire border area, most notably the Welds at Lulworth, the Arundells at Wardour, the Paulets at Basing House, the Montagus at Cowdray and the Howards, in the person of the Dukes of Norfolk, at Arundel. Winchester was quite a Catholic stronghold.[4] Indeed, the Catholic gentry were sufficient in number in central southern England and the West Midlands to influence the general tone of the area. It was in Wiltshire that the Canonesses would make their second English home in 1796. There was very little Catholicism in the south-west. The Chichesters at Arlington and the Cliffords at Chudleigh, both in Devon, were exceptions.

In East Anglia Catholic families were well-established and wealthy. But they were in an enthusiastically Protestant area and were more exposed to violence at moments of crisis than elsewhere, as had happened in 1642 in Suffolk and Essex. In the end their wealth, continuity of tenure and loyalty to the monarch earned the respect of their neighbours, though they were a little cut off from the rest of the Catholic gentry till the latter began to frequent London and provincial spas for the social season in the mid eighteenth century. Amongst them Lady Frances Jerningham was a well-known Catholic hostess ("Her Catholic Majesty" as she was irreverently known) whose salon in Boulton Row, London, in the 1790s enabled French émigrés to mingle with English Catholics ("The Cats" as she called them). Her country home at Costessey in Norfolk later gave refuge to the Blue Nuns.[5] The proximity of the East Anglian gentry to London ensured a fairly influential voice in Catholic matters. The Petres of Thorndon Hall and Ingatestone Hall in Essex were particularly successful in making their position and wealth felt. The Petres, the Bedingfields in Norfolk and the Brudenells in Northamptonshire were also pragmatically shrewd in their business dealings, avoiding gratuitous offence by the wanton enclosure or emparkment of others' land.[6] They realized that there was no sense in unnecessarily provoking Protestant hotheads. The Canonesses were to find their third and final home in Essex amongst these east of England Catholics, close to the influential Petres at Ingatestone and their own generous patrons, the Stourtons, at Witham.

Families such as the Petres were the centre of significant Catholic communities, some following the local lord's faith through genuine conviction, others needing a job or, as traders, hoping to gain business. In 1767, at the request of the House of Lords, the

Anglican Archdeacons' Visitations required their clergy to declare the number of papists in their parish. The results suggested a total Catholic population of about 50,000 in England as a whole, probably up to 80,000 (or just 2% of the population) if one allows for the imprecision of the survey, down from 115,000 in 1720.[7] In Essex there were 719 and almost half were in the parishes near Lord Petre's two seats at Thorndon Hall and Ingatestone Hall. The greatest concentrations were in the five parishes of West Horndon with Ingrave, East Horndon, Stock, Ingatestone and Fryerning. In total they accounted for 210 while another 147 were in neighbouring parishes. Smaller, but still significant communities, were to be found round Witham, where William, 16th Lord Stourton lived, at Kelvedon Hatch where the Catholic banker, John Wright was lord of the manor, and South Weald where the Manby family lived.[8] By 1780 the Witham Place congregation numbered 100.[9]

The industrial revolution, with its mushrooming towns, was just starting in the last quarter of the eighteenth century though the large Irish Catholic working-class immigration did not start until about 1790. That the leading members of the Catholic community were advocates of an upper-class household faith and of the same social class as the country's legislators was a major help in ending the penal laws. They were respectable, wealthy and articulate. Had large-scale Irish immigration started earlier it would undoubtedly have made things more difficult. In the 1780s there were only about 40,000 Irish in England. By 1834 there were 580,000, 5% of the labour force.[10]

Whilst there were Stuart Catholic claimants abroad enjoying French hospitality and posing the constant threat of an invasion to overthrow the Protestant succession, the penal laws were likely to stay in operation, albeit unevenly enforced. Although the two Jacobite rebellions in 1715 and 1745 failed, they did considerable harm to the interests of law-abiding Catholics. Mary, Duchess of Norfolk, in 1745 prayed God that this "wicked rebellion may soon be suppressed, lest it hurt the poor Roman Catholics".[11] However, in the long term the loyalty of the vast majority of the English Catholic nobility was noted. After 1745 the French lost interest in Jacobitism, expelled Charles Stuart from France and, in 1778 supported the rebellious American colonists, a much more effective whip with which to lash the English.

By and large Anglican clergy and their patrons were more concerned about the unsound theology of the growing numbers of Protestant Dissenters amongst the lower orders. They seemed much more of a threat to religious orthodoxy and social stability than the ancient but weakened enemy, the Catholics, whose numbers were small and possibly declining and whose leading members were respectable gentlemen and ladies, well-mannered, unprovocative, loyal to the king and seen increasingly at some of the best spas and assembly rooms in England. A letter to one of the Chichester girls says of her family, "they are still in Bath though the height of the season is passed".[12] As the Catholic Henry, 6th Baron Arundell pointed out to his friend Philip Yorke, 1st Earl of Hardwicke, "I have lived here above thirty years, and, thanks to the lenity of the government, without ever having had the least molestation given me".[13]

The reign of George II (1727-1760) was the first since the Reformation in which no fresh laws were introduced against Catholics though priests were still, from time to time, brought before the courts. An Act of 1699 had offered £100 (£10,900 in today's money) to anyone who brought about the successful prosecution of a priest which proved an inducement to bounty hunters and bigots. In 1771 James Talbot was the last priest to be arraigned but Lord Mansfield at the King's Bench put a cap on the efforts of a serial bounty-hunter, inappropriately named Payne (John Payne had been the martyred priest of the Petre household in the sixteenth century), demanding absolute proof that the accused had been ordained a priest and had also performed Catholic rites. Talbot was acquitted.[14] As such evidence could only be given by Catholics, an unlikely event, Mansfield's judgement effectively put a stop to further opportunist prosecutions. In any case juries also took a dislike to some of the cases that were brought and refused to convict.

In such circumstances there was general agreement in Parliament that the penal laws should at least be reduced. Bonnie Prince Charlie (the failed Stuart invader of 1745) did not die until 1788 but was a busted flush. The French would not support him and three popes in a row had refused to acknowledge him as King of England. The official disbanding of the Jesuits by Pope Clement XIV in 1773, at the behest of Catholic monarchs who did not like their missionary independence and direct accountability to the Vatican, also helped the legal cause of English Catholics as Jesuit priests had been identified as the true enemy in Protestant mythology. The final spur came from America where the British Government desperately needed Irish and Scottish troops to quell the colonial rebellion. In 1774 the Irish Parliament, a separate entity until the Act of Union in 1801, passed a law allowing Irishmen "of whatever persuasion to testify their allegiance ..." The oath only required a denial of the Pope's temporal power, not his spiritual authority. If this was now to be extended to Scottish Catholics it must also in all justice encompass England. A Catholic Committee of senior laity, led by Robert, 9th Lord Petre, negotiated with the Government.[15] No priests were involved in the discussion. The four self-styled Catholic bishops (a title used internally as it would have been too provocative if assumed officially; they were otherwise known as Vicars-Apostolic) were cold-shouldered by Lord Petre. This was to be a political, not a religious, discussion. Many Catholic magnates saw their families as the true guardians of Catholicism with priests likely to provoke hostile reactions. Priests were considered safest in a controlled position as virtual servants in noble households.

The Roman Catholic Relief Act of 1778 was passed with little opposition. An oath required Catholics to abjure the pretender, the so-called Charles III, and any other claimant to the throne, to declare that it was unlawful to depose or murder a prince and to accept that the pope had no civil jurisdiction in England. The penal laws on property were all lifted for those who took the oath at Quarter Sessions. The £100 priest bounty was also removed and Catholics could join the army without taking an oath but still could not hold commissions. Catholic education was still illegal.

Slight though the legal changes were there was a Protestant backlash in London with the Gordon Riots of 1780. Lord Petre's house in Park Lane was set on fire. Over 300 people were shot or died of their wounds and twenty-one rioters were executed. But the extremism of the capital was not representative of the country at large. The provinces stayed calm, save for the burning of a Catholic chapel in Bath by four London rioters who took a mail coach to the west country to fulfil their arsonist ambitions.

The Catholic Committee continued its energetic work to secure further relief but political instability caused delay. No sooner had William Pitt the Younger got himself established as Prime Minister with a secure Commons majority than the Prince Regent's marriage to the Catholic Mrs Fitzherbert made the Catholic question too sensitive to raise, especially as she had previously boasted three deceased husbands from the Catholic gentry. George III's first bout of insanity caused even more delays. Eventually in 1791 the second Catholic Relief Act was passed. Catholic chapels were permitted provided that they were not ostentatious and steered clear of steeples and bells. Rites, processions and robes must not be publicly displayed outside Catholic churches. There were to be no further prosecutions for teaching or instructing young people in Catholicism but no Protestant children could be admitted to Catholic schools. Funds could now be used openly to endow Catholic schools in England. However, laws against the use of money for "superstitious purposes" still impeded the growth of other Catholic charities. In 1793 commissions in the army and navy during service in Ireland were opened to Catholics. But these concessions would only apply to those who took an oath which was now simplified to resemble that used in Ireland.

William Pitt, as Prime Minister, favoured full Catholic Emancipation with enfranchisement, the right to sit in Parliament and the abolition of oaths, but he knew he would never get it past George III. The latter liked his chief Catholic subjects and had visited Lord Petre at Thorndon Hall but he took literally his coronation oath to defend the Anglican religion.

The timing of the 1791 Relief Act was propitious. Within three years the exodus of Catholic religious communities from France and the Low Countries to England was underway. Although the act forbade the founding of convents in England, a blind eye was turned. There was temporary sympathy in England for the displaced religious and priests though distrust of Catholicism lurked just beneath the surface. In any case, if one were to make a fine legal point, the Canonesses were relocating, not founding a convent, and their prime purpose was to teach children.

Catholics were still not equal in law with Protestants. Their rights were fewer and dependent on taking an oath. They were reluctantly tolerated but discrimination was still likely to occur. In time of danger or insecurity they were likely to be scapegoats and were commonly described as "outlandish", literally out of bounds and not belonging.[16]

But as far as the Canonesses were concerned the way was now clear for legal Catholic education in England for the first time since 1535.

Chapter 15

Migration

Liège to England 1794

In January 1794 Mr Clifton, the convent's Jesuit pastor who had succeeded Father Howard on the latter's death in 1783, working under a secular title while the Jesuits were banned, had already started planning an evacuation.[1] It could only be a matter of time before the French army resumed its invasion of the Low Countries. When it did boats would be impossible to acquire except at vast expense. Clifton therefore arranged with the convent's coal-merchant that he would make available two large barges which he used for river trade with Holland.

At the same time Clifton also hired a very large unfurnished house in Maastricht, a twenty mile river journey to the north (see Map 1), on a three month renewable lease, to which the nuns and their pupils could rapidly retreat if the occasion demanded. Furnishing the house beforehand proved more problematic. The Prince-Bishop objected to the nuns sending furniture on ahead as he feared it would cause alarm in the town and grudgingly consented only if it were done with the utmost secrecy. On January 26th 1794 valuable Church plate, ornaments and legal and financial papers were sent to Maastricht, but the secret leaked out. Locals demanded to know if the nuns had secret intelligence about French movements. As no assurance could be given they were then ridiculed by some and accused by others of having unfair supernatural communication. Some of the Liègeois threatened to seize any further goods the nuns might send off. "Mr Clifton was deemed as an augur of ills and the nuns deluded visionaries".[2] Things were getting so restless that the Prince-Bishop imposed a ban on any further movement.

After four months biding their time, Clifton's worst fears materialised. In May 1794 the French army entered the Low Countries and approached Namur. A general exodus started from Liège and the Prince-Bishop reluctantly agreed that the nuns could join it. They took as much food as they could though some of the corn had to be sold and beer was too bulky to transport. A large amount of coal and kindling also had to be abandoned as were the organ, fixed altars, the great clock and most remaining furniture and choir hangings. Maybe they would be able to send for them later.

In anticipation of the move parents of continental children had been asked either to remove them or appoint someone in the town to look after them. Naturally it would be safer for the English and Irish children to stick with the nuns and find a way out. Of the fifty-two children on roll in January 1794, seven had left by the end of April and, according to the pupil register, the remaining forty-five reduced to twenty-two by May[3] although the nuns' own account says that they left for Maastricht on May 29th with twenty-five children.

They decided to leave just before first light, at about 3.00 a.m. on a rainy morning, before the locals were up and about, having attended their last Mass a little after midnight. The Prince-Bishop declined to provide a guard but some French émigrés fleeing their hostile fellow-countrymen did the honours. With the known anti-clericalism of the French troops and tense relations with the local townspeople, it was agreed that the nuns should be as inconspicuous as possible. Each was supplied with a piece of black material about one metre square to wear over her head like the common people of Liège. They walked quietly to the boats with two horse-drawn coaches taking about ten of the infirm. To their dismay the promised large coal barges, each capable of taking a hundred people, were not there. In their place was a small and filthy open coal boat. It had to be supplemented by another boat that had to be unloaded leaving the nuns and children stuck on the quay side until 6.00 a.m..

They moored at Maastricht at 1.00 p.m. in heavy rain. It took the best part of a day to get the rain-soaked luggage from the boat. The exhausted nuns and children had to sleep on the floors of their new house or doze in chairs but, on May 30th, were delighted to find that the house was protected at the back by the town ramparts and also had a pleasant garden, though the barracks on the other side of the street were very noisy and disturbed prayer and worship.

At Liège things seemed to be quietening down. The French had not moved any nearer but the nuns were determined to stay put in Maastricht as there was no point in having to repeat the evacuation all over again. Attempts to secure more of their possessions left at the Faubourg d'Avroy were unsuccessful and, despite, leaving two maidservants, a man and a French gentleman to keep an eye on the place, it had been frequently broken into and there was some evidence of pilfering by servants before the main party had left. Maastricht was proving very expensive as it swelled with refugees but at least forward planning had ensured a roof over their heads.

In June 1794 the French advance began again and Maastricht was threatened. It was time to leave for Rotterdam. The coal boats had been retained and a house reserved en route at Ruremonde. Passports for travel through the Dutch United Provinces had been obtained in advance thanks to the efforts of the Princess of Orange and the English Ambassador at The Hague. Getting permission from the Prince-Bishop to restart their journey was more difficult, but was eventually guaranteed at the end of June through the intervention of Lady Clifford of Ugbrooke in Devon, a friend of the Prince-Bishop's and mother of Charlotte who was a novice in the Community. Rather pretentiously the Prince-Bishop attached a condition, that the nuns should come back to the convent when he judged it convenient "sous l'obéissance qu'elles me doivent" (under the obedience they owe me). One feels that he was more concerned with perceived affronts to his status than with the safety of those he was supposed to protect. Men who think themselves strong do not like to appear weak!

On July 8th at 4.00 a.m., after five and a half weeks at Maastricht, seventy-five people embarked on the next stage of this extraordinary odyssey – sixteen pupils (seven more had left to go home), thirty-two professed nuns and one novice, two clergesses, twelve professed lay sisters and two lay novices, one other adult boarder (probably Mr Berlize, father of one of the girls), Mr Clifton, Father Gervais Genin who was a French émigré priest (one of hundreds about to arrive in England) and seven men who had taken care of the house at Maastricht. The preceding hours were spent sitting in the garden as the furniture had already been sent to the boats which had, in fact, only been partly unloaded when they originally arrived in order not to delay any emergency departure that might prove necessary. The Jesuits from the Liège Academy, with whom the nuns were almost travelling in tandem, took over their house.

At the height of summer the river was shallow and the heavily laden boats were lying low in the water. Navigation was tricky and progress slow. Ruremonde was not reached until noon the next day, July 9th, so the night had to be spent on the boat. Fortunately old carpets and a few other very basic comforts made conditions slightly more bearable than on the original journey from Liège. It was a very hot, long walk to the house although the priest to whom it belonged provided some local wine on arrival. It took a long time for the furniture to come but only half-an-hour to discover that the house was infested with fleas, despite its apparent cleanness and recent whitewashing. Unfortunately it had recently been used as a military hospital. The fleas had made their entrance on the soldiers' clothes and found nuns and children equally tasty. Sleep proved impossible for the exhausted party – "from this moment we called this place the Flea House".[4]

On July 11th at 11.00 p.m., again a night hour to preserve as much anonymity as possible, the party sailed for Venlo. They moored at a remote spot outside the town, sent for provisions from a local inn, and dined al fresco. They stayed three days living on and off the boat until July 14th when, at long last, they were joined by three boats from Liège bringing the possessions they had left behind.

Their river journey recommenced on July 14th with Mr Berlize and Mr Clifton dealing with the numerous toll collectors at various points along the river. The water continued to be low. The convoy of five boats, which were chained together, provided more space for living and sleeping but, with their heavy loads, frequently scraped the river bed. Ideally they needed horses to provide extra pulling power but they were hard to get. When they did acquire them, only one or two boats could be hauled at a time.

Leaving Venlo at 4.00 p.m. on July 15th they arrived at Mouch (probably the modern Goch) on July 16th, again mooring and living on the craft outside the village. The local Protestants' curiosity about the nuns in their habits forced the party to keep to the boats. On July 17th they reached the village of Maeghen (modern Megen). The Poor Clares from Liège had passed that way the previous day and a local churchman had given them shelter. He was able to converse with Mr Clifton in their own common language, Latin, and offered the nuns shelter. But the party preferred to stay together on the boats which, however, could not proceed because the water was too shallow. Getting exercise proved to be complicated, with individuals sometimes getting lost in local woods and on another occasion having money demanded of them by a farmer for allegedly trampling his clover.

Eventually the journey continued to Wackam on July 19th and then the confluence with the Rhine delta near Dordrecht where they arrived at 5.30 a.m. on Sunday, July 20th. It was two hundred years since any religious had been seen in the city and it was considered safer to stay on the boats rather than to venture into the town for Mass. This did not stop the locals coming out to row round the nuns' boats and stare.

At last, on July 22nd at 7.00 a.m. they arrived at Rotterdam. It had been an exhausting and expensive trip. The river Rhine was thronged with refugees and provisions could be purchased only at exorbitant prices. At least there were a few friendly faces in Rotterdam. Two nuns, one of them a Mrs Plowden (a name that has featured earlier in this history – see Chapter 10) from the Prinsenhof in Bruges came to meet their sisters from Liège. They were dressed in secular clothes and the nuns decided to copy their inconspicuous style of a black gown with a large cape and long sleeves, buttoned down the front, a muslin double handkerchief with a double border and a black ribbon, and a large black silk hood, which, even after the migration, the nuns continued to wear in the choir. The lay sisters changed to a black and white cotton gown and their caps had just the one border. Four or five local Dutch mantua makers were employed to do the work.

The original intention had been to spend up to a fortnight recuperating in Rotterdam but it was so filled with refugees that no lodgings could be found. Again the locals thronged to see these strange religious in their boats.

An English merchant told the nuns about a ship, the *Smallbridge*, which was due to sail for England in a few days. The captain of the *Smallbridge* agreed an all-in fee of 130 guineas (£11,150 in modern values) for transport of people and effects which were contained in 800 oak chests.[5] The ship had put in to Rotterdam on May 29th, the day the nuns had left Liège, with serious damage sustained in a voyage from the East Indies. The repairs were on the verge of completion. The timing could not have been better. But the Liège party were in desperate need of clean linen and clothes. They had anticipated that the 180 mile river journey from Maastricht to Rotterdam would take only five or six days. It had taken two weeks. No one had more than one change of clothes and they dared not send their things to be washed as they were unsure when they would be sailing. Their attempt to go further up river into the countryside to get some privacy and a chance to exercise was thwarted by the tidal nature of the river and strong contrary winds so, in the end, they went aboard the *Smallbridge* where the captain made a tent on deck to separate the religious party from the crew and gave up his cabin to the Prioress and seven or eight other nuns. All the rest of the Community slept in the goods hold whilst the pupils had the passenger beds.

At last there was news from England. Charles, 17th Lord Stourton (who had succeeded his father William in 1781), wrote to offer the Community his house at Holme in Yorkshire but the nuns deferred a decision pending news of larger accommodation elsewhere.

The *Smallbridge* eventually left Rotterdam on July 29th. It was ready to sail earlier but the nuns needed time to get their new clothes made and provisions brought on board. When they eventually left they immediately became stuck on sands for a day and, by the time they got off, a contrary westerly wind meant that they had to anchor at Helvoetsluys from August 2nd. They were still there a week later together with a veritable armada of ships waiting to make the North Sea crossing. During their enforced delay a passing collier severed the anchor cable, the first of three narrow escapes their ship was to experience. On a more pleasant note the Jesuits from the Liège Academy, also waiting for favourable winds, visited the nuns on the *Smallbridge*. Father John Laurenson reported that "we found the generality of them better, considering the fatigues and hardships to which they had been so long exposed, than we could have expected. Most of them, however, were wan, sallow and tanned".[6] It was not until August 13th that the wind allowed them to set sail after two hungry weeks (they had purchased provisions for only ten days at Rotterdam), a great deal of sea-sickness caused by lying to in stormy weather and, at the end, rancid drinking water. They set out in a convoy accompanied by an English man-of-war to see off French privateers. They soon lost contact with the man-of-war but stuck close to a large English merchant ship whose pilot was familiar with the crossing.

At 3.00 p.m. on August 16th they arrived at Gravesend. The captain did not know the Thames estuary waters beyond this point and needed a pilot to see him up to London. The exorbitant offer he received, twelve guineas, (£1,030 in modern values), was refused. But at least the ship's party were able to buy some fresh fish and drinking water from local fishing boats. On August 17th another collier ship ran foul of the *Smallbridge* and a fire broke out in the captain's cabin when a candle overturned. Then there was a further two days' delay when English officials came on board to check that the nuns took nothing from the ship when they landed and to warn that no outward signs of their Catholicism, such as breviaries, should be flaunted.

The captain, without a pilot, decided to ride his luck and set sail again. At 4.00 p.m. on August 18th they arrived at Woolwich where they were in collision with a man-of-war. A small boat hanging over the side of the *Smallbridge* was smashed to smithereens. They avoided disaster but it was a close run thing. The sight of two sunken vessels with their masts protruding above water reminded them of what might have been. Mr Clifton may well have been glad to leave the ship at this point to make his way to London to see if he could sort out accommodation for the nuns, pupils and servants.

Just before Greenwich the captain at last managed to get a pilot who at 6.00 p.m. on August 17th, got them to an anchorage point opposite Wren's great Naval Hospital. That was as far as the captain was prepared to go. There were too many hazards in getting right into the port of London. At 1.00 a.m. on August 18th the party disembarked and made for the London house Clifton had found for them in Old Burlington Street, but it would take no more than forty-two people so, contrary to their hopes, they were split with twelve nuns, three lay sisters and twelve pupils having to go to another house in Dover Street, just a few minutes walk away. The servants and some lay sisters had been left on board the ship to take care of the transfer of effects which were conveyed to two Thames-side warehouses, permission having been given by the Prime Minister, William Pitt, for the nuns' goods, wine apart, to be exempt from duty. Nonetheless it still proved a costly business with warehouse fees, wharfage and customs' officers' fees coming to £100 (£8,180 in modern values).

The divided Community was reunited after ten days when Hugh, 6th Lord Clifford of Chudleigh, provided a house complete with chapel just two roads away in Bruton Street. At last the nuns were able to resume their regular hours and religious discipline.

Now serious house-hunting began. Henry, 8th Lord Arundell, offered Laherne in Cornwall but it was too small. So was Sir John Webbe's house in Dorset. The Duke of Queensberry's house at Amesbury in Wiltshire, Derking Abbey in Norfolk and Lord Gage's High Meadow in Gloucestershire, were all considered. Amesbury was the favourite but the nuns could get no response from the Duke of Queensberry. As time went on several of the nuns became sick through lack of exercise as no one ever left the house in Bruton Street except on business. Mother Teresa Dennett died there at the age of seventy and had to be buried privately at Pancras not, as was the Canonesses' custom, in the nuns' own burial ground clothed in a religious habit and with the Community accompanying her to the grave. This proved most distressing.

With no obvious solution on the horizon Mr Clifton set out to reconnoitre Holme Hall in Yorkshire. Charles, Lord Stourton, was eager to make it available as a stop-gap and even offered, with his customary generosity, to pay the first year's rent in any other property the nuns might take. Mr Clifton reported back favourably, two ships took all the furniture and other effects to Hull and the party went by mail coach to York at £3.5s.0d per person (£265 in modern values). The wet weather and poor roads slowed the journey. The nuns at the Bar Convent in York provided accommodation on arrival before the final twenty-five mile journey to Holme.

So, at long last, in November 1794, after four exhausting months the remnants of the Liège party arrived at Holme Hall on Spalding Moor, five miles from the nearest town, Market Weighton. Now the nuns could begin rebuilding their Community and school, starting with the thirteen pupils who had completed the odyssey from Liège – the three Miss Plunketts from Dunsany in Ireland, Louisa Fermor of Tusmore in Oxfordshire, Miss Gerard of Garswood in Lancashire, Miss Skerritt of Dublin, two Miss MacDonnells of Edinburgh, Miss Eyre of Sheffield, Miss Leckonby of Preston and three French girls, Mademoiselle Berlize and Mademoiselle Olivier from Lorraine, and the much endangered Louise de Choiseul from Angers[7], who was now safe from the terrors of the French Revolution.

Chapter 16

Neither Here nor There

Holme Hall and Dean House 1794-1798

The first winter at Holme Hall was severe. The garden was a wilderness and, without a harvest of home-grown vegetables, food was at first hard to come by.[1] None could be bought in the neighbourhood. Suspicious locals were convinced that the presence of this alien community would push up prices to their own detriment. The rumours that the nuns were Frenchmen in disguise led to some agitation to light the beacon as an indication that an invasion had started. On at least one occasion the nuns had to leave off singing Vespers because of the number of local Protestants crowding noisily into the Chapel to witness this bizarre event.

Things gradually settled down. Charles, Lord Stourton, gave extra land so that two or three cows could be kept. A Protestant lady at Pocklington, seven miles away, sent a basket of vegetables every week until the nuns had established their own garden and there was a small orchard which would produce fruit in season. The two acre walled garden provided an enclosure in which the nuns could exercise. When a belated offer of the house at Amesbury came from the Duke of Queensberry it was politely declined. The remoteness of the Yorkshire moors was welcome after four years of turbulence and at long last the Community was able to restore its religious discipline. Significantly, Charlotte Clifford was the first of the Canonesses to be professed in England, on March 12th 1795, an event that Susan Hawley would have cherished. The Cliffords continued to be trend setters. Thomas Clifford was to be made a baronet in 1815, the first Catholic elevation since the seventeenth century,[2] and Henry Clifford was to be one of the first recipients of the Victoria Cross during the Crimean War.[3]

The Jesuits from the Liège Academy were not far away from Holme Hall, having settled at Stonyhurst across the Pennines in Lancashire, on land given by the Welds of Lulworth. The priests rode over to make a visit to Holme Hall in September 1794. A former priest, Mr Barrow, who was about to visit Liège to see if he could tie up business matters for the Jesuits, undertook to try to collect rents for the Canonesses or, alternatively, to sell whatever land he could to ease their parlous financial situation.

The school temporarily resumed its activities with ten pupils but, with the nuns and girls having to sleep in one room, conditions were unacceptable and parents were asked to take their daughters home. This caused a temporary panic amongst some of the client families as a rumour spread that the nuns were poised to emigrate to America. Mr Clifton, now weakened by a serious illness which hit him not long after the arrival in Yorkshire, set out to look at two larger houses – Wrox Hall in Warwickshire and Dean House near Salisbury, the latter recommended by the Arundell family who lived at nearby Wardour Castle. Wrox Hall was too small and Dean House, although larger than Holme Hall, was still not spacious enough comfortably to accommodate the Community, servants and pupils. The nuns would have to lodge in the very confined attic rooms and the building in general was in a poor state of repair. But, at least, the school would be able to resume its work. The nuns quickly decided to accept a tenancy but it would be yet another stop-gap.

Another long and expensive journey was necessary and the nuns had very little by way of regular income. Friends stumped up £500[4] (£34,750 in modern values). On October 21st 1796 the furniture went by sea from Hull to Southampton accompanied by five lay sisters and two servants. On October 23rd three nuns went by mail coach to be at Dean House when the furniture arrived. The landlord's promise, that coals would be laid in and repairs made, had not been fulfilled and there was no friendly patron, like Lord Stourton at Holme Hall, to put things right. The nuns' furniture, which they had been led to believe could be transported by water to within five miles of Dean House, was stuck at Southampton. The local roads were so bad that farmers would not hire out their horses to pull barges on waterways as they needed the animals for their own purposes, so everything had to be transported overland by pack horse and carts at great expense. The rest of the Community came by stage coach from York to London as there were no direct routes across country to Salisbury. The French priest, Mr Genin, was badly injured when his stage coach overturned. It took two weeks to complete the transfer of the major part of the Community. The conclusion of the journey on November 5th was an unpropitious time for Catholic nuns to be travelling. Fireworks were thrown by Protestants who rejoiced at this convenient target for their anti-Popery celebrations. The final part of the journey from Salisbury to Dean House was on such a muddy and flooded road, that it was difficult to get coach drivers who were willing to brave the journey. The Prioress finally arrived on November 12th and Mr Clifton on November 15th enabling a full religious life to recommence.

The first winter was harsh. The Community had no coal, just quickly burning wood. Building repairs were going so slowly that the first pupil, Henrietta Goldie from Edinburgh, was not admitted until the middle of June 1797.[5] The landlord grudgingly leased another six or seven acres to the Community but at an exorbitant cost about three times the normal rate. One of the nuns noted that the Anglican parish church was so near the house "that we could with ease hear the singing and preaching ... it was a very unpleasant circumstance for us".[6] But it was not all doom and gloom. Despite the difficulties we have a fascinating handwritten account of school life, *Days of Yore*, by Henrietta Goldie.[7] For the first time we have an actual insight into what school life was like.

When she started Henrietta had six mistresses, confirming that only a minority of nuns were engaged in teaching at any one time. She had what she called a head mistress, Mother Francis Xaveria Trant, who looked after her general welfare, came regularly to her morning and night prayers and was always present at dinner and supper time helping Henrietta to her various dishes. Mother Agatha Laurenson gave Henrietta a music lesson twice a week for an hour and listened to her reading in English and French three times a week for half an hour – "learn to read slow; all other graces will follow in their proper places" was the motto. She also gave her a lesson of writing four times a week for half an hour, with some success, if the handwriting in *Days of Yore* is anything to go by. Mother Mary Buchanan Smith gave flower-painting lessons three times a week. She was an excellent artist but "a sickly, middle-aged person". Sister Anne Teresa (sister of Lord Clifford and aunt to the two Clifford girls who in August became Henrietta's companions) taught drawing of heads – "she had a very winning manner of teaching ... my first drawing was of an old Jew with a long beard and nightcap, drawn on light brown paper with black, red and white chalk". Later that year Henrietta's mother brought her a turbaned head of a Sultana to draw. Sister Aloysia Austin (Ann Clifford) gave Italian lessons twice a week on Tuesday and Thursday afternoons. Because Catholic books were scarce she also compiled a general history text which was still in use a century later.[8]

On Henrietta's sixteenth birthday in August "my five mistresses came to dine and take tea. They also walked with me between meals. All this I considered a great treat". For a visit of Lord and Lady Clifford who were bringing their two daughters from Devon to start school, Anne Maria aged nine and a half and Christina aged eight, Henrietta prepared an eight page life of Alfred the Great and a written description of a voyage along the east coast of Spain from Perpignan in France to Algiers in North Africa, at the end of which she blazoned the arms of the Clifford family and

Lady Clifford's family, the Arundells. She also gave them a little speech of welcome in French. Later in August Margaret Smith from Woodhall in Northumberland arrived. She had two aunts amongst the nuns and spoke with such a strong regional accent that she was called "little Scotchy". With four pupils they were now able to dance minuets on the lawn. In September Catherine Nickell, a cousin of two more nuns, arrived. She was eight years old and a poor reader.

Much of the learning was by rote copying. In October "we learnt by heart a French conversation and a sacred history intermixed with geography which we repeated before some of our mistresses". Every now and then Father Clifton gave some religious instruction in the Chapel and Henrietta said the Catechism to her head mistress four times a week between 12.30 p.m. and 1.00 p.m., after which the mistress would read aloud from *Instructions for Youth* translated from the French work written by the Reverend Charles Gobinet. On Tuesday and Thursday afternoons Henrietta read to herself for half an hour from the life of a saint "or other edifying book" such as *Novelle Morale* (Moral Stories) or Tasso's *Gerusalemme Liberata* (Jerusalem Delivered) in addition to the Italian lessons mentioned above. Physical exercise was that which was deemed appropriate for a young lady – walks in the grounds or when the weather was bad, Friars' Ground, a sort of running and catching game played indoors, as well as country dances after supper, one nun playing the accompaniment and another dancing with the pupils. A skipping rope was later introduced, with two holding and two skipping. It was all very genteel.

In November 1787 Mary and Anne Wright arrived, aged sixteen and fourteen respectively, orphan sisters who were in the care of Thomas Wright, the Essex banker from Brentwood. Their aunt, Ann Wright (Mother Aloysia Joseph), was one of the nuns. Then came Mary Anne Tuite from St. Croix in the West Indies, another orphan, interestingly from the same Caribbean Island as one of the nuns, Ann McEvoy (Mother Aloysia Staislaus) whose brother, Michael, was soon to buy New Hall. Mother Agatha Laurenson taught all eight girls arithmetic three times a week as well as music, geography and history. She could speak five languages fluently (English, French, Latin, German and Italian) but "it was not the fashion for young ladies to learn German and Latin; none of us took lessons in them". History teaching involved Mother Agatha giving lectures once a week from which the girls were expected to write notes in their leisure time, starting with the history of Charles XII of Sweden and Tsar Peter the Great of Russia. On another day they studied the four northern countries (Norway, Denmark, Sweden and Russia) using maps and on Saturdays had lectures on the globe. Short lessons on heraldry ensured that the girls understood many of their family histories, a socially desirable asset with so many of the great Catholic families intertwined by marriage. To perfect their written style they wrote letters in English and French on alternate weeks with an Italian letter or exercise every week. On Saturday afternoons, after work on the Catechism and some private moral reading, Saturday duties began – personal hygiene and washing, and looking out proper clothes for Sunday. Henrietta complained that they had little time for needlework – Mondays, Wednesdays and Fridays from 3.30 p.m. to 5.00 p.m. - during which time they took it in turns to read aloud in French.

In December 1787 eighteen year old Lucy O'Toole and two more sisters, Letitia and Margaret Whyte, aged eleven and seven, all from Ireland, joined the school. Each girl's mother had recently died. As Henrietta makes mention of her own mother but never her father she may have been in a similar situation, with just one living parent. The pattern continued on New Year's Eve when the orphaned sixteen year old Isabella O'Donnell joined the school. It would be interesting to know how many of the girls over a longer period of time were orphans or had just one living parent and therefore the extent to which the school was seen literally as an extended family. The evidence is lacking. But the fact that so many girls in this small sample had relatives amongst the nuns reinforces the view that this may have been an underlying trend. Protestant girls in such bereaved circumstances were often sent to live with relatives in the extended family. The school provided a Catholic alternative.

Besides lessons there were moments of relaxation. Every two or three weeks the girls enjoyed Nun-night for an hour in the evening in the room where the Community assembled. And then there were the great feasts. On November 21st, the Presentation of the Blessed Virgin Mary, all mistresses took tea with the girls and the young nuns did the same on December 5th, 6th and 7th. On December 18th the girls ceased their studies, until after Epiphany, with an oral examination of what they had learned over the previous six weeks.

The Christmas period was an essential part of their spiritual education but mixed with good fun. On Christmas Eve the older girls went to midnight mass followed by mulled wine with the nuns. With bed at 2.30 a.m. and wake up call at 7.30 a.m. on Christmas morning for High Mass at 9.30 a.m., it was a tiring day with early bed at 8.00 p.m.. December 27th was Holy Innocents Day. At noon the girls processed to the Community's room led by the two smallest, Margaret and Catherine, adorned with a black silk hood and a handkerchief, to look like little nuns. In a rather gentle version of the custom of the Lord of Misrule, the youngest asked, "Reverend Mother please to give us all the recreation of Holy Innocents. I will take care of the Community whilst you keep warm in the Infirmary". The nuns withdrew leaving the youngest child in charge. The girls then had all their meals with the nuns.

Thereafter the girls prepared three plays for Kingstide on the Sunday following the twelfth day of Christmas. Their first play was a little French drama with extracts from *L'Ami des Enfants* and *Les Soeurs de Lait* (Foster Sisters) but it was not entirely convincing – in the latter "the two Miss Wrights ... seemed far too young to be foster sister to Léonora [one of the Clifford girls] and their appearance [the Cliffords] was too aristocratical to be the children of a Paysanne". The other two plays were *Jubilee* and *Talisman* written by a nun, Felicitas Carcoran, who had died at Liège. On the Monday, Tuesday and Wednesday they were allowed to play cards, the only concession during the year to this unseemly activity, and during the fun the nuns supplied punch and plum cake. School recommenced on January 22nd 1798.

It is clear from Henrietta's account that the girls were now divided into three classes according to age and she was in the First Class. By this time her mother had located a French professional dancing master and half the girls took lessons from him twice a week. History classes had progressed to a study of the great Catholic monarch, Emperor Charles V, and his contemporary, Francis I of France. Their third great contemporary, Henry VIII, something of a villain in Catholic history, was understandably ignored. Geography now concentrated on the southern countries of Europe. Some of the girls also had to learn set piece conversations on interesting subjects which they had to repeat to their mistresses.

The days were long. The girls rose at 6.00 a.m. (6.30 on Sundays and holidays). After prayers and breakfast they had three quarters of an hour to prepare written or memorised pieces of work. Mass was at 8.00 a.m. followed by lessons until 11.00 a.m. when dinner was brought to the refectory. After dinner there was an hour's recreation during which they walked or took indoor exercise. During this time they could also sit and talk or play a game (not cards) but were not allowed to do anything that might be construed as study. At 12.30 p.m. there was Catechism or the reading of an improving book, for half an hour on Tuesdays and Thursdays and for an hour on other days. This was followed by the writing lesson on weekdays and then, Saturday excepted, by drawing or painting flowers. After these lessons tea took nearly an hour. On Thursdays there would then be a Benediction. Sometimes they took an additional walk when the weather was fine. At 5.00 p.m. on weekdays they recited aloud part of the Rosary and then had three quarters of an hour to prepare for the next day's lessons – probably more rote memory work or a written piece, as in the early morning. Supper was at 6.00 p.m. after which there was an hour and a half of recreation with walking or dancing according to the season. Then they would converse in French with two of the nuns before the Angelus bell summoned them to night prayers and bed at 8.30 p.m.. The little ones went to bed at 7.30 p.m.. The night prayers concluded with a French meditation.

Henrietta left Dean House after exactly a year on June 18th 1798. By this time the nuns were on the look out for a better place to make their permanent residence. There was some pressure from their friends and families to take over the Duke of Clarence's former house, Clarence Lodge, at Roehampton, ten miles out of London.

The Duke, the future King William IV, had been appointed Ranger of Bushey Park in 1797, a sinecure with a substantial country house a mile from Hampton Court and sold Clarence Lodge as he desperately needed the cash. He had paid 12,000 guineas for it in 1789[9] (£1,176,000 in today's money). In 1798 it was on the market again. One of the main advocates for the purchase was Michael McEvoy, brother of Anne McEvoy (Mother Aloysia Stanislaus). He had promised £4,000 (£315,960 in modern values) towards the purchase of any suitable premises, though one feels that the asking price of such an expensive property would probably have been well outside his budget had negotiations got that far and would have required significant injections of cash from other benefactors. Clarence Lodge would also have been too near the centre of civilisation for the Community to maintain its privacy. Nonetheless the Chapter, in the absence of any other suitable alternative, retained an interest but deferred final judgement as there were legal issues concerning land ownership that needed to be resolved.[10] During this delay they were informed that New Hall, in the village of Boreham, just north of Chelmsford in Essex, was available and would be more suitable. When the Community's friends, including Michael McEvoy, went to see it they were totally converted. A visit from Mr Clifton confirmed their judgement.

Since 1794 the nuns had lived in seven houses, several barges and a ship. In the process they had travelled hundreds of miles in great discomfort and frequent danger. The school had been significantly reduced, then temporarily closed in Yorkshire and had recovered to fifteen pupils by the end of 1798 when they left Wiltshire for New Hall.

They were about to find their true home.

Chapter 17

Coming Home

New Hall, the House 1713-1802

So what had happened to New Hall since the Dukes of Albermarle owned it?

Sadly it had fallen into neglect during the insanity of the 2nd Duchess of Albermarle, Christopher Monck's widow. Her second husband, Ralph, 1st Duke of Montagu had married her in 1692, and was even prepared to dress as the Emperor of China to satisfy her insane requirement that she would marry only a monarch.[1] He was nothing but a fortune hunter after a rich widow's pickings so there is some rough justice in the fact that he died in 1710 and she lived another quarter of a century.

Widowed for the second time, the Duchess sold New Hall in 1713 to Sir Richard Hoare at the end of his year as Lord Mayor of London, under the condition that she be allowed to live in it until her death. Sir Richard was son of Richard Hoare who founded Hoares Bank in 1672 in Cheapside in London. Today C. Hoare and Co., its descendant, is the only private bank of that era still surviving. Sir Richard was knighted by Queen Anne[2] and struck lucky in the South Sea Bubble speculation of 1720, selling shares at a tidy profit which enabled him to buy Stourton House on the Wiltshire/Dorset border[3] from Thomas, 14th Lord Stourton, when he came into the title. Without delay Sir Richard demolished it and, with the help of Capability Brown, built a new Palladian house next door, Stourhead, with beautifully landscaped grounds.

Perhaps Sir Richard had intended that New Hall would have been that showpiece. But his speculative success in 1720 and the fact that the mad Duchess lived until 1734 meant that Stourhead became the focus of attention and New Hall disappeared from his plans. By the time of the Duchess' death New Hall was dilapidated and written off as a bad investment. It passed to a younger son, Benjamin Hoare. Rather than renovate New Hall he built Boreham House nearby, yet another Palladian property, designed by James Gibbs, and took some of the best fixtures and fittings from New Hall to equip it. In 1737 Edward Harley, 2nd Earl of Oxford, described how "we went to see the ruins of New Hall ... The House was all uncovered, the floors taken up and sold, all the chimney pieces gone and all is to be sold as fast as there are bidders". Local farmers had also pillaged some of the brickwork to enhance their farmhouses.[4] The famous chapel window was hidden by ivy and that too was sold in 1742.[5]

In 1738 Benjamin Hoare sold the redundant New Hall to John Olmius. He was a grandson of the Dutch trader Hermen Olmius who had become a naturalised Englishman in 1675.[6] As a successful merchant he invested his profits in nine Essex estates, including Cressing Temple, perhaps intending one for each of his nine children. One of them, John, became deputy governor of the Bank of England and his son, another John, was the eventual purchaser of New Hall. He at once began work on the house as can be seen from the 1738 date on the downpipe hoppers. He dismantled the courtyards and the service buildings to the east. Without a courtyard in front of it the Earl of Sussex's beautiful Elizabethan north wing became a self-contained house. It was remodelled with a new entrance and deeply projecting bays were inserted between the existing windows. Repairs and renovations were done to the Tudor brickwork. On the east side he cannibalised Tudor bricks to rebuild the service quarters round a courtyard to which access was gained through a doorway, reused from Henry VIII's gatehouse. No expense was spared on the interior with panelling and plasterwork in the latest fashion. The current Chapel and a surviving bedchamber are fine examples.[7]

Away from New Hall, John Olmius was a political wheeler-dealer who was MP for Weymouth in 1737 and Colchester in 1754. He married Anne Billiers, daughter of Sir William Billiers who was Lord Mayor of London 1733-1734.[8] Like many a nouveau riche he coveted a peerage to which end he devoted himself to supporting Sir Robert Walpole, Britain's first Prime Minister, and in the 1741 General Election acted as his agent in some dirty and disputed contests, not unusual for those times of small electorates with few controls on bribery. But he had hitched his horse to the wrong wagon. Walpole fell from power in 1742 and Henry Pelham and his brother, Thomas, the Duke of Newcastle, proceeded to dominate politics with the former managing the House of Commons until his death in 1754, and the latter, with some of his Whig colleagues in the House of Lords, controlling a wide range of pocket and rotten boroughs to produce government majorities at elections over the next twenty years. Like many out-of-favour politicians Olmius gravitated to the Leicester House Court of the heir to the throne, Prince Frederick, on the assumption that sudden illness could at any time carry off George II leaving the new monarch keen to reward his supporters with offices and titles. But that plan backfired when the Prince died in 1751. In 1757 Olmius sent a long-shot letter to the Duke of Newcastle soliciting a peerage as an acknowledgement of his "family, fortune and principles".[9] He was not successful. In 1760 George II died. This signalled the end of Newcastle's dominance and the arrival of George III's favourite, the Earl of Bute, as the man who pulled the political strings. In June 1762 Bute became Prime Minister and Olmius was created 1st Baron Waltham of Philipstown, an Irish peerage that did not carry a place in the House of Lords and thereby permitted continued membership of the House of Commons. Ironically Olmius died in October 1762 before he could enjoy the sweet taste of success.[10]

He was succeeded by his son, Digue Billiers Olmius, 2nd Baron Waltham. He fought the 1774 Maldon election on an anti-Catholic ticket. His election poster proclaimed:

"No Popery, No Arbitrary Power!

BUT

Lord Waltham, with Liberty and the Protestant Religion!"[11]

He did not win that one but succeeded ten years later in 1784. He died at New Hall on February 10th 1787 deeply in debt because of his expenditure on the house and grounds which included the creation of a lake behind the house and a very large greenhouse.[12] The short-lived Waltham peerage also became extinct on his death. New Hall passed to his sister Elizabeth Olmius who had married John Luttrell, the heir to the Earldom of Carhampton. The marriage was held by special licence at New Hall.[13] Luttrell, from the family that owned Dunster Castle near Minehead in Somerset, changed his name to Luttrell-Olmius. His own estate was Luttrellstown Castle in the Irish Pale where the Luttrells were one of the most significant Catholic families.[14] Elizabeth died in 1797 and was the last to be buried in the Waltham Mausoleum, an octagonal building that stood in the north-west corner of Boreham churchyard till 1944,[15] the church being too full of Sussex tombs to take yet another family. John Luttrell-Olmius, as beneficiary from her will, took the decision to offload New Hall. Selling to a Catholic order would not have bothered him half as much as it would have done his deceased brother-in-law!

In 1798 New Hall house was valued at 2,000 guineas (£165,880 in modern values) and included a considerable amount of land. After some negotiation the price was increased to £4,000 (£315,960 today) to include a total of fifty-eight acres of land which would ensure the privacy that was crucial for an enclosed order. Michael McEvoy paid the money "for which I entail no kind of obligation for myself or family, except that as being considered a Founder for the general good of the Community and of Religion".[16] The nuns agreed to buy some of the furniture in the house and the timber on the land, for an extra sum of £489 (£38,630 today). The nuns' possessions were conveyed overland to New Hall at a cost of just over £239 (£18,880 today). A small advance party of nuns arrived at New Hall on January 25th 1799.[17] Reverend Mother Aloysia Clough arrived on February 1st. Mass was said for the first time on February 3rd. The depth of snow kept the rest of the Community at Dean House until February 21st. Ultimately everyone had arrived by March 3rd though tables and chairs had to be auctioned to pay carriage costs.

The house at New Hall was the most spacious yet but was still crowded. Most of the rooms were given up for the school. All the apartments at one end of the house were taken by the nuns and, at the other, by the pupils. A new building containing thirty-eight nuns' cells (each 10 x 8½ x 9½ feet), two infirmaries (presumably one for nuns and one for pupils) and some storage and office rooms, was opened on May 29th 1799. Work also began on converting the Great Hall into a Chapel, minus a room which was partitioned off for a Refectory. In the interim the nuns' workroom was used as a place of worship. The Chapel was finished and blessed on August 14th 1799.

The house had been described to the nuns as being in excellent repair, though it needed some expenditure to make it suitable for habitation by such a large group. The very dry summer of 1800 enabled the roof to be re-leaded. The old lead was sold and paid for the cost. At the rear of the house there was a canal, a relic of the old moat, and this was drained for the safety of the pupils. The drains had also not been cleared for years.

There was only one well for drinking water. The pipes that took the water round the house did not extend to the pupils' end and so water had to be carried there by hand. However there was a spring about twenty yards from the building and a pipe was laid to divert the water for school use. The springs which provided water for the rest of the house came from adjacent farmland still owned by John Luttrell-Olmius and, when New Hall had been bought, no legal protection had been included to guarantee continued water access. In 1802 Luttrell-Olmius informed the nuns that he intended to sell these neighbouring farms and he advised them to get a proper deed drawn up that guaranteed water access before he put the land up for sale. The nuns actually wanted to buy the four fields through which the pipes passed and in which the spring lay, but legally the farm had to be sold as one entity. The nuns were lucky to have a co-religionist as such an accommodating neighbour.

The oven was also a problem. It was large enough for a family's needs but not for this vast community that now filled the premises. In 1800 a new bakery was built out of a stable with an oven large enough to bake sixty loaves at a time. In the same summer Mrs Laurenson, from Witham in Essex, mother of Mary Laurenson (Mother

Mary Sales) and Father John Laurenson (of the Liège Academy and now Stonyhurst College), fitted up two rooms for herself over the bakery, at a cost of £37 (£1,900 in modern values), so that she could board at the convent. They were ready in November 1800 and must have been kept snugly warm by the bakery.

A controversial incident involved the chopping down and sale of the wood from the double avenue of lime trees, which may have been the originals planted by John Tradescant, a mile in length leading from the main London road to the house. In the nuns' defence they had not purchased them with the property. They had agreed only to leave them standing until a purchaser for the wood had been found. Presumably the profits went to John Luttrell-Olmius. Local feeling may well have run high – the trees were described as "the pride and boast of the neighbourhood" and the wood was sold at a low price.[18] If they were the original Tradescant trees they would have been quite hollow and at the end of their lifespan, so perhaps they needed to be cleared. The 1805 Ordnance Survey map shows the double avenue quite clearly but as the survey was carried out in 1799 these would have been the old trees. Clearly the avenue was replanted as White's Directory of 1848 refers to a "noble avenue of trees".

The nuns may have left Liège but they still had a lot of capital tied up in property there. In 1801 the war between England and France came to a temporary end with the Peace of Amiens which, as one of its minor clauses, allowed all English properties in French controlled territories to be restored to their former owners. The nuns gave Power of Attorney to Mr Barrow, who was still working on behalf of the Stonyhurst Jesuits, to do whatever he could on their behalf. He managed to get the convent and its properties officially restored and the nuns received some portion of their rents before war broke out again in 1803. During the ensuing twelve years' conflict the old convent buildings were occupied by families whose houses had been destroyed. When peace returned in 1815 Liège was incorporated into the Kingdom of the Netherlands which was under the Protestant House of Orange, one of a series of enlarged barrier states surrounding France intended to thwart the resurgence of any future French territorial ambitions. The Dutch authorities were insensitive in the treatment of their Catholic subjects in Belgium and refused to allow the nuns to realise capital or collect revenues unless they chose to return to open a school. The nuns declined the offer so the Dutch authorities seized the convent's property in 1823.[19] By the time Catholic Belgium rebelled and gained its independence in 1830 the property had been dispersed.

But Catholic Liège was all in the past. The future would be in Protestant Essex.

MAP 4:
The Canonesses in England

Chapter 18

La crème de la crème

New Hall families 1799-1829

School numbers quickly picked up. The nuns arrived at New Hall in January 1799 with eighteen girls. Numbers rose by steps to forty-six by December and for the next thirty years they still averaged forty-six, though this covers up a significant drop from 1819-1824 for reasons unknown (see Table 4). [1]

Table 4:

Average monthly pupil numbers 1800-1829

1800	56	1806	47	1812	50	1818	50	1824	32
1801	62	1807	48	1813	52	1819	36	1825	41
1802	55	1808	41	1814	57	1820	32	1826	37
1803	60	1809	39	1815	57	1821	31	1827	44
1804	55	1810	39	1816	59	1822	35	1828	44
1805	47	1811	45	1817	58	1823	29	1829	42

There were now many more Catholic schools with which New Hall had to compete though marketing was a concept unknown in early nineteenth century education. Catholics had been used to keeping their heads down for the last 265 years and relied on the grapevine to find out about schools, quite easily done when the major families intermarried so extensively. This grapevine probably still functioned well in the nineteenth century with recommendations for the school contained in letters that do not survive and family assemblages on anniversaries and Holy Days. Thus a brief advertisement in the 1803 Catholic Directory[2] demurely announces that "the Ladies from Liège have opened their school in a healthy situation where airy and commodious apartments are neatly fitted up for the immediate reception of young ladies. Conditions may be had by applying to Mrs Clough as above". Note the care in avoiding Bridget Clough's proper title, Reverend Mother Aloysia, even in a document aimed at Catholics, for fear of flaunting styles of address that would offend Protestants.

There were at least twenty-five alternative English schools for Catholic girls at the turn of the century led by the Bar Convent at York and the English Benedictines of Hammersmith, old established schools that had defied the penal laws and got away with it. The former English Community of Brussels and the ladies from the Prinsenhof, Bruges, went to Winchester. The Ladies of the Order of St. Austin from Louvain settled near Blandford in Dorset. The Benedictines from Cambrai were relocated in Liverpool, those from Ghent in Preston, from Montergis in Brandon in Norfolk and from Paris near Shaftesbury in Dorset. The Teresians from Antwerp found a home at St. Columb in Cornwall, those from Hoogestraat at Wimborne in Dorset and from Lier at Auckland near Durham. The Poor Clares from Dunkirk made their home near Worcester, those from Gravelines at Gosfield in Essex (later moving to Buckingham), from Rouen at Haggerston Castle in Northumberland and from Aire at Watlington in Oxfordshire. Nine other schools that did not seem to be run by religious orders were advertised, mostly in London and the Midlands. Of the girls' schools that were run by religious orders one was priced at 35 guineas (£1,900 translated from 1800 to modern values), two at 30 guineas (£1,620 today) and the rest between 20 guineas (£1,080 today) and 26 guineas (£1,405 today).[3] New Hall, at 44 guineas was, in price terms, at the top of the pile. Its fees had doubled from those of Liège. Much of the increase would have been caused by England's higher costs of living and war-time inflation. In real terms there was not much difference. 22 guineas at Liège in 1790 was worth £1,955 in modern values, 44 guineas at New Hall in 1800 was worth only £2,378.

These schools were also geographically well spread. Parents could find a school relatively close at hand though, as at New Hall, the presence of aunts, cousins and sisters amongst the nuns and fellow-pupils would have been an influence. However the Canonesses of the Holy Sepulchre had the monopoly in Essex. The English Poor Clares from Gravelines, enjoying the hospitality of the Marchioness of Buckingham at Gosfield Hall, in 1814 fulfilled their original intention of making their home at Buckingham itself[4] which left New Hall as the county's sole Catholic school for young ladies.

When one examines the surnames in the pupil registers there is a constant reminder of the traditional Catholic gentry and aristocratic families, many of them legendary in the history of Catholic recusancy. To illustrate these connections it is worth looking at the Liège intake as well as that of New Hall.

The Arundell, Blundell and Chichester families had suffered for supporting Royalist forces in the Civil War. The Arundells of Wardour in Wiltshire had lost their land but it had been bought by the non-combatant Catholic Welds of Lulworth who held it in trust for them.[5] Catherine Arundell was at New Hall from 1811 to 1812 and a wave of seven more Arundell girls arrived in the middle of the nineteenth century. A Weld girl attended New Hall from 1812 to 1816 and fifteen more were to come during the next hundred years. Nicholas Blundell had lost his lands in the Civil War but staved off poverty because his wife retained hers.[6] Two Blundell sisters were at New Hall from 1802 to 1804 and 1806 to 1809. The Blundells later intermarried with the Coppinger family from Ireland[7] who provided two New Hall daughters from 1812 to 1815. But the Blundells were one of the noted Catholic families who conformed to Anglicanism thus ending the New Hall connection. Four Chichester girls from Arlington in Devon (1780-1782, 1781-1783, 1783-1786, 1802-1807) came from a classic recusant family whose sequestered lands in the Civil War, as in the case of the Arundells, were bought by friends and then leased back to the family.[8]

The most prolific family were the Cliffords, nineteen of whose girls attended the school in Liège, Yorkshire, Wiltshire and Essex. There were only twelve years in the seventy-two years from 1777 to 1848 without a Clifford pupil. Lord Clifford, another Devonshire recusant, from Chudleigh, was a loyalist who, like Lord Petre in Essex, raised a militia at his own cost in 1798 at the height of the French invasion scare.[9]

Two families had contrasting experience with the double land tax. The Constables of Everingham and Burton Constable in Yorkshire invented a clever way to escape it by borrowing large sums of money from friends on the security of their lands.[10] They may well have been represented at Liège by three Constable girls in the second half of the 1770s. The Darrells of Calehill in Kent were not so lucky and were hit badly by the double land tax on their share of the Little Chart estate.[11] Nonetheless there were four Darrell girls in Liège variously between 1780 and 1791.

Three of the great Catholic aristocratic families, the Petres, Stourtons and Howards are represented, the latter only just, with one Howard girl spending nearly five years at New Hall in a split stay between 1808 and 1816. This vast family provided the Dukes of Norfolk but their young ladies were generally educated elsewhere. A Petre girl from Bellhouse in Essex was at New Hall from 1808 to 1816, four had been educated at the school in the early eighteenth century and fifteen others were to pass through the classroom doors over the next seventy-five years. There were two Stourton girls in the 1720s, two more in the 1760s, and three in the 1790s from the family of this generous benefactor and nine more Stourton girls followed up to 1864.

Girls with surnames of persecuted priests are also to be found. Lady Teresa Plunkett attended Liège from 1779 to 1780 (the Plunketts were also Earls of Fingall),[12] with four other Plunkett girls variously there between 1786 and 1795, all, perhaps, related in some way to Oliver Plunkett, Archbishop of Armagh, who was falsely executed in the aftermath of the Popish Plot.[13] Charlotte Talbot, at Liège from 1780 to 1781, may well have come from the wealthy and prominent Catholic family that provided the Earls of Shrewsbury and two late eighteenth century Catholic Vicars-Apostolic, one of whom, in 1771, was the last Catholic to be prosecuted for his faith (see Chapter 14). An active priest who escaped the clutches of the law was Thomas Brockholes, whose vigorous proselytizing in Wolverhampton earlier in the eighteenth century earned the town the nickname "Little Rome".[14] Frances Brockholes and her sister, who were at New Hall from 1813 to 1814, may well have been related to him.

The Cisalpine Club formed in 1792 (and not disbanded until 1830) was certainly well-represented by surname in the Liège and New Hall pupil registers. This private club, under the 9th Lord Petre's chairmanship, continued the work of the Catholic Committee that had negotiated the terms of the Catholic Relief Act of 1791 by ensuring that the laity continued to have the upper hand in the governance of the English Catholic Church.[15] Their members saw themselves as the sensible pragmatists who had ensured the survival of Catholicism. This was to be the high point of their power, soon to be altered by the large Irish Catholic immigration which shifted the balance of power from the heads of rural houses to the missionary clergy in the industrial towns.

Of the twenty-two nominated members in the Cisalpine Club[16], many of them peers, twenty had surnames in common with girls in the school (see Table 5).

Of the twenty-six elected members fourteen had surnames represented in the pupil registers. Two of them were junior branches of the Catholic peerage families[17] and the rest are shown in Table 6.

While there may not have been a direct daughter or other relationship in all these cases, and cadet branches of the main title holder might spread out far and wide, nonetheless it is reasonable to assume that most of these girls were directly or indirectly associated with the Catholic peers, baronets and major gentry.

That New Hall's young ladies represented the cream of Catholic society could not disguise the fact that England was not necessarily a welcoming place for the nuns. Initial sympathy for these religious victims of French regicide Republicanism hid a deep dislike of Catholicism which soon resurfaced. Nonetheless the nuns shared in the rejoicing at Nelson's victory at Trafalgar in 1805 with the singing of the Te Deum and, like many Catholics, were staunchly loyal to the Crown.

Table 5:

Possible pupil connections with the nominated members of the Cisalpine Club

(* = Catholic peers)

9th Lord Petre*	Fifteen Petres	1799-1876
11th Duke of Norfolk (Howard family)*	A Howard girl	1808-1816
6th Lord Clifford*	Nineteen Cliffords	1777-1848
17th Lord Stourton*	Twelve Stourtons	1790-1864
8th Lord Arundell	Eight Arundells	1811-1864
15th Earl of Shrewsbury (Talbot family)*	Four Talbots	1780-1842
8th Earl of Fingall (Plunkett family)	Thirteen Plunketts	1791-1898
Baron Camoys (Dormer family)*	Two Dormers	1774-1783
Earls of Westmouth (Nugent family)	One Nugent	1802-1804
8th Viscount Taaffe	Three Taaffes	1776-1829
2nd Viscount Southwell	Five Southwells	1785-1862
Sir Henry Doughty-Tichborne [sic]	Two Titchbornes [sic]	1775-1816
Sir Charles Smythe	Three Smythes	1787-1819
Two Burke families	Ten Burkes	1781-1863
Sir Gerald Dalton-Fitzgerald	Three Daltons	1788-1794
	Five Fitzgeralds	1803-1882
Sir James Power	Eight Powers	1788-1841
Sir Patrick O'Brien	Ten O'Briens	1787-1854
Sir Henry Barron	One Barron	1812-1813
Sir John Ennis	One Ennis	1815-1821

Table 6:

Possible pupil connections with the Cisalpine Club

(non-peerage families)

Sir Walter Blount	Ten Blounts	1804-1891
Charles Butler	Three Butlers	1813-1824
William Fermor	Two Fermors	1788-1794
Sir John Lawson	One Lawson	1817-1818
John Townley	Two Townleys	1812-1818
Rev. Charles Bellasyse	One Ballasyses [sic]	1800-1805
Thomas Heneage	Two Heneages	1792-1794
Stephen Tempest	Two Tempests	1813-1822
Thomas Stapleton	Two Stapletons	1817-1834
Thomas Hawkins	One Hawkins	1793-1794
Henry Swinburne	One Swinburne	1802-1803
Dr Thomas Nickell	Two Nickells	1797-1807

During the Napoleonic wars there were constant fears of a French invasion of the Essex coast. In April 1804 Anna Maria Blount (later Prioress 1844-1869), a thirteen year old new girl, and her sister, Agatha, started at New Hall. Their uncle remonstrated with their father for "sending those two poor girls to school in Essex where the French were sure to land".18 Troops were garrisoned at Chelmsford for that reason. Father Clifton invited the commanding officer to the convent and asked him to place it under his protection. The officer who, like most Englishmen, had not seen a nun before reckoned he had never been engaged in such a formidable encounter.

There were other local uninvited visitors keen to satisfy their curiosity. Mother Mary Ann Head said to one such, "I am a nun. In seeing me you see all". Whether through disappointment or relief, the intruder responded, "Well, if they are all like her, there is not much to see". Another intruder was less phlegmatic. Mother Aloysia Austin Clifford's morning walk in the grounds in full habit caused an innocent labourer to flee screaming in terror at the sight of what he thought was a ghost. However, except for early morning Matins the nuns did not return to wearing their full habit until 1812.19 Discretion was the better part of valour.

In April 1806 the New Hall farm began with the purchase of another fifty-one acres of land at a cost of £2,100 (£115,860 in modern values). Twelve more acres were purchased in September for £540[20] (£29,800 today). All of this land was at the north side of the house (i.e. behind the house as you approach it up the avenue) and came from the old park. At the same time greater privacy for enclosure was achieved on the east side of the house where the road to Boreham had passed through the convent yard and orchard. It was now diverted to the east side of the pond. However enclosure was less absolute than in Liège as there was no grille through which nuns had to converse with visitors. Instead they would now walk with them in the grounds.[21]

But an era was ending. Some of the principal actors in the transplantation of the convent and school died - Father Genin in 1807, Father Clifton in 1812 and Reverend Mother Aloysia Clough, the first of New Hall's Prioresses, in 1816.[22]

Victory at Waterloo meant that Britons no longer associated the Catholic presence at home with a military threat from abroad. In 1829 Roman Catholic Emancipation extended the vote to Catholics, as well as the right to sit in Parliament and hold civic offices and military commissions. They were still excluded from the throne and, until 1871, from the ancient universities. But unlike 1780 there were no riots in protest. Things were changing slowly.

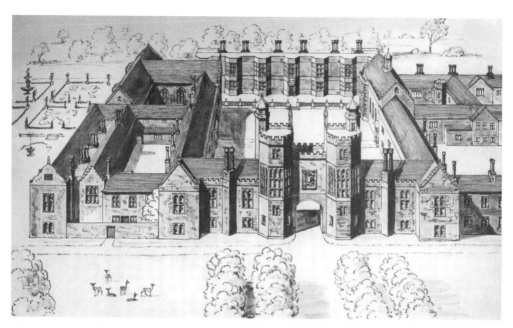

Artist's impression of Beaulieu, courtesy of the Reverend Ian Dunlop. It shows how New Hall might have looked in Elizabethan times. The wing in the north at the rear of the courtyard is the main school building.

View of the front of Beaulieu as engraved for the Society of Antiquaries by George Vertue 1786. The Henry VIII coat of arms is visible above the gate

Engraving of Lord Waltham's House from the south, late eighteenth century

Engraving of Lord Waltham's House from the north with lake and boat, late eighteenth century

Photograph by Annabel Brown

Stone Dragon
It watches over the school from the front lawn.
This piece of Tudor insignia was probably one of
a pair looking down from the gatehouse parapet

Photograph by Annabel Brown

Cellar in the Tudor basement of the east wing

1738 hopper.
Proof of the year in which John Olmius, who
became 1st Lord Waltham, started his
renovation of what remained of New Hall

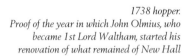

Archway that was at
the front of Henry VIII's
palace and moved to the
east side in 1738.

Tudor basement windows
can be seen through the
— arch on the left

Photograph by Annabel Brown

The Chapel sometime beween 1872 and 1881. The pictures in the Chapel panels were painted by Sr M. Ann Teresa Purcell.

Tennis net and older girls c.1914

Under the Cedars c.1917

Senior Class Room

Blue Room dormitory

Music Room

School Infirmary c.1914

The school 1934, showing current entrance door on the right

Chapter 19

A Genteel British School

The Young Ladies 1799-1829

New Hall was much more British in its intake than had been the school in Liège. Although, in England, the nuns' pupil registers[1] now rarely recorded places of origin, the surnames and other known family connections of those who entered the school in its first thirty years in Essex show that nearly 30% of the girls probably had Irish and Scottish origins with 61% probably from English families and the remaining 9% from Catholic Europe (Spain, the Low Countries, France, Germany and Italy) with one from the Caribbean.

The mean length of stay in this early period at New Hall was two years eight months, an overall increase of nine months on Liège. The British girls still stayed longer, two years eleven months, compared with the mean length of one year four months for their continental peers. We have starting and leaving dates for most of the girls. 9% stayed for less than a year (compared with 24% in Liège), 48% for between one and three years (45% in Liège), 25% for three to five years (21% in Liège), 10% for five to seven years (8% in Liège) and 8% for over seven years (3% in Liège). The massive reduction of short-stayers can be attributed to the reduction in continental pupils who accounted for most of the transitory appearances in Liège.

We also know the ages of the vast majority of the girls when they entered and left the school. Such details were much more spasmodically given in the Liège registers. At New Hall in the first thirty years 67% started between the ages of eleven and fifteen and 21% between the ages of seven and eleven. The rest comprised a small number entering at what we would call today nursery age or as late teenagers, the latter using New Hall as a finishing school and inevitably staying very briefly.

117

Looked at from the other end of the spectrum 49% left at the age of between sixteen and eighteen and 26% left at the ages of fourteen and fifteen. Thus three-quarters of the girls left as mid to late teenagers having developed sufficient learning and polish to be launched on the social scene and the marriage market. 17% left at the ages of eleven to thirteen, leaving 8% either starting very young for a short stay (caused in some cases by illness or family circumstances) or staying on until they were nineteen or twenty. In one case a Miss Carter was at the school for just under eleven years and left when she was twenty-three.

Up to 1890 these figures were to remain very stable (see Table 7). During the nineteenth century the school remained predominantly British with a slight decline throughout the century in the numbers from Scotland, Ireland and Wales. Consistently three-quarters of the girls stayed on until their mid or late teens, with a shift to late teens in the second half of the nineteenth century. Starting ages scarcely varied at all throughout the century. The numbers staying for three years or longer also remained much the same, although the numbers staying for less than a year crept up steadily towards the figure that had been common in Liège which showed that, as the century progressed, more British girls were seeing New Hall as a finishing school. The mean length of stay fluctuated a bit but always stayed between two and three years and British girls stayed on average six months to a year longer than their non-British counterparts. So even though pupil numbers varied considerably, their places of origin, length of stay and ages of starting and leaving remained remarkably constant.

Between 1799 and 1830 ten Gillow girls appear on New Hall's books. They were from a long-standing Lancashire Catholic family who were leading cabinet-makers and upholsterers based in Oxford Street in London and Lancaster. The aristocratic Stourtons sent five girls. Several Irish Catholic families sent large contingents – Murphy (twelve), Browne (seven), McCarthy (seven), MacCann (six), O'Connor (five), Roche (five) – and the Scottish MacDonnells, a military family, sent six girls. The Angelo family, possibly Italian, sent five. In thirty years 469 girls were admitted with just 242 different surnames, an indication of the large size of families with, on average, nearly two girls to each name.

In the first three decades at New Hall some of the preoccupations of the parents as expressed in individual requests reinforced the school's identification with the upper strata of society. Melior Weston (1798-1804) was "to drink wine, cocoa in the morning and tea in the evening". Her contemporary Miss Addis "must pay great attention to her carriage and to learn fine works". Some were to be spared anything that might smack of horny-handed toil – Miss Hill (1799-1801), for example, "is not required to do any work". The Perry sisters (1809-1814) and Ryan sisters (1810-1813) "are both to take port wine after dinner".

Table 7:
Pupil origins and lengths of stay 1770-1889

	1770-1794	1800-1829	1830-1859	1860-1889
From Wales, Ireland, Scotland	15%	30%	28%	24%
From England	29%	61%	57%	63%
From Europe	53%	9%	14%	12%
From other continents	3%	0%	1%	1%
Mean length of stay − all	1y 11m	2y 8m	2y 2m	2y 10m
Mean length of stay − Brit. Isles	2y 11m	2y 9m	2y 4m	2y 10m
Mean length of stay − Europe	1y 4m	2y 0m	1y 11m	1y 10m
Stayed less than 1 year	24%	9%	14%	19%
Stayed 1-3 years	45%	48%	45%	36%
Stayed 3-5 years	21%	25%	25%	26%
Stayed 5-7 years	8%	10%	10%	10%
Stayed over 7 years	3%	8%	6%	9%
Started at ages of 7 to 10	not known	21%	22%	20%
Started at ages of 11 to 15	not known	67%	66%	66%
Started before 7 or after 16	not known	12%	12%	14%
Left at ages of 16 to 18	not known	49%	46%	56%
Left at 14 or 15	not known	26%	29%	19%
Left at ages of 11 to 13	not known	17%	16%	15%
Left before 11 or after 19	not known	8%	9%	10%

The elder Townley (1812-1816) "is to take strong coffee for breakfast and in the afternoon when she has the headache. She is never to take wine unless the young ladies are treated. She may not go out with anyone except the Dowager Lady Stanley and to her grandpapa Mr Townley". Miss Weld (1812-1816) "is to drink pure water without any burnt toast put into it. She is to have fruit in the afternoon when it can be procured". A slice of toast soaked in boiling water was highly recommended for invalids but was clearly not thought much of by the Welds.[2]   On the other hand some girls had a little more of the ordinary about them, such as Miss McCarthy (1813-1817) who "is to make all her own clothes except her frock" and Miss Titchborne (1814-1816) who was to apply to "... mending her own clothes ..."

To be fair some of these dietary requests may have been linked to perceived health requirements as is explicitly stated with the afflicted Miss Balfe (1815-1818) who "is subject occasionally to a delicacy in her bowels. She is to take a glass of port wine every day at dinner". Port and porter, a kind of stout, were viewed as a general tonic which may have been desirable for menstruating girls.

The Stourton girls were either genetically inclined to weakness or had over-fussy parents. Of both Anna Maria and Teresa (1822-1829) it was noted that they should "not abstain two days together. They are to have porter every day. They are crooked". Appolonia (1824-1826) and Charlotte (1826-1832) "are both delicate. They are to eat meat every day". In the end each of the latter two "went away for her health".

The description of girls as being "crooked" is not uncommon, perhaps referring to posture and physical weakness that may have been aggravated by a physically inactive life and the stultifying effect of stays which had all sorts of negative impacts on proper growth as the upper half of the body was artificially confined. Some are advised not to do embroidery, presumably because stooping over a frame would make a bad situation worse. Thus for Miss Corballis (1826-1827) "the strictest attention is to be paid to her shape and carriage as essential for her health which is very delicate. She is to be required to sit erect at all times and it is the wish of her parents that any part of her study that requires her to stoop or lean should be avoided". Miss Barker (1827-1831), a local girl from Little Hallingbury, "has a defect in her shape. She is subject to faintness and is not allowed to kneel long".

Independence was not a virtue. Miss Mostyn "is not to write to anyone without inspection. She is of a lively volatile disposition and consequently requires strict management but not scolding. If much thwarted, she becomes disgusted and will not do anything. She is to have a pair of stays every six months and more frequently if requisite and the back should be made so as to give support and they should be very wide across the chest. She is to go out to nobody but Miss Ryan". This free spirit was too unladylike. Censorship and physical restriction were the remedy.

The parents of Eleanor Weld (1822-1830) gave very strict instructions for her health and social protection. "In the winter rhubarb and magnesia or, in the heat of summer, Epsom salts in the quantity of half an ounce with a teaspoonful of tincture of senna have been found to be the best medicine for her. She is not constitutionally subject to any ailment but every little cold requires attention or brings on bad coughs. She has been used to take for them an emollient of one gram of ipecacuana in treacle twice a day. She is not to go out to anyone".

This detailed prescription is more than matched by a letter from John Talbot about his daughter Anne who started school in 1835.[3] She is "to get a glass of sherry in water at dinner ... I wish the greatest attention to make her avoid rain and damp of any kind, particularly in the fact that her chest is delicate ... She also has a bad stomach and must be confined to a plain nourishing diet and to avoid fruit ... I wish her to be permitted at convenient times to write short letters to her friends. The reason I say this is that I fear too much writing would injure her health. I am particularly anxious she should write a good hand and be perfect in arithmetic and the keeping of small accounts as absolutely necessary in female education". In the event of illness the nuns are also to summon a named doctor from London "to counsel with the medical adviser of the establishment". None of these requirements was written in the pupil register (a black mark for one of the nuns!) but the twelve year old Anne managed five years at New Hall with no recorded mishaps. The Talbots were not the only ones who wanted a London doctor. The parents of the Grainger sisters (1805-1810) asked that "if either of them is particularly ill, as for example the measles, Dr Nickell is to be consulted". This may not be as unreasonable as it seems. There were plenty of quacks about and it was safer to stick with someone you knew and trusted such as the eminent doctor from the Cisalpine Club.

These examples accurately reflect contemporary attitudes to genteel ladies. Girls of affluent families were kept within domestic confines until they married when they passed almost immediately from an extended childhood to adulthood probably with no experience of ever having been out on their own.[4] At New Hall all their walks in the grounds were in the company of nuns. Female frailty was also taken as read.

If the doctors were not at hand the nuns had their own book of medicines which were carefully recorded to deal with coughs, diarrhoea, stomach upsets, consumption etc.. As there was no pharmaceutical industry until the twentieth century, the nuns' potions comprised mixtures of spirits, and, culled from their garden and surrounding countryside, roots, fruits and vegetables. For rheumatism they recommended eight ounces of shredded burdock root in three pints of water mixed till it reduced to a quart, with the patient taking a teacupful twice a day for two months at least. For "a decline" they prescribed two handfuls of stock boiled in two quarts of water; then a stick of liquorice and half a pound of each of honey, refined sugar and raisins had to be added, topped with two heads of garlic; the liquid would be strained off, stopped in a bottle and a teacupful taken morning and night.[5]

Some of the views on diet seem equally strange but are merely reflective of the wisdom of the time. Mrs Beeton's *Book of Household Management*, although published in 1861, codified the customs and etiquette that had been around for some time. She says that a child should lead a well-ordered simple life. Wholesome food was not only nutritious but morally edifying. Strong-tasting food, especially for girls, could arouse passion and be troublesome in puberty. Fruits and vegetables could be hazardous. Expensive, delicious foods were a self-indulgent temptation to be avoided.[6] Mrs Pedley, author of *Infant Nursing and the Management of Young Children*, reckoned that children fed on meat attained a higher intellectual ability[7] (or perhaps the uneducated poor could not afford much meat?) The girls at New Hall were certainly given plenty of meat. The school's *Regulations for the Kitchen* stated that "the young ladies must always have either boiled meat, cold meat or pie, or something equivalent, and roast meat every day. They may also have [meat] balls or potted meat but not instead of any of the above-named things". The exceptions would be abstinence days when there was fresh fish, pickled salmon or salt fish in season and the main feast days when poultry or game would be offered.[8]

The household accounts that had concerned Mr Talbot were, in fact, very important for a woman's self-esteem. This was the one area of domestic life where she was totally in control. Sloppy account books and arithmetical inaccuracy could lead at best to financial chaos and, at worst, to pilfering by dishonest servants. The probability of getting a good education in this aspect of a woman's life was high at New Hall. With nuns, in effect, running a major business and having an internal ruling that, teaching apart, no office may be held for longer than five years, there was a fair sprinkling of arithmetically adept women who would have had some experience of financial management.

However all social classes were equal before the scourge of smallpox.[9] It is interesting that virtually all the girls admitted to New Hall between 1799 and 1830 had had smallpox. Was this deliberate policy or did it reflect the fact that many who had the early inoculations actually contracted the disease mildly? It was reckoned that only 5% escaped it without preventive treatment.[10] We know that inoculations in county towns and populous villages were common by the 1770s.[11] Having said that, the nuns do discriminate between the disease and its prevention as Miss Segrave, admitted in 1810, is recorded as having had inoculation and the Coppinger sisters in 1812 as having had vaccine pox.

A series of letters in 1798-1799 from Mr R.J. Gandolfi to his twenty-three year old novice daughter Maria, who was a nun from 1799 to 1850, throws interesting light on the issues of the time. The war looms large in his mind – "we must now all turn out to defend ourselves and fight the savage hordes that threaten to invade us ... It is a great consolation to see such unanimity among all ranks of the Nation".[12] Mrs Gandolfi seems to fit the stereotype of the wilting woman who literally enjoys frail health – "we are so unfortunate as to not be able to prevail on her to ride. She always adduces some cause or other to get off". He also comments on the 1798 rebellion in Ireland and the desperate need for peace.[13]

As Maria moves towards profession his letters provide some insights into convent finances:

> "I am informed that formerly £500 [£46,340 in modern terms translated from 1790 values] or thereabouts used to be the sum generally given with a person entering the religious state but this was ... in countries where everything was so much cheaper than in England ... I don't think even £800 [only £41,200 in 1800 values] would be ... at all unreasonable. The annual sum at 5% would be £40 [£2,060 today] and the maintenance of a person in your situation could not certainly be rated at less ... The sum should stand in the names of two or three trustees so that, in the case of any dissolution or separation of the Community, you might have the sole right and title both to the principal and the interest ... On your demise the whole principal and interest would of right devolve to the Community. You mention also a pension of ten guineas a year [£540 today] for your proper spending".[14]

He then asked Charles Butler, secretary and legal adviser to the Cisalpine Club, to draw up the legal documentation. The final trust deed dated July 12th 1799[15] invested double the amount suggested in the letter, £1,666 13s 4d in 3% Consolidated Bank Annuities with Lord Charles Clifford, John Vincent Gandolfi the Younger and Bridget Clough (the Prioress, Mother Aloysia) as the three trustees. He made an identical dowry for his other daughter, Dorothy, in August 1800.

This seems a great deal of money compared with the £300 settlements back in the early eighteenth century. But the debilitating effects of recent war-time inflation had devalued money by about 40% compared with fifty years before. However, even allowing for this, the Gandolfi settlement is generous, realising an annual income of £50 to the convent (£2,575 today). It is also interesting that Maria is to have a significant personal income, so the strictures on a nun's own disposable cash imposed by Reverend Mother Christina Dennett in the 1770s seem to have been eased. That, of course, may have been due to family pressures. It is clear that Mr Gandolfi had a view about the life-style, even within a convent, that a person "in your situation" should expect. Indeed, since the convent's foundation in 1642 there had been two classes of nuns – choir nuns and lay sisters. The choir nuns required a good level of education and significant financial backing; they provided the spiritual and liturgical heart of the convent's life, ran the school and filled the major posts of responsibility, from the Prioress down including care of the finances (Procuratrix) and teaching. The lay sisters, who were from lower social strata, tended not to have had any significant education and undertook much of the manual work. Within the social structures of the time it would have been expected, even in a convent, that the high-born nuns would have some element of comfort appropriate to their class.

But although the Gandolfi settlement suggests that the convent was in good financial health events were soon to shatter that illusion.

Chapter 20

Financial ups and downs

New Hall 1830-1859

The Catholic population of England was burgeoning with Irish immigration into the industrial towns of the north and midlands, although the number of English Catholics was also increasing at a faster rate than the general increase in the population. In 1700 two-thirds of Catholic clergy had been employed in rural landed households. In 1850 over three-quarters served in missions in English industrial towns independent of the landed interests. The Board of British Catholics, set up in 1808 to represent Catholic views, fell under clerical control and representations were made to Pope Gregory XV in 1837 for the restoration of a full episcopal hierarchy. He prevaricated suspecting that Protestant England was not yet ready for such a shock, especially in Queen Victoria's accession year. In the meantime Roman Catholic Emancipation in 1829, which secured the right to vote and sit in Parliament, was the work of Irish Catholics rather than the English élite who had negotiated the legislation of 1778 and 1791.[1] The Cisalpine Club had had its day though the Duke of Norfolk and Lords Petre, Stourton, Clifford, Arundell and Camoys, all familiar Liège and New Hall names, could now take seats in the House of Lords.

Pupil numbers at New Hall seemed to reflect this aristocratic depression. Intake was very uneven from 1830 to 1859, ranging from twenty-seven to fifty-nine, and averaging only forty-one, well below the peaks reached at the end of the time in Liège and the early years in Essex, though the congregation of local worshippers assembling in the Chapel was encouraging, reaching 158 in 1829.[2] Nor were the aristocracy any longer significant benefactors as they had been in the previous century. Their relative lack of engagement was reflected in reduced income from benefactions which in the 1820-1850 period totalled £5,525 (or £385,425 in modern values). The average amount received annually was about half the level of a century before, although there was a significant rise in the 1850s when benefactions doubled.[3]

Occasional troughs in pupil numbers can be explained. For example, in 1848, at their lowest point, England was in the midst of the Chartist agitation and there was much unrest. A major cholera epidemic also hit the country in 1848 and 1849. For both these reasons it might have been safer to keep girls at home but there were seven years of decline that followed this low point. A continued threat from cholera, including a major outbreak again in London in 1854, may have had some impact, but cannot be the sole explanation. There may have been other reasons. The row over the neighbourhood poor school opened by the nuns in 1844 for Protestant and Catholic children, in the context of a resurgence of national anti-Catholicism in the 1850s, seems to have created a particularly unpleasant atmosphere locally, while the financial crisis caused by the collapse of Wright's bank in 1841 may have consumed the finances of some Catholic parents. We will return to both these issues later in this chapter. Whatever the causes these troughs would certainly have had a significant impact on income, especially from 1848 to 1855.

Table 8:

Average monthly pupil numbers 1830-1859

1830	38	1836	34	1842	55	1848	27	1854	33
1831	41	1837	37	1843	46	1849	31	1855	35
1832	40	1838	43	1844	43	1850	30	1856	45
1833	42	1839	49	1845	43	1851	32	1857	46
1834	31	1840	57	1846	47	1852	33	1858	56
1835	34	1841	59	1847	41	1853	32	1859	50

Within the varying pupil numbers certain family names continued to be well-represented. Four de Domecq sisters, of the Spanish wine-making dynasty, arrived on the same day in 1838. Almost certainly from Ireland there were seven Burke, four Dolan, five Plunkett, six Rorke, five O'Loughlin, five O'Donnell, five Lynch, four Maguire, eight Murphy and four Moran girls, many of them probably inter-related as sisters and cousins; from England seven Arundell, four Gray, four Hercy, seven Lescher (Sidney Lescher was one of the founders of *The Universe* that later merged with the *Catholic Weekly*), five King, five Lyons, four Mason, five Middleton, four Parker, four Petley, four Roskell, four Weld and four Lightbound girls; and from

Scotland five more MacDonnell girls. There were also five Purcell girls possibly from the USA where the Purcells provided an Archbishop of Cincinatti. In this three decade period 456 girls were admitted with 241 different surnames, a very similar ratio of girls to names as in the preceding thirty years, confirming that families remained large.

By chance we know a little more about one of the less exalted girls from the diary of Clarissa Bramston, wife of the vicar of Great Baddow near Chelmsford. Her best friend, Miss Lawlor, was the aunt of Elizabeth Lawlor (1833-1835), "a very nice, intelligent, little wild Irish girl", whose health became so bad that, at the age of ten, she had to return to Ireland. Clarissa visited New Hall frequently between 1833 and her death in 1844 and made good friends amongst the nuns. The different creeds of these educated women were no impediment to friendship. They may have been helped by the fact that the Reverend Bramston had been a curate in Oxford where his vicar had been John Henry Newman who was to become a significant figure in English Catholicism. Bramston and Newman were firm friends. On September 6th 1834 Clarissa records that she "took Mr Newman to New Hall and introduced him to the nuns ... Mr Newman left us with a most pleasing impression of his visit; a lovely specimen of a real English clergyman, deep piety, gentle manners, a very cultivated mind".[4] Newman at this time was Vicar of St. Mary the Virgin, the University church in Oxford and was about to become central to the Oxford Movement that sought to recall the Church of England to the catholic doctrines of the early church fathers. He had already published his first tract on this subject in 1833. It is doubtful whether the nuns were able to foresee that their much-liked visitor was to split the Anglican Church, join the Catholic Church in 1845 and become a Cardinal in 1878.

At least one intrepid pioneer emanated from New Hall in this period. Isabella Arundell (1841-1846) left at the age of fifteen to continue her education at Boulogne where, in 1851, she met the explorer Richard Burton. At this stage Isabella was described as "a quiet girl ... of the convent type" although the observer clearly did not know that she was already a confirmed cigar smoker.[5] She eventually married Burton against her parents' will in 1861. She shared his explorations in the Middle East and Africa and became a significant author, notably her *Inner Life of Syria, Palestine, and the Holy Land*. After Burton's death she wrote his biography[6] but destroyed his translation of the *Scented Garden*, a celebrated treatise on Oriental erotica, together with his journals, as she realized that a prudish Victorian England was not yet ready for such revelations. Without the money she might have made from these publications she died in poverty.[7]

Some girls went to settle the expanding British Empire. Mary-Anne Hercy (1831-1833) married Charles Clifford, an early settler, and later administrator, in New Zealand, who went originally as a sheep-farming pioneer with his cousins William

Vavasour, Henry Petre and Frederick Weld (there were two Clifford, two Vavasour, five Petre and four Weld girls at New Hall in this period). In 1859 Filumena Phillips, who started at New Hall in 1846, married Frederick Weld. She subsequently followed him to Western Australia, Tasmania and the Straits Settlement in each of which he was Governor and, in the process, gave birth to twelve children.[8]

There was also some movement in the other direction. Two girls from Australia, one from India (all three with very English surnames and therefore probably daughters of British colonial administrators or merchants) and two from Mexico, the Jenkins sisters (1846-1850), added a slightly more cosmopolitan flavour to the school. The latter two had been born as Protestants, but had been baptised in Mexico by a Catholic priest and had come to New Hall with the dual intention of being educated and received into the Catholic Church.

The longest stayer in this period was Dolores Stanardo from Spain, who was a pupil from the age of three to fifteen (1832-1844). Two Irish young ladies, Miss Power and Philomena Loughnan, were the oldest, leaving at the age of twenty-two in 1838 and 1854 respectively.

Some parents continued to register their concerns for their daughters' health. Miss Dunbar (1831-1832) "is apt to faint when kneeling too early ... rising does not agree with her". Many girls may have shared the problem without such a convincing reason! Appolonia Middleton (1834) was delicate and "not to study too much". Miss Congreve (1837-1838) was "to have a full diet of meat, little butter and plenty of milk, very little fruit, cooling medicine once a fortnight". Physical weaknesses occasionally surfaced – Miss Ayre (1837-1839) was "to attend to her carriage as one shoulder is a little out" and Constantia Clifford (1837-1848) was "not to learn drawing until she holds her head more erect". The Gillespie sisters (1853-1854) were "to pay great attention to the shape" and were to take "no medicine but the homeopathic" showing their parents' aversion to the blood-letting and leeches that still prevailed as common treatments. From the parents' point of view the conventionally demure, devout and accomplished young lady was still the required end product. Isabella Arundell's untypically robust and independent character, which defied all stereotypes of the frail woman, had clearly been contained within conventional bounds at school, unlike poor Miss Ramon de la Quintana (1858-1860) whose "temper is to be attended to and corrected" and Miss Bathouis who, in 1856, was twice sent away for bad behaviour and not seen again.

Had Miss Bathouis brought a testimonial of good conduct from a previous school? This was one of the requirements of an 1850s prospectus[9] which also indicated that the fees were £46 (£3,480 in modern values) or £40 (£3,025 today) if under twelve years of age. Extra fees were still chargeable for music, drawing, singing and dancing for which masters were brought from London. German and Spanish lessons also cost extra. The costs for extra subjects were mostly in the region of £4 p.a. (just over £300 today). The common curriculum was similar to that of the previous century comprising French, Italian, writing, arithmetic, geography, the use of the globes, history, heraldry, botany, drawing, flower painting, and plain and ornamental needlework. The main changes were the addition of Latin as an optional extra and the introduction of mineralogy, philosophy and mythology, probably for the Great Class.

Uniform was pink print in summer and bright red merino in winter with a tippet lined with silk. On Sundays and fast days white was worn with a blue sash or belt. In about 1852 blue was adopted for Sundays and in 1870 came into use for all year wear. The black silk hoods, worn for Confession and Communion, had probably been used at Liège and were not peculiar to this school or religious order.[10] And for the first time, in the 1850s, there is mention of an official summer holiday, from mid July to mid August.

In 1848 White's Directory,[11] a history and gazetteer of the County of Essex, records that "nuns are engaged in the education of about fifty young ladies of the Roman Catholic faith [roughly accurate numbers for 1846 but certainly not 1848]. Mrs Blount [Mrs is a term of respect for an older woman, not necessarily signifying married status] is the Reverend Mother, the Reverend Francis Lythgoe director of the nuns and the scholars, and the Reverend Francis Brownbill, Chaplain … The Great Hall is elegantly fitted as a chapel for the nuns, scholars and Catholics of the neighbourhood … The grounds comprise about thirty acres and are mostly enclosed by a wall and approached through an iron gate on the Chelmsford Road where a noble avenue of trees extends to the mansion. Among the trees are several fine cedars … The farm buildings and the priest's house are at a distance from the Hall in the northern part of the grounds". This dovetails with the nuns' own history which says that Reverend Mother Teresa Joseph Blount (Prioress 1844-1869) enclosed a garden for the nuns and put an enclosure wall around the grounds to keep out stray cattle, while Father Lythgoe was instrumental in getting the local hunt not to come across the convent grounds as "the ladies object to being intruded upon".

The history also notes that an old stable provided a dining room for the priests and a school for children from the neighbourhood. This "poor school", which started in 1844, raised a good deal of "No Popery" feeling in the villages round New Hall. The Anglican clergyman at Springfield, a neighbouring village to the north of Chelmsford, "as well as the nearest Squire" visited the convent and tried to intimidate the Prioress into closing the school. The 1899 historian observed that "the interviews were stormy but she seemed rather to enjoy them". Both Protestants and Catholics attended the school, all learned the Catholic Catechism and said the same prayers. Opposition subsided when it became clear that Protestant children were not forced or even urged to become Catholics. However, there was some local glee when a village child turned out not to like the school. The Boreham National School Log Book for June 1865 records, "S. Dawson left – gone to New Hall School ... [where] she never attended more than a third of her time, consequently knows next to nothing. From Popery good Lord deliver us".[12]

However well-meaning the opening of the school it came at a touchy time for Anglicanism. The Oxford Movement had seen the secession of major figures such as Newman to the Church of Rome. The old respectable and private English Catholicism which had kept the Pope at arm's length was being replaced by a more aggressive, triumphalist and devotional faith with a flamboyant Continental style of worship and a strong attachment to Rome. In this atmosphere the establishment of the Catholic hierarchy in 1850, with Cardinal Wiseman as the first Archbishop of Westminster, sparked off a furious anti-Popery diatribe by *The Times* and by the Prime Minister, Lord Russell. The emerging Church was seen as a threat to the English way of life, more so because of its association with Irish immigration. "The liberty of Protestantism has been enjoyed too long to allow of any successful attempt to impose a foreign yoke upon our minds and conscience".[13] Perhaps some of this national unpleasantness, with its own local variant on the issue of the "poor school", contributed to a feeling of insecurity and lower pupil numbers at the main school. However that may be, the nuns were confident enough to invite a visit from the Jesuit Father General Jan Roothaan in 1849 during which he gave an address to the school in French and in 1851 Cardinal Wiseman himself visited the school en route to opening a church at Witham, the first of three such visits to New Hall.[14]

The free school for local children had twenty-five pupils in 1860[15] and was then probably near its peak. In 1899 the history of the Community records that "the little grain of mustard-seed has never become a large tree, as the school has never numbered more than thirty, and, since many schools flourished in the neighbourhood, it has dwindled down and at present numbers only eight".[16] There was also a Catholic church and school in Chelmsford from 1847 and other competition would have come in the first place from the increasing number of Anglican National Schools set up locally and then the Board schools after 1870. A letter from Father Heery in 1906 explained to an enquirer that "the school is kept by the nuns simply for the sake of the people employed on the farm".[17]

While White's Directory paid tribute to the handsome avenue it did not add that it was now bisected by a railway line and level crossing. The London to Norwich railway began from the London end in 1837 and needed to cross New Hall's land in order to link Chelmsford with Colchester, leaving two-thirds of the estate north of the line and the other third sandwiched between the line and the main London road.

As with the era of canal building in the late eighteenth century, railway development provided an opportunity for landowners who sat astride the projected line to sell their land dearly. On the London to Chelmsford stretch William, 11th Lord Petre of Ingatestone Hall, successfully held out for £20,000 for land and £100,000 for compensation, (a total of £8,180,000 in modern values) and Henry Labouchère of nearby Hylands Hall netted £35,000 (£2,380,000 in modern values) although their combined properties affected only six miles of line. Another major landowner, Sir John Tyssen Tyrell at Boreham House demanded his own private station as part of his land deal so that, until he died, he should be able to stop any train on which he wished to travel. He lived until 1877 hopping on and off trains from the shed that made do as a station.[18] The fifty-one miles of track from London to Colchester cost the Eastern Counties Railway £600,000 in land and compensation (£40,600,000 in modern values). Services to Colchester opened in March 1843 when the first train steamed past New Hall.[19]

The 1899 historian says that the nuns were blamed for not claiming larger compensation than £300 (£20,000 in modern values). This self-criticism may be a little harsh. While the Petre, Labouchère and Tyrell gentlemen (all peers or MPs) had the political and financial resources to strike good deals and knew that the railway company would probably settle rather than fight expensive legal cases that would delay the line's completion, life was not like that for lesser landowners without significant financial reserves. Even Wadham College, Oxford, which owned land at Fryerning near Ingatestone , found the whole thing to be an expensive gamble. They employed local land agents, the Parkers, to protract proceedings as long as possible in order to raise the price of their land but in 1838 the Warden of Wadham wrote, "we are so pressed now into a corner that we seem to have nothing to do but to accept the terms they choose to give".[20]

It was also in 1838 that compensation appeals were being heard for the Boreham area. The *Chelmsford Chronicle* assiduously reported these cases, heard at the Saracen's Head in Chelmsford by a jury described on June 1st by counsel for the railway company as "common sense sort of men who are acquainted with agricultural matters". At that same session counsel reported that 101 out of 111 cases in Boreham had been agreed with the landowners without recourse to the law. New Hall would have been one of these. Two major complainants in June 1838 spent much money on surveyors and lawyers without getting anywhere. On June 15th the newspaper reported that Mr Anthony, a London solicitor who owned land in Boreham, claimed £1,608 (£109,600 in modern values) but the jury awarded him only £858 (£58,470 today). On June 22nd it was reported that Lord Western, who owned land between Kelvedon and Rivenhall, claimed £13,369 (£911,000 in modern values) but he was awarded only £2,559 (£174,400 today). The jury seemed unsympathetic to attempts by the well-off to screw ever more money out of the railway company and there are no reports of small compensation claims being brought to court. The costs would have been prohibitive.

The criteria used to resolve these cases give some sort of yardstick by which to assess whether the nuns had missed a trick. At the apex of society some major landowners received compensation because the railway line could be seen from the front windows of their grand residences, but one would have needed to be on the roof of New Hall to get a view of passing trains. However, the main thrust of arguments presented to the jurors was about simple agricultural matters. Bridges to join separated pieces of land would, it was claimed, require an extra horse to haul the carts. The jury agreed with counsel that the horse should be priced at the normal market value. Cattle were cut off from water sources. But, as the company was obliged by statute law to provide alternative water sources, the jury saw no need for further compensation. The railway would need to be fenced. The jury disagreed where the railway ran on an embankment and rejected the cost of new fencing where old fencing could be reused. The land was undervalued. The jury agreed that the claimant's London surveyor did not know much about local land values. Split farmland would take longer to plough because it was in smaller parcels. The jury, with its farming experience, was unconvinced. In this light it is difficult to see how New Hall, run by nuns who were predisposed to Christian charity and honesty, could have made a case for further compensation. Farming activities were carried out well away from the railway, largely close to and north of the convent building and provided only about 4% of the convent's income each year. It could also be argued that the railway company had been reasonable in providing a level crossing with a special New Hall signal box next to it from which the signalman would open and close the gates. A comparable case with a level crossing would be that of the Anglican clergyman, the Reverend S.J. Nottidge,[21] who received £360 for land and £360 for compensation (a total of £46,000 in today's money) at Cressing in 1847 during the building of the Braintree-Maldon line. His compensation was calculated on the potential danger to his cattle that a level crossing posed. By contrast New Hall dairy cattle were well away from the danger zone and the risk to intelligent nuns and girls would have been negligible, especially as their daily lives were spent in an enclosed property half a mile away and the girls did not go out unaccompanied.

The criticism of the nuns' business acumen may have been coloured by a much more disastrous event three years later, the collapse of Wright's bank, not unconnected with the railway expansion we have just been considering. All had seemed well under Reverend Mother Mary Regis Gerard (Prioress 1816-1844), from a wealthy Lancashire landowning family that had made its fortune from coal. She brought to the convent large sums of money which she intended to spend on a new convent building.[22] The money was kept with Wright's bank in Chelmsford which went bankrupt in 1841 when it was discovered that, over four years, John Wright had embezzled £126,833[23] (£8,100,000 in today's money) for private speculation, probably in the railway boom.

The Wrights were a Catholic family and had many Catholic clients. Seven Wright girls attended New Hall in the period up to 1836 and an Ann Wright had been professed at Liège in 1766. This banking disaster had dire effects on Catholic church building in general as potential benefactors saw their savings wiped out.[24] Its effect on New Hall was immense. In 1841 the nuns had £26,439 in Wright's bank (£1,690,000 in today's money). They lost the lot but recouped something during the next twelve years with token creditor's payments amounting to £2,854[25] (£215,250 today). Even so that left a net loss of £23,585 (£1,474,750 today), which killed off hopes for new convent buildings. The only consolation was that it was the loss of a bonus rather than of core revenue so that the actual continuation of the school was not threatened. In such circumstances hindsight may have generated the thought that a better deal from the railway company three years earlier could have been secured. But even if the compensation received had been doubled the extra would have knocked only 1.25% off the net loss caused by the bank's demise. It may have been not entirely coincidental that at this juncture New Hall lost two Prioresses. Reverend Mother Mary Regis Gerard died in 1843 and her successor Reverend Mother Aloysia Austin Clifford in 1844. The strain of the financial crisis would not have helped them cope with their ill-health.

By 1860 the nuns appeared to be making some recovery from the financial disasters of the 1840s. A questionnaire from the Catholic authorities filled in by the nuns, probably in 1860,[26] showed that the convent had £38,500 in investments (£2,880,000 in today's money) which provided an income of £1,700 p.a. (£127,000 today), net profit from the farm of £180 (£13,450 today) and £240 from annuities on investments made by nuns' families (£18,000 today). On the other hand income from nuns' dowries was not what it once had been. There were thirty-seven choir nuns and fourteen lay sisters but only twelve paid the expected dowry of £4,000 (£300,000 today) and twenty-five had no dowry at all because "each one is received according to her need".

The nuns were also having tax problems. Twice they had appealed against income tax assessments which appear, from the accounts books, to have been levied on income from bonds and stock.[27] In 1848 they had been charged £300 tax on profits (£22,000 in modern values) and, on appeal, had the amount reduced to £20 (£1,460 today). In 1856, with higher taxes caused by the Crimean War, they had been charged £500 (£33,100 today) reduced after appeal to £11 (£728 today). Legal counsel's case for the nuns was probably based on the advice given in 1799[28] when William Pitt had first introduced income tax. That original advice said that the nuns were partners, in the sense of a company, only with regard to the school but that the convent's profit beyond that (from the farm and investments) was jointly owned by all the nuns and that each nun's share was so small as to be worth very little tax. This may well have been the basis of their successful appeals. However in 1860 they were being charged £100 (£7,475 today) "to which we concur rather than submit the expense and trouble of appealing". Clearly lawyers would have cost as much as the potential tax rebate so the nuns decided a fight was not worth the candle.

Whatever the financial ups and downs there was enough cash to re-roof the house in 1855 when the tall chimneys were also built. In the process the stone dragon, formerly on Henry VIII's gatehouse, and since its destruction on the roof of the house, was moved to its present position on the front lawn.[29] These building works were achieved largely through three major donations in that year from a legacy from Miss Canning, and gifts from Mrs Coney and Miss Gandolfi which amounted to over £100,000 in modern values. Indeed Miss Gandolfi was a generous benefactor from 1845-1866 during which time she gave over £318,000 in modern values.[30]

These had been financially troublesome times or was it just the will of God, as Reverend Mother Mary Regis Gerard described it? With any luck the young ladies in the school would have been blithely unaware of all the turbulence that had surrounded them.

Chapter 21

A Steady Ship in a Moving Sea

New Hall 1860-1889

For many years parental requests had been associated with relief from fasting. Although fasting was obligatory for those between the ages of twenty-one and sixty the exemptions were considerable. Delicate women were one such nominated group together with the sick and convalescents. So were day labourers and, interestingly, those involved in brain work where weakness might result in poor output. In any other case formal dispensation was required from "lawfully constituted superiors".[1]

That parents felt obliged to ask for dispensation from the nuns suggests that in some devout families children nonetheless observed fasting, receiving just one full meal at midday in Lent and on other specified feast days.[2] Or it may have been a protection to ensure that growing daughters did not engage themselves voluntarily in fasting. So Edith Aspinall (1864-1868) was never to abstain "and to take cocoa rather than tea", while Alice Bedingfield (1871-1874) was to abstain no more than once a week and was to have "a glass of claret for dinner and one for supper and an egg for breakfast". Others like the Cary sisters (1884) were to abstain on Fridays only. Frances Mahoney (1865-1866) was one of those who was not to abstain for more than two days consecutively. Not only was Miss Sherlock (1869-1872) not to abstain but she was to eat meat twice a day.

Beer, porter and wines were clearly still seen as tonics. Winifred Haggerston (1869-1873) was "to have wine whenever she abstains or feels the want of it" and "to have a bath once a week". Fanny Fitzpatrick (1877-1881) was "delicate and requires care". She was "to abstain only once a week [and] to take porter at dinner". Not only was Katherine Gordon (1865-1870) not to abstain but "she is to take beer", pay "great attention to her deportment" and "take a bath as often as possible". Florence Kelly (1887) was under strict instructions "to have hot meat for breakfast, porter or claret for dinner, is not to abstain and is to avoid morning fasting". But no one could quite match the connections of the de Cirat sisters from Spain (1881-1883) – "they have leave from the Pope to take meat on all abstinence days". It must have been a very complicated process for the nuns making sure that everyone did as they were supposed.

As we have seen baths feature frequently in parental requests. Spaniards Paulina de Regina (1871-1875) and her sister Sacha (1871-1881) were "to have a cold bath every day and wine for dinner". Of the Arbazuz sisters (1865-1868), also from Spain, it was noted that "their shape requires much attention" and they were "to have a bath as often as once a week if possible". Lily Dunne (1870- 1871) was "to have a cold bath every morning summer and winter". She only lasted one winter at New Hall! The Haggerston sisters (1869-1871 and 1871-1873) were to bath once a week and Mary McDonnell (1866-1870) once a fortnight. For Mary O'Toole (1865-1869) it was much more specific – "she has weak ankles which are to be bathed in salt water frequently". The business of taking baths when hot water had to be carried some distance and poured by hand into metal tubs was an arduous affair requiring much organisation, and was therefore relatively infrequent by modern standards, as is implied in the parental request for Mary Walmesley (1865-1874) who was to take "a bath as often as possible i.e. once a fortnight". Quite what was entailed in the request for the exotically named America Weber is not clear – "to take mineral water and a particular kind of bath every week" – but as she stayed for only nine days in November 1880 no one would have had time to find out.

Girls' health problems still feature in requests. For Laura Cologan (1865-1867) "great attention is to be paid to her figure; she is not to lace or unlace her stays herself". Weak eyes meant that the dangers of reading in dim candlelight were forbidden to Miss Lassaletta (1864-1869) while Margaret Powell stayed for only three weeks in 1879 because her sight was so poor. The unfortunate Mary Leeming (1869-1872) "suffers from weakness in her back ... is to be frequently on the board and sit in an easy chair, not to kneel much; not to learn dancing; not to write much or apply much to any study; to see the doctor once a month". That all sounds very agonizing. Annie Molyneaux (1863-1864) had less visible problems – "everything to be done for her improvement there being a deficiency in the mind which causes a habit of absence and want of memory attributed to an attack of fever some years ago", while Eileen and Annie O'Connell (1885-1893) brought with them attacks of fever ague that they had contracted in India but without the mental complications.

Numbers continued to oscillate, from sixty in 1874 down to thirty-two in 1888 (see table 9). The most frequently represented family names were six Barry, four

Brand, four Dawson, eight Ellison, five Kendal, five Leeming, five Morris, four Murray, eleven Petre, four Read, five Riddell, four Roope, four Roskell, four Russell, four Scholes, four Seymour, four Smith, four Smythe-Piggott, six Vavasour, four Walmesley and five Weld girls, probably all English; four Cronin girls, a good old Scottish name; and almost certainly from Ireland, four Dolan, six Fitzpatrick, five Kelly and four Murphy girls. Altogether the 409 girls admitted in this thirty year period came from just 209 different family names, maintaining the ratio of nearly two to one.

The longest stayer was again a Spanish girl, Sacha de Regina, for just over ten years. The oldest leaver was Belinda Fitzpatrick at the age of twenty-two after eight years at the school. The two youngest new residents on the New Hall estate in this period were not pupils at the school but Peter and Jane Vincent, two orphans who were adopted by the Community. We know that Peter was three years old. Two of the labourers' wives, Mrs Parkes and Mrs Phillipson took charge of the children and the Community paid all their expenses. After seven years they were placed in orphanages which, sadly, would have separated them by gender.

Table 9:

Average monthly pupil numbers 1860-1889

1860	44	1866	42	1872	60	1878	45	1884	42
1861	37	1867	37	1873	59	1879	39	1885	41
1862	41	1868	33	1874	60	1880	33	1886	44
1863	43	1869	38	1875	53	1881	37	1887	37
1864	39	1870	37	1876	47	1882	39	1888	32
1865	40	1871	49	1877	44	1883	46	1889	37

Reverend Mother Teresa Joseph Corney (Prioress 1869-1873) oversaw new building alterations and additions, started in 1869 and finished in 1870, which seemed to indicate that the Community had recovered from the financial shocks of the 1841 bank collapse. Two new dormitories were converted in the west wing of the house by removing room partitions, passages and a staircase, one dormitory on the ground floor, the other immediately above it. Each had sixteen cells with hot and cold water and waste pipes, but the latter were unconnected and water had to be removed in pails. More girls could now be admitted and numbers rose to sixty or thereabouts from 1872 to 1874. However, the 1899 history says that nuns found this to be too many and decided to limit the numbers to fifty as had been the custom before though, between 1843 and 1919, that number was reached on only six occasions and most of the time they were a long way short. In forty-seven of those seventy-seven years the number fell to forty or below.

Other buildings improvements saw hot water radiators introduced in the school and the chapel, with a comment that the rooms on the north side had always been very cold. Between 1869 and 1872 a completely new building was erected. It housed the ambulacrum (a place for nuns to walk indoors), a music room, a small dormitory, two chapels for devotional groups, one for the Sodality of the Angels and the other for the Children of Mary, and some administrative rooms.[3] It may have been this building spree that caused a major rise in benefactions from a modest £3,487 (£258,000 today) in the 1860s to £7,987 (£570,700 today) in the 1870s. This rate of giving was sustained in the 1880s with £5,242 (£405,000 today) and the 1890s with a massive £12,008 (£955,200 today). Unlike a century before the gifts were not heavily reliant on a limited number of very generous aristocratic benefactors but relied largely on bequests. These accounted for nearly two-thirds of all gifts. The timing of such large windfalls was inevitably irregular.

While New Hall seemed content with an education that had changed little since the 1770s, the world of English female education, so long in the doldrums, was beginning to stir. The North London Collegiate College had been founded in 1850 by Miss Buss and Cheltenham Ladies' College in 1853 by Miss Beale. In 1868 the long dormant boys' grammar schools, whose archaic trusts still bound them to a classical curriculum, had been investigated by the Taunton Commission. The Endowed Schools Act of 1869 followed. It permitted boys' schools to modernise their curriculum and allowed the Endowed Schools' Commissioners to redirect ancient endowments to girls' education "so far as conveniently may be".[4] Progress was slow. The sheer task of preliminary inspection had been enormous and some existing girls' schools, in which government had never taken much interest, became nervous of letting outsiders in to have a look. One said "we have always been private in our home and desire so to remain, in spite of the march of intellect in the nineteenth century".[5] Convent schools were not included in this survey but would probably have taken the same view.

On the male side of the fence endowments were in the possession of boys' schools and, where that endowment was small and the boys' school barely financially viable, nothing could be diverted. Such were the cases at Chelmsford and Colchester. In reality the task of dealing with 700 to 800 grammar schools and 3,000 endowments was more than a few Commissioners with four clerks and a messenger boy could handle.[6] As each grammar school had to have a new scheme, individually negotiated and published, backwoodsmen amongst their governors could employ delaying tactics. Nonetheless forty-seven endowed girls' schools and six co-educational schools emerged.[7] The nearest to New Hall were at Grays in south Essex and in east London at Stepney, Greenwich and West Ham.[8] Within thirty years inspections showed their success. Only in Wallingford in Oxfordshire did the girls' school do markedly less well than the boys. In a number of cases - Mansfield, Loughborough, Newcastle-on-Tyne and Burton-on-Trent - the boys' grammar schools were seen as second rate compared with their new sister schools.[9]

The curriculum the Commissioners recommended for girls in these newly endowed schools comprised English, history, geography, French or German and mathematics, as well as Latin and some form of physical science. This more or less matched what New Hall offered in the common curriculum save that New Hall was confined to biological science, offered Italian instead of German but retained German and Latin as optional extras and, of course, its own complete religious experience and doctrinal instruction. The Commissioners were keen on Latin which they saw as "a means of mental culture and strengthening of the intellect". Latin eventually became a regular class lesson at New Hall from 1887.[10] So girls in secular secondary schools were to learn much the same as boys with drawing and music (still regarded at New Hall as core accomplishments but confined to class singing in secular schools) far down the list. Lord Lyttelton, the major influence in these decisions, made concessions to the domestic side and put in needlework "which, on the whole, I think girls have a special aptitude for, in themselves and in their circumstances". Other vocational subjects were rare.[11]

Alongside these newly endowed girls' and co-educational schools there emerged the Girls' Public Day School Company, formed in 1872 with the intention of setting up independent local girls' schools if there was sufficient demand as measured by local people buying shares in the Company.[12] The first Company school opened in Chelsea in 1873 followed by others in Notting Hill and Croydon and the first Company school outside London opened at Norwich in 1875.[13] Over thirty schools had been launched by 1900, all in areas where there was no competing girls' endowed school.[14] Maria Grey, one of the Company's founders, also formed the National Union for Improving the Education of Women in 1871 and kept the question of endowments before readers of *The Times*. She pointed out that the annual income from grammar school endowments was £300,000 (over £21,000,000 in today's money) - "when we find it shown in the last Census that the proportion of women supporting themselves by professional work is to men in professions as 1 to 7, and their share of educational endowments is 1 to 92, it does not appear unreasonable or extravagant to ask for some rectification of this enormous inequality ..."[15]

At the time all this activity in the Protestant world may have seemed distant for New Hall. After all the nuns had been in the vanguard of girls' education for over two hundred years. But the reforms of the 1870s were creating a new climate that would eventually require a response. When Queen Victoria assented in June 1871 to schemes establishing the first endowed girls' grammar schools at Keighley and Grays, it signalled the dawning of a new age. Girls' education was moving gradually towards the content and quality of that given to boys.[16] In 1858, the Cambridge and Oxford Local Delegacies of Examinations had come into being to set external examinations for the grammar schools and in 1865 the first girls took these new examinations. It would be sixty years before New Hall followed suit.

Once women were allowed to attend university then women teachers would also be able to match the men in intellectual training. Girton College (1869) and Newnham College (1872) opened at Cambridge and the first women were examined there in 1882. Lady Margaret Hall (1878) and Somerville Hall (1894) opened at Oxford with the first women examined in 1884. London University, founded in 1832, was ahead of both of them with women first being examined in 1878. As a consequence we see the first headmistress "graduates" (Cambridge stingily awarded certificates and did not award full degrees to women until 1948; Oxford degrees for women came in 1920). Miss Bebbington of Tiffins at Kingston-on-Thames (1891) had the history tripos, Miss Hamm of Simon Langton, Canterbury (1896) had been to Newnham as had Miss Creek of the High School, Birmingham, who was also a London graduate. Miss Hall, headmistress of Maynard School, Exeter (1888) had first class honours in the Cambridge Women's Examination and had studied at the Sorbonne.[17]

In 1902, an Education Act enabled the new County Councils (formed in 1888) to levy a rate for secondary education. More girls' grammar schools followed, or high schools as they were known following the title adopted by the Girls' Public Day School Company, with Chelmsford and Colchester County High Schools opening in 1906. This expansion in quantity and quality would be a challenge to which New Hall would need to respond if it were to emulate the best that was on offer to girls in secular schools while, at the same time, maintaining the unique spiritual experience of its own environment.

Just as things had to change sooner or later in New Hall's approach to education, so the nuns found that their association with the Jesuits also came to an end. Although the Canonesses were Augustinians the Jesuits had served as their chaplains since 1642, even when the Jesuit Order was officially disbanded by the Papacy between 1773 and 1814. The nuns' spiritual exercises were based on the Jesuit model. But in 1884 the Jesuits' Provincial withdrew the Order's support as being inconsistent with their mission. The nuns' appeals to Cardinal Manning and Rome achieved nothing. In 1887 Father Heery was appointed as chaplain and served the convent for the next thirty-eight years.[18]

Chapter 22

Decline

New Hall 1890-1914

The Catholic Encyclopaedia of 1913 reported on the state of Catholic education at the end of the first decade of the twentieth century.[1] It acknowledged that there had been major advances in girls' secular education but said that allegations that the standard of scholarship attained was not so high in Catholic as in comparable non-Catholic schools were no longer true, as a general levelling up had taken place during the last ten or twenty years. The evidence came from public examination lists.

The Encyclopaedia's list of schools also illustrated the competition for Catholic girls that now existed. There were over two hundred Catholic girls' secondary schools in England under the care of about sixty different religious orders. It listed as some of the best known and most successful of these schools those of the Institute of the Blessed Virgin Mary at the Bar Convent, York and Cambridge; the schools of the Sisters of the Holy Child Jesus at Mayfield, St. Leonard's, Preston, Harrogate, and Cavendish Square, London; the schools of the Faithful Companions at Isleworth, Liverpool, Birkenhead, and Clarendon Square, London; the schools of the Sisters of Notre Dame of Namur at Liverpool Mount Pleasant, Northampton, and Norwich; the school of the Religious of St. Andrew at Streatham; the Servites' school at Stamford Hill; and St. Ursula's, Oxford. It noted that many of these secondary schools had attached to them pupil teacher centres, where valuable preliminary work in the training of elementary schoolmistresses was done, and that many of them served also as "practising schools" in which the students of Catholic and other training colleges gave model lessons in the presence of their instructors and Government inspectors.

New Hall was not part of this broad advance. In the 1890s and 1900s very little had changed and there was a damaging decline in pupil numbers (see Table 10). Frances Russell (1894-1898), later returning to New Hall as Sister Antony Magdalen, attributed this decline to the long tenure of Reverend Mother Aloysia Austin Butler (Prioress 1873-1912). "She was very small and autocratic at least in her old age ... She had become old-fashioned and out of touch with modern requirements and the school had gone so far down it was seriously thought it would have to be given up". [2] The result was that pupil figures from 1910-1912 were the lowest since 1775-1776.

Table 10:

Average monthly pupil numbers 1890-1913

1890	36	1895	36	1900	33	1905	30	1910	18
1891	36	1896	37	1901	30	1906	29	1911	15
1892	37	1897	46	1902	26	1907	31	1912	17
1893	37	1898	42	1903	27	1908	24	1913	14
1894	29	1899	36	1904	32	1909	20		

There are also indications of splits in the Community in the notes that Father Sidney Smith made on his 1899 visitation.[3] One nun says that sisters were afraid to speak in Chapter. A second says she did not get on with the Prioress but this may have been a collision of incompatible wills as she also complained that "people with little sense [are] allowed to vote in Chapter". A third says that "the Prioress does not understand sickness". A fourth complains that "correction is hard in Chapter". A fifth comments that the Prioress "is too hard on lay sisters" and the doctor confirmed that one in particular was overworked. The Novice Mistress said that the Prioress was "too hard on the sick". The Procuratrix said that the Prioress "storms at those who disagree with her". In addition the Community was bitterly divided between the older and younger nuns over a change in Church music. In 1903 Pope Pius X had ordered a return to the traditional Gregorian chant of the Church, withdrawing the Ratisbon chant which the nuns had been using though, "I don't think anyone really knew how to sing the Ratisbon ..." All the young nuns favoured the Solemnes Plainsong with the older ones in opposition – "I have never seen the house so near a complete split [from] which it took a long time to recover".[4]

In 1912 the Prioress decided to resign. Mother Joseph Sales Kendal was elected in her place (Prioress 1912-1918) but "saw no use in anything but spirituality" so new educational thinking was delayed. She was also hampered by her predecessor who, until her death in 1915, "never quite got accustomed to not holding the reins which caused some difficulties".[5]

Overall during these twenty-five years there was an increase in the numbers of pupils staying for five years or more (this may have been the result of more girls of colonial administrators and settlers coming to board), the net result being that a higher proportion were leaving in their late teens. But within this trend the school continued to move back to the Liège pattern, with 22% starting at sixteen or seventeen and attending briefly for a "finishing school" course. Indeed Dorothy Smythe-Piggott (1909-1911) commented that her education was "glorious for those fortunate enough to do the Grand Tour"[6] with the implication that it would not have been so appropriate for those with more prosaic needs and no independent means.

The longest stayer was Beatrice Innes (1902-1917) for nearly fifteen years though she had an unfair head start arriving at the age of two. As the pupil register noted when she arrived, "she is to be made the charge of a lay-sister for the present who will act as her nurse; she is to remain in England as the Indian climate is injurious to her health".[7] Her mother came from India to nurse her for one year but otherwise Beatrice was brought up within the convent and its school. The second longest was Aline Coventry (1905-1916) for nearly twelve years, her parents also resident in India, indicating the way in which imperial expansion was increasing the need for boarding education. The oldest leaver was Mathilde Alvarez from Spain at the age of twenty in 1896.

There were 196 girls who entered the school in this period with just 116 different surnames of which the most common were Blaxland (a major Australian Catholic name) and Coventry (an Indian colonial family) with five girls each, and Arathoon, Eyre, Leahy and Warrington (the latter seem to have come from Canada) with four girls each.

Contagious disease was always a fear for boarding schools. Ever since pupil records began at Liège the nuns had been assiduously checking on whether the girls had had smallpox (or a preventative smallpox vaccination), measles or whooping cough before they entered the school. Scarlatina was added to the enquiry early in the nineteenth century. Pupils who subsequently contracted any of these diseases would have to be isolated from the others.

Diphtheria was a particularly fearful disease and one of the leading causes of childhood death. It was a bacterial infection of the nose and throat which could cause difficulty in swallowing and, in extremis, suffocation, paralysis and heart failure. Isolation of infected pupils would be crucial as the disease was spread by coughing infected droplets or shared use of utensils. It was reckoned that one-tenth of all children would catch the disease and there was no generally available vaccination until the 1920s. There was a major scandal at Chelmsford Grammar School in 1888 when accusations were made that a pupil fatally infected with diphtheria had not been attended to or isolated quickly enough. The accusations proved to be unfounded but showed how vulnerable schools were.[8]

In September 1893 New Hall experienced an epidemic of scarlet fever followed immediately in October by a fatal outbreak of diphtheria. The pupil register records that three of the five Blaxland girls already at New Hall had had diphtheria before they came to the school which gave them some immunity. Tragically Antonia Britten, aged fifteen and sisters Mary Kendal, aged seventeen, and Ursula Kendal, aged eleven, all died of the disease. The latter two were nieces of Sister Aloysia James Kendal who was First Mistress of the school.

The school had to be closed temporarily for three months for the first time since the heavy snows of 1814, while the drainage system, itself quite new, was examined and replaced. It was believed that the extraordinary heat that summer may have affected the sewers[9] so the nuns played safe with a complete renewal. Frances Russell (1894-1898) later recollected that cold running water was also provided to clean the soapy pipes that were felt to be a possible source of infection.[10] A letter in January 1894 from the Essex Medical Officer for Health certified that "sanitary arrangements have been remodelled on the most approved modern principles. No expense has been spared. I have also examined the water supply in the springs from which it is obtained and found it of excellent quality".[11] A further precaution was to fumigate pupils on their return to school. They spent two minutes in the cook's room in a choking atmosphere created by sulphur on hot coal. This was supposed to kill the germs caught on the journey or during the holidays, though this practice seems to have ended some time before the First World War. Parents were encouraged to keep their children out of public places in the week or two before returning to school to avoid infections. The under sixteens also underwent "head scraping" on Saturday afternoons in the perennial search for the embarrassing, but much less harmful, head lice.[12]

Helen Britten not surprisingly left the school when her sister died of diphtheria but Margaret Codrington, the delightfully named Pansy Jump and Rose Murphy also decided to leave on account of the outbreak and did not come back. Evelyn Roope went home, developed a mild version of the disease and eventually returned. Kathleen Maguire developed diphtheria at school but survived. In the circumstances the sudden drop in pupil numbers in 1894 was not surprising. There was another outbreak in 1900 but this appears to have been mild in its effect. All told this was not a healthy period. Mary Lynch had died early in 1893 from the effects of whooping cough. The house was not well-heated and six of the nuns died in the very harsh winter of 1894-1895.[13] Agnes Russell died in 1898 after surgery for appendicitis which the pupil register notes was the first instance of this illness at New Hall. Mabel Ryan died of meningitis in 1901.

Frances Russell's recollections[14] give us a good idea of life at school in the second half of the 1890s. Baths were taken weekly, with a nun regulating the bath taps from outside the cubicle but hair was probably washed only once a year. Girls were not obliged to wear uniform but most did. They all wore their hair in plaits.

She also confirms that the school was still divided into three classes (as in Henrietta Goldie's time a hundred years before), Great, Second and Third, the latter also known unofficially by the nuns as Brats' Class. Each class had two mistresses, one for all the subjects taught in English, and the other for French. Girls sat at box desks in a double row with lighting provided by paraffin lamps. The Great Class, the most advanced class (probably comprising girls over sixteen) learned Latin, general history, English literature, the history of Italian and Dutch painters, architecture, chemistry and logic in their core curriculum – "all smatterings no doubt but they laid a foundation". Arithmetic was generally not taught beyond the second class but Frances Russell notes that Miss A.M. Buchanan, an Oxford graduate, taught arithmetic from 1896 to 1897, the first recorded instance of a lay graduate on the staff, although this did not yet set a trend. Set against this evidence of modern thinking, the nuns were still using home made history texts for teaching that had been compiled a century before.[15]

In these pre-electricity days the girls' hours made the most of daylight. They rose at 5.45. Mass, at which Holy Communion was taken, was at 6.30. The girls were expected to attend this service two or three times a week. Those not going walked down the avenue with the First Mistress but only in summer and autumn. Then there was breakfast and another Mass at 8.00. The lessons of the common curriculum began at 9.00 starting with questions on the lesson learned the previous evening and possibly a run out of doors at 10.00, then more lessons, dinner at 11.30 and recreation at 12.00. If, during the morning, French became a little tedious Sister Mary Austin McSwiney, the French Mistress, could always be diverted – "she hated Napoleon and all his works and if one did not know the lesson it was quite safe to say something about him to make sure it would not be heard". At 1.00 there was one of three alternatives depending on the day of the week – either a lecture on Church doctrine and history with catechism, miracles and parables learned by heart, or readings from a spiritual book by the First Mistress, or religious instruction from the Chaplain. In the afternoon there was drawing with a Master who came once a week or with two of the nuns who specialised in religious paintings. Frances Russell complained that "drawing was not well taught, at least by modern standards". Tea was at 3.00 followed by half an hour of free time "when we could go out, talk or read". Time to talk was, in fact, strictly rationed. Silence in dormitories and passages was absolute as also in the refectory, except at tea-time.[16] Everyone went to Compline at 5.00 and then there was study, sometimes in the form of reading while walking down the avenue, followed by supper and finally recreation until 8.00.

Evening recreation would be taken outside in the summer. In the winter it always began with a set of quadrilles "after which we walked round and round the room holding the nun's apron for ten minutes or so". Very occasionally the Prioress gave permission for dances such as the waltz or polka, otherwise known as "round dancing". Dances were learned on Tuesday afternoons from a dancing mistress brought from London. On all occasions, when such risqué activity took place, the First Mistress had to be present to ensure that partners were restricted to holding each other by the forearms. Otherwise recreation consisted of playing the piano and singing or sitting in the bow windows or round the table sewing and knitting. Sometimes the nuns told a story – "Sister Mary Philip [Kendal] used to make up very good serial ones". Very occasionally the girls were allowed to play games but never cards (except at Kingstide). At the end of recreation there were Night Prayers and then the girls went up one by one to say goodnight to the First Mistress, shake hands with her and get her blessing.

On Saturdays the girls wrote letters from memory. A passage from a book of letters would be read aloud slowly for fifteen minutes while the girls listened. Then it was read a second time at a good pace while they copied down what they could and then read very quickly for a third time during which they tried to fill the gaps. Finally they would have to write up a fair copy.

For the first time there is some evidence of games. Apart from the morning run at 10.00 midday, recreation provided twenty minutes in which girls could play rounders or basketball (as netball was then called) in winter, or tennis in summer. By 1905 a drill sergeant from Chelmsford was giving the girls physical drill,[17] a common feature of many schools and something of a substitute for the lack of a gymnasium.

Exams were towards the end of each term, mostly written but some were oral. One contemporary, Margot Jackson (1910-1915) said that they lasted for two weeks and that the oral inspection on religious subjects was frightening as girls had to be word perfect on the Catechism. It may have been worse for her as she and her sister were not Catholics but were to receive instruction. Nonetheless Margot said that "I felt like a piece of chewed string when it was all over".[18] A day or two before breaking up in the summer Place Day saw badges given for good conduct. The badge was a long blue, white or red silk ribbon (in ascending order of merit) with a Sepulchrine cross also in ribbon. It was worn over one shoulder on Sundays the following term and was valid only for that term

The main feasts and celebrations seem to be much the same as in Henrietta Goldie's day at Dean House, with many of the same customs carried over from Liège – St. Stanislas, patron saint of Novices, on November 11th "when the custom was to visit the Noviceship and stand on a certain board which apparently 'squeaked' if you were going to be a nun";[19] Presentation on November 21st (with the famous Presentation Tart, up to fourteen inches in diameter, of double pastry and strawberry jam) and , in the evening, 'Rush in the Workroom', a form of General Post, "in which

nuns and fishes used to make up names for themselves as part of the game"[20];
Christmas, Holy Innocents and Kingstide in December and January with the famous
Kingstide plays; tea in the nuns' refectory on Mothering Sunday; Holy Week and
Easter; St. Aloysius in the summer term when, in the so-called wilderness area, which
was in fact a hay meadow, girls took over hay stooks and made nests[21] as well as being
treated to new potatoes and peas for dinner, strawberries for tea and yet another large
fruit tart; Corpus Christi (when the trees would be decorated) plus a new event in
May, the Knill Procession in thanksgiving for the recovery from illness of Mary Knill,
daughter of a former Lord Mayor of London who had built the Pavilion in the
grounds for the nuns.

Since the 1840s the girls had called themselves "fishes"[22] (the nuns took a while
yet to adopt the term) because, tradition says, Anne Boleyn used to send fish from the
New Hall ponds to Henry VIII when he was in London as "New Hall fishes were
second to none",[23] a great story that ought to be true! Most of the girls still stayed at
school over Christmas and New Year to enjoy the celebrations and activities when
relationships with the nuns became less formal. Frances Russell said that each of the
fishes had a favourite nun known as her "Angel" and they were her "crackies" –
"without this you were hardly New Hallish". As soon as a girl reckoned she "owned" a
nun someone stood on a chair, rang a bell, called out "Proclamation fishes!" and
announced the fact. In New Hall jargon a girl had then been "proclamated". Now that
this had occurred she could talk privately to her "Angel" and had rights of access
before other girls, so it would seem the nuns were complicit in this arrangement.
After she had left she might get letters from her "Angel". The adoption of an "Angel"
came into its own at Kingstide, though not without its criticism. Frances Russell
commented that "a group of fishes with their 'Angel' went apart into some room,
usually in semi-darkness, and sat around more or less in silence with her talking
quietly ... We loved it but I heard it said later that all this love of the nuns tended to
sentimentality and taught us to flirt. However that may be, New Hall was a
wonderful seed-bed for religious vocations. In just the four years I was in the school,
eighteen became nuns". Seven joined the Canonesses and eleven went to other Orders.
Indeed, while Sister Aloysia James Kendal as First Mistress was fairly rigorous
intellectually, her own blood sister, who became Reverend Mother Joseph Sales, "saw
no use in anything but spirituality" which may have exacerbated the problem of New
Hall's declining numbers in an era when parents may have wanted more than this for
their girls.

Easter seems to have been "rather a sore point as some went home but those
who stayed did lessons". According to Pearl Bourke (1894-1898) only a very few whose
homes were in or near London were allowed to go home at Christmas or Easter. She
also regretted the lack of adventure - "gym and games in the modern sense were

unknown. Wet grass was regarded with utter horror by the authorities".[21] In the summer wild purple and white violets grew in profusion and the girls used to make up bouquets for the nuns. At the end of the summer term a special treat would be to go out of doors with the nuns and eat raspberry vinegar and gingerbreads. It was still all very genteel.

Two additional festivities were the celebration of Queen Victoria's Diamond Jubilee in 1897, with meals outside under the great oak tree (destroyed by enemy bombing in 1943), and then three days of centenary celebrations in July 1898 when the Old Fishes gave a new altar for the Chapel. Mary McDonald (1876-1880) organized the subscriptions but tragically died at the school on the day of the first Mass, probably of an epileptic fit. Cardinal Vaughan, Archbishop of Westminster, came for the final day to present prizes at Place Day when tableaux representing scenes from the history of the Order were presented.

It would be fair to say that while New Hall continued to fulfil its spiritual aims its broader educational provision was slipping behind the times. Parents who felt this too confining seemed to be voting with their feet and going elsewhere.

The First World War, Britain's first experience of total war, was about to revolutionise the role of women in society. It would end with the first women getting the vote. How would New Hall respond?

Chapter 23

The Great War

New Hall 1914-1918

We can trace the impact of the early events of the war from the diary of Sister Ann Frances Trappes-Lomax.[1] On August 4th 1914 Britain declared war on Germany. On August 5th "trains were running all day with hardly a pause. In the afternoon we heard cannon. It shook the cells". That may have been the artillery range at Shoeburyness. The dangers of war came early to the convent. On August 7th "Sister Magdalen Philip Crewse's nephew was in the cruiser that was sunk by a mine but he was saved". Shortages could be foreseen, so on August 14th "Reverend Mother gave out at Chapter that the old system of picking up sticks for firewood was to begin again".

With the need to deploy troops in south-east England to protect against a German invasion, New Hall received a visit on August 28th from two officers of the 7th Battalion Worcestershire Regiment, one of them the Chaplain. The diarist gleefully recorded, "he was awfully nice and very pious and High Church. I had him nearly all the time". The 7th Battalion were Territorials, part-time soldiers, who had been on their annual summer camp at Minehead when war was declared and had then moved via Worcester to Danbury.[2] Whatever their military skills, their public relations were finely tuned. They had picked their reconnaissance team well and the Chaplain had made a hit! There was immediate feedback from this visit. Two days later "a soldier came to ask if he and seven others could come to Mass ... He fetched the others ... We gave them plums and gingerbread ... The sergeant said there were eight Roman Catholics in the Regiment". So the Worcesters were not entirely unknown to the nuns when, on September 2nd, "thirty soldiers [arrived] to be billeted ... in the school and an officer in the outquarters". However, the timing of their arrival seems to have taken the nuns by surprise as they were all in retreat as the soldiers approached - "we all turned out to cut bread and butter for their tea". The soldiers slept in one of the dormitories and were scheduled to be at New Hall for just two weeks prior to the start of term.[3]

Their stay at New Hall was short but long enough for good friendships to be formed. On September 10th "the soldier's cook exhibited his rifle bullets to an admiring audience". On September 15th "the regimental band came ... with drums and bugles. It was heavenly. We put off dinner and all stayed out till twelve when they left ... We gave them beer and two buckets of pears". The men, mostly from Kidderminster, made a red Kidderminster carpet for the Chapel and in return were given handkerchiefs by the nuns. The Worcesters subsequently suffered heavily in the trenches of France and Flanders. Sister Mary Peter Davies poignantly observed that "many a New Hall hankie must have been found on dead and wounded men".[4]

At this time of high excitement mingled with fear the soldiers were able to confide their thoughts to the nuns. Mother Mary Philip Kendal was a confidante for many of them, so much so that, after the war, those who had survived brought their girl friends or wives to be introduced.[5] However, after a month at Danbury the battalion was moved to Maldon for six months prior to going to France.[6] On September 18th, the day before their departure, "the band came just before ten playing a heavenly march ... There was a great rush for apples but the greatest for prayer books. They all wanted them ... They took every book from the box in the Church. They left playing *Marching through Georgia*. We talked to the men until 8.00". Some were veterans of the Sudan and South African Wars. The man the diarist talked to "had been through Egypt and South Africa in a cavalry regiment and saw the 21st Lancers charge at Omdurman ... He was shut up in Ladysmith".

Air raids were a new feature of warfare. The Zeppelin air ships started their bombing raids in 1915 and their route to London brought them in over the Essex coastline. Precautions were taken in anticipation. On October 13th 1914 the diarist notes that "we had curtains down at Matins on account of the Zeppelins! As in Chelmsford lights are not allowed except in very small quantities after sunset and our lights are most brilliant". Later in the war the diarist records that, on April 1st 1916, "a Zeppelin flew right over the house and dropped a bomb near Springfield Gaol in Chelmsford. I slept through it all – lots of nuns were very afraid". There was another raid two days later. Navigation for the Zeppelins was solely by compass and sight. Not only light but clock chimes could betray possible targets. On April 4th "a policeman came to say we were to stop our clock at night on account of the Zeppelins. It will stop at 7.45 p.m. till 7.45 a.m.. No bell will ring till 6.00 a.m.".

For some of the Catholic Belgian walking wounded who were sent to England for treatment the convent would have been a reassuring sight. On November 29th

1914 "two Belgian soldiers who had been wounded came to Confession and Holy Communion. They are staying with the Governor of Chelmsford Gaol whose daughter is a pupil". One wonders whether they knew Liège and the Faubourg d'Avroy which, by that time, would have been under German military occupation. On other occasions in the next few years more wounded Catholic servicemen would pay a visit to the convent. The Worcesters, at Maldon until the end of March 1915, were too far away for regular visits. But on December 20th 1914 "eleven soldiers came in after Vespers. Eight stayed for tea. Four were ours from Maldon". One nun remembered that "some of the Tommies in the neighbourhood came to tea in the Parlour and quite a number used to come on Sundays".[7] How generously the nuns could feed military visitors as war shortages bit home is not clear, for, on November 3rd 1914, we learn from the diary that there are "very small portions nowadays".

The nuns were having to accommodate their rules of enclosure to the reality of war. One gets the feeling that, with their own relatives on active service, they were pleased to have some contact with the fighting men, to be able to show practical and spiritual friendship and to welcome Catholic soldiers into their Chapel. Even so, as much of the enclosed life as possible was preserved. Nuns could not stay in the Little Garden if men came to work there and when the doctor came a bell rang to give them a chance to get out of sight. There was a telephone but only for outgoing calls. The nuns still never went out beyond the grounds. Dentists came to visit and operations were done in-house by visiting surgeons. One nun remembers watching a hysterectomy operation in the Infirmary as late as 1926[8] The last in-house operation that the current members of the Community can remember was in 1932. By 1936 it became common practice for nuns to leave the enclosure for medical or dental treatment.[9]

The nuns were generally cautious about change. In 1916 the Government introduced British Summer Time to make more effective use of daylight hours. The nuns refused to follow suit. New Hall clocks remained one hour adrift on the grounds that 3.00 a.m. would have been an impossible time to rise. The logic of this argument is difficult to follow. They would have lost an hour's sleep only once a year, but the Community eventually caved in after the war when changing the clocks became a permanent feature. From 1920 national and New Hall time were as one[10] though the clock still struck at seven minutes past the hour to signal the times of divine office for the nuns.[11]

The war also had its effect on the school. The average monthly number on register rose to twenty-six in 1914, thirty in 1915, thirty-seven in 1916, thirty-two in 1917 and thirty-seven in 1918[12] reaching the highest figure for twenty years but still well short of being full. Much of the increase was due to the war with nearly a quarter of the intake coming from the Low Countries and France. Just as the nuns had left Belgium to seek refuge from war in 1794 so they were now to give shelter to young ladies following a similar route. The war also ended the longstanding link of the Phillipson family with the convent. They had been resident at New Hall when the nuns arrived in 1799 and had remained in service ever since – "there had been Abraham and Long James and Long John who was followed by his son Albert". Albert died suddenly in 1915 without children and his nephew went off to fight in the war.[13]

Amongst the European war refugees to come to New Hall were Veronica, Cécile and Dora Doehard who arrived in late October 1914 following the German attack on Brussels. Annette, Annunciata and Antoinette Regan (1914-1915) were also probably from the Low Countries and like Anne and Jeanne Vercruyssen (1915-1918) had been sent to England from Belgium for safety. Jeanne became a Canoness in Belgium after the war. Esther and Gabrielle Seghers (1915-1917) fled Ostend when it was bombarded by German forces. Hélène, Josephine and Marriette Thonon (1915-1916) lost their mother through friendly fire. The pupil register calmly records the awful facts – "the family was driven before the Germans for some hours; their father was then sent prisoner into Germany but was released after three months; their mother was exposed to French force and was shot on August 24, 1914; the children themselves suffered imprisonment in Dinant; in February 1915 Monsieur Thonon with his six children took refuge in England". Juanita Prochnow (1916-1917) and her sister Carmita (1916-1920) were the daughters of a German of Polish descent born in Berlin. As he was of military age he had been interned on the Isle of Man. The children, for convenience and protection, used their mother's Spanish maiden name of de Montilla. If the royal Battenbergs needed to change their name to Mountbatten, then lesser mortals needed to be even more careful about making their German connection too obvious.

The pattern of entries still showed some parents sending daughters en bloc at the same time to the school. In addition to the war refugees there were four Calder, Carey, Daly, and Weld girls. However, for the first time, there is significant evidence of the admission of Protestants and also of weekly boarders. Elizabeth Blake (1914-1920), Lucille Perry (1918-1919), Alison Gray (1918-1919), Hazel Ward (1916-1918) and her sister Joan (1918-1921) were all weekly boarders while fellow Protestants Nyria Hawkins (1918-1922) and her sister Vera (1918-1920), Barbara Woodhouse (1915-1919) and Geraldine Roffey (1917-1922) were full boarders. As Protestants none were required to attend Religious Instruction or Catechism, though they did attend Chapel, and arrangements were made for Geraldine Roffey to attend Boreham Anglican Church on a Sunday. There were also two day pupils for six months, Dorothy and Vera Seel (1916) whose father was second in command at the General Headquarters of the 65th Lowland Division based at nearby Boreham House.

Overall, during the years of the war sixty-four girls were admitted with thirty-six different surnames, indicating that families were still large. That was to be one of the many facets of life that would change after the war.

A prospectus from the war years[14] shows that fees had soared to £60 p.a. (£3,450 today) and £50 for those under twelve (£2,880 today). This would have reflected the price-rises caused by war-time shortages when inflation had halved the value of the pound. In certain respects the education on offer was very familiar – "usual branches of a thorough English education together with French and Latin ... and plain and ornamental needlework". But it also mentions the study of logic, apologetics, social questions and the history of art, one assumes for the older pupils in the Great Class. The first three were certainly new developments. The extras included some of the old favourites – musical instruments, private singing, dancing, drawing, Italian or German – but also showed some signs that the school was making marginal movements into the twentieth century with typewriting, shorthand, scientific cutting-out, cooking, games, and Swedish drill. The overall aims were summarised - "great pains are taken to cultivate the minds and individual tastes of the pupils, and above all to form their characters and give them a solid religious training". For the first time in a prospectus an official three-term year begins to emerge – the "scholastic year is divided into three terms although pupils may remain at school during the Christmas and Easter holidays at a charge of £1 per week" (about £55 today).

On the spiritual front the Community and school lost their direct link with the Archbishopric of Westminster when, in 1917, the Diocese of Brentwood was created. That very summer the new Bishop of Brentwood, Bernard Ward, visited New Hall, following on from Cardinal Bourne who had visited every year since 1904. In 1918 Reverend Mother Joseph Sales Kendal died and the Chapter elected a new Prioress, Reverend Mother Aloysia Magdalen Dolan. She was the last Prioress to be elected for life and was much more worldly with a love of dancing, music, colour and beautiful dresses.[15] She was aware of the need for New Hall to accommodate itself to post-war realities. As the niece of Alfred Austin, the Poet Laureate and not an Old Fish, she was able to take a broader view of New Hall and its needs. "Modern Times had begun". [16]

Chapter 24

Modernisation

New Hall 1919-1939

In December 1918 a cheeky new publication appeared, the *Fishes Pool*,[1] a home produced magazine of witty drawings and articles penned by budding journalists who used fishy noms-de-plume such as crab, hake and shrimp. This happy and serene inner world of New Hall's children was oblivious to the fact that the continued existence of their school was seriously in question.

It seemed that nothing would ever be the same again after the devastation of the Great War which had, in any case, caught New Hall at a particularly low ebb – out-of-date, internally divided and without much appeal to its potential customers. One nun later reflected that "pupils had been young ladies destined for life in society with marriage as their normal vocation. For this their education had been eminently suitable. War had played havoc with family incomes and a whole generation of men had been decimated. Many girls would have to make their own way in the world. An up-to-date education would be demanded by their parents".[2]

This judgement overstated the effect of the war, though it is true that the recent carnage amongst the families of the upper social classes had been large. Young officers were first over the top in Western Front offensives and often first to fall, so that one fifth of peers' sons failed to survive the conflict.[3] The old Catholic families had many to mourn with the loss of three Petres, two Welds, two Weld-Blundells, three Cliffords, one Fitzherbert-Brockholes and two Plowdens[4] just to mention some of the families whose daughters had over the years been the nuns' pupils.

On the other hand, the financial position of the landed aristocracy and gentry, the backbone of New Hall's traditional clientele, had long been declining, severely eroded by the glut of wheat production following the opening up of the North American prairies in the 1870s which caused a long-term slump in world wheat and agricultural land prices. At the same time political parties had to be more responsive to the new mass electorate enfranchised by the 1867 and 1884 Reform Acts. Thus, the Liberal Government of 1905-16 implemented a range of social and financial legislation to provide greater protection for the poor, financed by new measures of progressive taxation including a supertax on high incomes and increased death duties, the latter promising to eat further into landowners' declining incomes as each generation passed. In 1911 the ending of the power of the Conservative-dominated House of Lords to defy the legislative wishes of the House of Commons, after they had unwisely tried to frustrate Liberal reforms, reinforced the decline in the hereditary supremacy of the landed interests. The combined effects of agricultural depression and higher taxes led to many estates being sold off, including the Jerninghams' Costessey in Norfolk and the Gerards' Garswood in Lancashire.[5] In Ireland there was an added nationalist dimension when the emergence of the Irish Free State in 1922 led to huge land losses by the major Anglo-Irish families.[6] In these circumstances high-born women needed to be more economically productive as women in general had been during the war. Indeed the important economic and voluntary roles that women had played in the war did as much as the suffrage movement to win the vote for some women in 1918 and all of them in 1928, underlining the fact that it would no longer be exclusively a man's world and that women's rights would demand more attention, including their need for an education that fitted them for a role that was more than just ornamental.

This new world must have been difficult to comprehend for the Canonesses dedicated, as they were, to the vision of their founder and a type of education that had changed relatively little but now needed more emphasis on the secular side to match the needs of a twentieth century society with which, by the very nature of their enclosure, they had only tangential contact. After the disasters of leadership that led to the school's rapid pre-war decline, the first major step was to decide whether to continue at all. But, emboldened by the Bishop of Brentwood's support and the vigorous leadership of the Prioress, Reverend Mother Aloysia Magdalen Dolan, the Chapter decided to press on and the necessary steps to ensure the school's survival were taken remarkably quickly.

It was one of the apparently more innocuous pieces of legislation that posed an immediate problem. The 1918 Fisher Education Act, which raised the school leaving age to fourteen in state schools, seemed to be another unexceptionable step on the road to a fairer society. But in seeking to enforce statutory attendance the government needed to ensure that private schools were efficient alternatives, given that this was the same criterion on which the courts made a judgement should parents wish to educate their children at home. The Act required private schools to register centrally and, in 1921, added compulsory inspection to determine whether they were efficient. Many quickly availed themselves of this opportunity as it was a good marketing ploy to be able to head one's prospectus with "Inspected by the Board of Education".[7]

New Hall now had a major problem. It did not conform to new regulations concerning the minimum size of classrooms and dormitories and the nuns, although cultured women, were not qualified in specialist subjects, particularly in physical sciences, higher mathematics and games, nor specifically trained in teaching so that the curriculum would not pass muster in an inspection.[8] The issues would have to be tackled head on.

The 1920 Prospectus[9] was therefore of a different order from its predecessors. Fees increased to £80 (£2,190 today), nearly double the pre-war level, but the value of the pound had slumped by nearly a half since 1914 and pupil numbers were still low. But, more to the point, the school was now academically aspirational in a way that had not been seen before. The Prospectus announced that "pupils are prepared for the Universities, the Royal Academy of Music and the Royal College of Music. The Royal Drawing Society and London Institute of Plain Needlework examinations can be taken". The school still aimed "to give the pupils a solid religious training and to form their characters" but added the more modern proviso that it should be "with due regard to their mental abilities and individual tastes". Uniform was also brightened up in 1920. Winter navy blue dresses would now have red collars. In summer light blue check dresses replaced plain blue.[10]

For the aims of the Prospectus to be realised new buildings were essential. Plans were made for extensions to provide general classrooms, music rooms, a gymnasium and a science laboratory equipped for teaching physical sciences (the old laboratory was very small and could only handle botany),[11] all lit by electricity rather than incandescent gas and paraffin lamps. The nuns would also have some new cells. On November 17th 1923 Bishop Doubleday, who had succeeded Bishop Ward in 1920, laid the Foundation Stone under which was placed a sealed bottle containing some rock from Mount Calvary, some stone from the Holy Sepulchre, a relic of the Blessed Thérèse and some earth from her grave, and other sacred medals and pictures. The buildings were opened with a Pontifical High Mass by Cardinal Bourne, Archbishop of Westminster, on June 23rd 1925, having cost about £32,837 (£1,230,000 today), the money raised by an appeal which closed in April 1929.[12] The *Fishes Pool* in 1924 had given its own report on the emergence of the new building which rose "to an imposing height ... totally changing the north aspect of the house". A new courtyard had the old building on the south side, classrooms and bedrooms on the east, an art studio and hall to the north and a huge gymnasium hall with a large stage and gallery to the west, and, to the west of all of these slightly set back from the old building frontage, twenty-five new single and double bedrooms. A statue of the

Blessed Thérèse, to whom the building was dedicated, was placed in the niche on the west front.[13] It was a splendid way to re-dedicate the school and make a fresh start on the 125th anniversary of the nuns' arrival in Essex. The extra bedrooms and renewed interest in the school meant that, from 1925, the school ceased to take weekly boarders and appeared to make full boarding mandatory for girls already in the school. Daphne Barratt, one of the Protestant weekly boarders, left in 1925 for that reason.[14]

Cardinal Bourne said at the opening of the new building that New Hall "represented a very old and very important tradition" but added "those who had come from the school always had the same charming home-like spirit". However, he stressed that "they would not be content with that" and, echoed the Prioress' catchphrase that "they must move with the times".[15] As if to show that New Hall's future would combine the best of the new and the old, the new House System was introduced, with the two houses named after the Blessed Thomas More and the Blessed Margaret Pole,[16] while, with an eye to tradition the old red uniform was restored after several decades of blue, but with a nod to modern fashion by allowing girls with red hair to wear brown.[17] One teacher enthusiastically approved. "School uniform was very impressive especially when a party of girls was seen in the avenue going for the Sunday walk with one of the nuns – bright scarlet tunics and blazers with the distinctive cross of the Holy Sepulchre badge showed up well against the background of greenery".[18]

While it was decided that the First Mistress would always be a nun, in 1923 additional lay staff were appointed. The decision was very painful for the Community who, apart from employing dancing and singing masters, had always undertaken all the teaching themselves.[19] One can imagine their concern that they may have compromised on the original vision of Susan Hawley and their fear that they would begin to lose an element of control over the educational process. But as the Prioress said "these [secular] mistresses are able to give more time to their work and keep more in touch with up-to-date methods than is possible for the nuns".[20]

The first two lay teachers were Miss Simmons, a former headteacher of a Church of England school and her assistant, Miss Emily Hughes, both of whom had lost their positions when they became Catholics. Within a year Miss Hughes had joined the nuns as a novice. Another very important appointment was Winifred Dolan. She had been an actress, a profession that earned the severe disapproval of Reverend Mother Aloysia Austin Butler (Prioress 1873-1912) who cruelly banned her from visiting the convent to see her sister.[21] Now that self same sister was the Prioress and Winifred joined the staff to teach two days a week and take private elocution pupils. The new buildings contained a hall that could seat three hundred, an ideal venue for her Shakespeare productions which were to make New Hall renowned for its theatrical standards. *A Midsummer Night's Dream* was her first production staged at the opening of the new buildings. For this and future productions she secured the services of Joe Parker, formerly on the staff at Drury Lane Theatre, London, who came for six weeks each year to build sets, and Mr Crow, a leading scenic designer from London theatres, who, over the next nine years, did three weeks work a year at New Hall for the annual Shakespearian plays as well as the 1934 pageant to celebrate the Prioress' golden jubilee as a nun.[22] Winifred Matthews, one of the early lay science teachers who arrived in 1925, remembered that the other lay teachers were Jessie Meek (English and Latin), Sybil Hunter (PE and Maths), Eileen Shelley (History and Geography), Daisy Thunder, an Old Fish, (Music) and Mildred Daly (French).[23] Miss Simmons was paid an annual salary of £200 (£7,475 today) and the others £100.[24]

There certainly seemed to be a new get-up-and-go atmosphere in the school. A Prospectus from about this period was in booklet form,[25] replacing the old out-dated single sheet, and shows a view of the front of the school and the great cedar tree. Science and Mathematics are listed amongst the subjects studied and, again, stress is laid on the examinations to be taken. For the first time extra-curricular activities are mentioned – the excellent library, lantern lectures, recitals by professional musicians, sports and riding. The problem of communicable diseases still remained and parents were required to provide a certificate of health at the start of every term signed by one parent or the family doctor, without which the girl would be kept in quarantine until it was received. For the first time there is mention of a half-term holiday, though only from 1.00 p.m. on the Saturday to 9.00 p.m. on the Sunday. Failure to return to school on time or leaving before term ended carried the promise of a deduction of 100 marks! The basic fee was 135 guineas a year (£4,925 in today's money), a significant increase that raised fees in real terms to twice the 1920 level. But it was the only way of building up capital and lay staff had to be paid.

The same zest comes through in the *Fishes Pool*. Hockey was being played on a full-sized field with internal matches featuring, literally, the English versus the Irish and, more imaginatively, Oxford versus Cambridge and St. John versus The Holy Sepulchre. Hockey had to be given up in March to let the grass grow for tennis which had five courts enabling everyone to play at least one set a day. The old drill had been replaced by more popular exercises with bean bags, beam work and rope climbing. There was also athletics where the conventional sprints and jumps were supplemented by the brick race (walking twenty yards on two bricks without the feet touching the ground) and, for the youngest children, eating buns off lengths of string tied to cedar tree branches, though none of these compared for excitement with the feats of Philippa Leahy's and Pamela Casson's brothers who were apparently big game shooting in Africa. The *Fishes Pool* reported on the visit of the East Essex Hunt in 1922, where an unfortunate black cat was mistaken for the fox, but survived! They also rejoiced in starting a fortnight late in January 1924 owing to electric light being put in the old building, demonstrated that the Feast of the Presentation had come on a bit as a celebration with the addition of a six mile paper chase and a Jazz Band and reported on two very attractive tea-rooms in London run by Old Fishes. However, Spring 1924 proved a drab term with measles and 'flu epidemics raging so that "classrooms were nearly empty".[26]

In 1925 the Oxford Local Examination was introduced and New Hall became the centre for Chelmsford so that the girls did not have to go to London for the tests. This was a first step but at a relatively low level of academic rigour compared with the new School Certificate for sixteen-year olds which tested a five-year course of education in an English subject, a foreign language, a science or mathematics, drawing, music and handicrafts. That would wait another eight years. On the other hand the school needed to start somewhere while it was still building up its facilities and qualified staff.

In July 1926 the *New Hall Chronicle*,[27] professionally printed outside the school, took over from the *Fishes Pool*. It carried in its first edition an advertisement for New Hall peppermint rock at twopence a stick made by Hawkes Brothers of Chelmsford and urged its readers to take up the last offer to buy postcard views of New Hall as it was before 1925. We also learn that a German measles epidemic reduced outside tennis matches to just two, both against Mrs Collins' teams from Hatfield Peverel. Cricket was also played but, strangely, only when it was too wet for tennis.

Then in 1927 the school was inspected by His Majesty's Inspectors of Schools. Winifred Matthews said "there were many preparations ... Two nuns from the Holy Child Convent and Training College in Cavendish Square, London, visited ... and gave us valuable help. Miss Frodsham, headmistress of a large school in south London ... joined the staff for discussion. My report following the inspection was that 'I had some powers of inculcating knowledge,' " a judgement that seems somewhat damning with faint praise.[28] The inspectors gave "encouragement and advice on the standards of work"[29] but the certificate of efficiency was not yet granted. The official comment in the *New Hall Chronicle* of July 1928 said that recognition could not be given "until we had carried out certain improvements in the curriculum and schemes of work". The inspection may have exhausted everybody, for the *New Hall Chronicle* reports that it was followed by a severe outbreak of chickenpox and measles, one of the worst the school had ever known, which led to the addition of a trained nurse on the staff. There was also a slight relaxation of rules, whether as a result of the inspection or not is not known. The school's aim, it was said, was one "of developing character first and foremost, and of producing the woman who acts from a sense of duty and is guided by a sense of honour rather than by mere whim or from fear of punishment. To gain that end we have relaxed many of the lesser rules and restrictions ... to train our children to acquire self-control".

In 1928 the *New Hall Chronicle* reported that the school was being reorganised into three boarding houses – Seniors, Intermediates and Juniors. Seniors were to have a wireless but Intermediates and Juniors would have to make do with gramophones. Each boarding house would have a House Mother, one of the nuns, who would always be there. Two new societies were founded, Parrot Pot (art) and Melting Pot (English, history and science) where papers were read and discussions ensued or there were practical demonstrations. These were in addition to the guides and brownies (started in 1923) and debating that had been going on for some time. The official voice of New Hall (probably the Prioress) complained that there was still a weakness in mathematics which was not up to examination standard and, not for the first or last time in a school, that "the children are too inclined to think that knowledge can be acquired without effort on their part; that all they have to do is to be present in class. This seems to be the common tendency of the present day ... when every girl wants to be independent and earn her own living". So perhaps the nuns were still struggling to come to terms with changed social mores.

In the winter of 1928-1929 the *New Hall Chronicle* says that lacrosse began as a new sport and hockey matches were taking place against outside teams – Buckhurst Hill School, Ongar Ladies and Ipswich High School. We also see the beginnings of New Hall's tradition of charitable work with support for a Catholic mission on Chusan Island caring for abandoned Chinese babies. Winifred Dolan's drama productions were still going strong. The *Essex Chronicle* of November 29th 1929 reported that "the pupils of New Hall ... continue on their triumphant Shakespeare way. For the past six years they have produced a Shakespeare play and on Tuesday/Wednesday their presentation of *Macbeth* crowned their successful career so far", though the leads appear to have been taken by adults including Miss Dolan herself. However in 1932 the *Essex Chronicle* had to admit that "these clever young people will never surpass their acting"[30] as shown in New Hall's eighth Shakespearian production, *Richard II*. Winifred Dolan may have agreed and turned to *The Mikado* for her next effort.

In 1930 the Annual Conference of Convent Schools was established and two nuns from New Hall attended, another example of how the demands of the twentieth century world would make strict enclosure difficult to sustain. In 1932 the two-day Conference was held at New Hall which hosted 270 nuns from fifty-two orders. One nun quizzically observed that "a special train was chartered from Liverpool Street to Chelmsford. The commuters at Liverpool Street were open mouthed at all these queer people in queer dresses – all were in their original habits – and a band of journalists appeared with their cameras. There was a kind of 'hide and seek' played round the platforms as in those days nuns 'did not get photographed'! Nor did they like the publicity".[31] The 1930s paparazzi got two bites at the cherry when, because it was term-time, the visiting nuns had to return to London on the evening of the first day to sleep.[32]

The concept of enclosure faced another interesting challenge in 1931, the first General Election at which the nuns were enfranchised. Their choice of candidate was easy. The Labour Party had, in the past, opposed denominational schools and its attachment to the Red Flag as a symbol smacked too much of Communism with all its atheistic practices. The Conservative Party supported denominational schools. So "our man" was the Conservative and the nuns were urged by the Church to use their vote. Nearly all of them decided to go to Boreham School polling station and the story is best told in their own words:

> "It was a tremendous event as not only most of the nuns had never been in a car but most had never left the Enclosure since their entrance years before ... Miss Dolan was there to be our chaperon and to protect us against all aggressors. We were going very early so no one should be about the voting booth to see us. Remember, a nun had never before been seen in Boreham and it was feared we might be mobbed. Some of us went in our own car and some in a shooting brake sent by the Tory candidate. Margaret Francis [Trappes-Lomax] who had rather grand ideas, was quite upset at his having sent nothing smarter. Opposite me in the brake was Mary Dismas [Weld] who never lifted her eyes so as not to see the world. I tried to see all I could. Mary Winifred [Hughes] sat in front next to the chauffeur because she was among the latest from the world and could face the situation. Mother Mary Magdalen [Falls], the stickler for enclosure, was thoroughly enjoying the drive and shaking with laughter at the jolting of the car. When we got to Boreham, Sister Frances [McConville] had to be disembarked while we all stood round waiting, all still in silence. She was from Donegal and it was said she had never worn shoes before entering. She was old, enormously fat and crippled with arthritis so that she could hardly move but was quite determined to come and do her bit. So she was pushed from the back and pulled from the front and heaved down the steps, all the while making pious ejaculations at the top of her voice, with the policeman standing by watching. And so the New Hall Community worked for God and our country and helped to get our man in, and then came home to breakfast. We had also made New Hall history".[33]

The election saw Labour fall from power and the start of fourteen years of government by the Conservatives. So the nuns probably felt it was a good day.

The car in question was a Fiat which, just after the war, replaced the luxurious Sunbeam that had been a gift from Mary Beech, sister of one of the nuns. The nuns considered the Sunbeam to be too showy for a convent.[34]

Meanwhile back in the classroom the *New Hall Chronicle* of 1932 announced that from 1933 girls would be entered for the Cambridge School Certificate as well as the London Matriculation Examination which, if successful, could provide credit towards an eventual London degree. Now the school was moving into serious academic territory. As the official statement in the school magazine said, "everyone realises nowadays that a child, in order to be equipped for a career, must have a School Leaving Certificate" though tempered this statement with the qualification that "we also realise that exams are no test of true education". But in 1934 less confidence was shown by the Prioress – "the majority do certainly seem to realise the importance of carrying away a School Leaving Certificate ... but they do not seem to appear to think it matters what is written on that certificate! A blank certificate ... is really little more than a confession of weakness ... Too much helter-skelter to make an immature snatch at a School Certificate at the age of fifteen or earlier ... not only stands to the discredit of the candidates in all discerning eyes but also of the candidate's school".[35] The pupil register supports this concern. The mean length of stay since external examinations were introduced in 1925 had risen slightly, but only to three years, although the School Certificate was a serious five year course. Presumably parents paying good money felt that their girls ought to have an early stab at the examination just in case they fluked success. But it clearly was not working.

In 1934 Reverend Mother Aloysia Magdalen Dolan celebrated her golden jubilee as a nun. The pageant of New Hall was produced in her honour. The 1935 Prospectus, the first glossy production, reflects a new confidence and possibly quotes from the script of the pageant – "Happy the heirs of England's glorious history whose feet are set in such a place. New Hall has been the home of saints, the resting place of kings and the daughters of kings. From it princes have gone forth to find a throne and queens to lose a crown ... From that to matters more prosaic – but who shall say less important? Eating, playing and sleeping; here are matters which receive the earnest attention of the wise parent on consideration of school life...".[36] And so on!

But the Prospectus' upbeat tone disguised the fact that all was not well. Pupil numbers of sixty-four in 1932 had plummeted to forty-one in 1935.[37] In March 1936 one of the nuns wrote to Arthur Doubleday, the Bishop of Brentwood about a rumour "that our numbers are decreasing so that it will prove necessary to close the school".[38] Rumours create panic and, she said, at least fifteen more were talking of leaving while the new intake for September 1936 was reluctant to commit to the school. The letter said that the Prioress was ready to resign if the Bishop and the

Community wished it. There also appear to have been serious splits within the Community involving the then Sub-Prioress who "expressed views with which I have no sympathy ... as regards the School".

These pressures were probably the last straw for the Prioress who resigned in 1936 through ill-health. Sister Mary Christina O'Donnell was elected as the new Prioress for life though the new constitution in 1948 subsequently changed that to three year terms when she was re-elected twice for a further six year period, up to 1954.[39] Later in 1936 Reverend Mother Aloysia Magdalen Dolan died. In October 1936 the *New Hall Chronicle* said of her, "how many times have we heard her say 'we must move with the times?' " Her eighteen year tenure of office had certainly seen many modernising changes at New Hall but not without an echo of the past as Jesuit chaplains had been reinstated after the death of Father Heery in 1925.[40] However, towards the end she sounded tired and impatient. Under the new Prioress the tone of the official commentary in the *New Hall Chronicle* is less haranguing and more encouraging.

On June 17th 1938 New Hall received its first royal visit since James II, 252 years before. Queen Mary was performing other duties in the neighbourhood and, at her own request, paid a fleeting visit to New Hall. The avenue was lined with New Hall pupils and employees as well as children from Boreham School. Because she was behind schedule the Queen spoke briefly with the Prioress from within her car before being whisked off to Ingatestone Hall and back to Langleys at Great Waltham for tea.[41] Always a prim and severe person, the Queen did not impress the servants. Eileen Lodge, one of the maids, remembered the event. "She didn't get out. The car stopped outside the Chapel. I remember this very elegant lady without a wrinkle on her face. But I thought, what a miserable old lady – she didn't smile".[42]

Eileen had come from London in 1933 as a fourteen year old maid. She was struck by her first sight of "this beautiful place. I thought it was somebody's palace". To her it seemed a life of luxury for the girls – "some were lovely young ladies, some a little snooty. I was in awe of them ... They were lovely girls but they didn't clean their shoes, they sat for their meals and everybody waited on them ... I polished their cutlery and they had silver goblets with family crests on ... On Saturday afternoons I washed their hair ... No one washed their own hair". She remembered that the lay teachers came down for morning prayers in black mortar boards and gowns and that, at this stage, she thought the nuns did not do any teaching. The girls had a good choice of meals – "their dream sweet was chocolate tart – they would all go mad". A favourite pupil was Bridget O'Connor (1930-1940). She was very thoughtful and kind, with "a sense of mischief and fun", and used to give Eileen little gifts "with such warmth and affection". She later became Prioress in 1966. But, in general the maids had "no sense that they were part of the family of New Hall".

This situation may appear dated to the modern eye but most moneyed households were used to having servants. Such class divisions were typical of the time and were also reflected in the lay sister/choir nun distinction in the Community and the availability of private rooms for a limited number of pupils at extra cost. There was also probably a distinction between the women and men servants. The former were directly subservient to the nuns. The latter were more independent in their work on the estate, many of them living in tied cottages and, in the cases of the Parry and Phillipson families, serving the nuns for two or more generations. In 1909 Joseph Parry was given fifty florins (£5 or £365 today) by the Prioress to celebrate fifty years at New Hall, a dinner at his own house and later on a supper at the convent for all the men, all paid for by the nuns. In 1914 Charles Devenish, the gardener, was treated to twenty-five florins and a supper with the men to celebrate his half-jubilee.[43]

Eileen was one of a large group of domestic staff. In 1937 there were eleven domestic servants of whom six, like Eileen, were school maids, two others worked in the outquarters, two in the laundry and one in the linen room. The maids all lived in small servants' dormitories. In addition there were three handymen, five gardeners, five farm hands and two poultrymen with all but two of the gardeners and the two poultrymen living in cottages on the estate.[44]

In 1938 the first nun was sent to be formally trained as a teacher when Sister Magdalen John Earle went to the National College of Domestic Subjects in London. From that time on all nuns involved in teaching were properly trained and were able to enter more fully into the educational work of the convent.[45] This was not before time. Oxford and Cambridge had been open to Catholics since the Test Acts were repealed in 1871 and in the 1890s the Vatican had lifted its disapproval of Catholics attending secular universities.

The overall effect of the last twenty years' changes had led to a healthy improvement in school numbers, apart from the blip in the mid 1930s (see table 11). The longest stayer was Joan Merrells from Weeley, near Clacton, for just over eleven years. She later was professed as a Canoness. The oldest leaver was Elizabeth Norman at the age of twenty-one in 1934.[46]

But families were no longer coming in such large numbers even though in the inter-war period there were five Cantopher, four Baker and four Russell girls. Overall the 329 girls who joined New Hall in these twenty years had 244 different surnames, an average of 1.3 girls per surname, considerably down from the constant 1.8 to 1.9 of earlier periods. The effectiveness and availability of contraception had increased significantly in the 1920s. Its effects were apparent in these statistics. This would be a new issue with which the Catholic Church would be, and still is, confronted.

Table 11:

Average monthly pupil numbers 1919-1939

1919	**44**	1923	**49**	1927	**63**	1931	**60**	1935	**41**
1920	**49**	1924	**53**	1928	**61**	1932	**64**	1936	**46**
1921	**39**	1925	**53**	1929	**59**	1933	**56**	1937	**53**
1922	**46**	1926	**54**	1930	**59**	1934	**47**	1938	**59**
								1939	**63**

For the first time since the 1790s the school had experienced two decades of sustained growth. It had survived one real closure crisis after the war and a phantom one in 1935. Just as it was managing to come to terms with the new world of the twentieth century it was once more confronted by the dislocation and horror of war.

Chapter 25

Evacuation

New Hall and Newnham Paddox 1939-1946

Britain declared war on Germany on September 3rd 1939. At 3.00 a.m. on the morning of September 4th the air raid warning sounded and the nuns spent an hour and three quarters in the cellars. It was a false alarm but good practice for what was to come. The girls returned on September 24th and were kept company by some city evacuees who stayed for six months.

The nuns' religious routine had to adapt to war-time requirements. The Prioress, Reverend Mother Mary Christina O'Donnell, gave the Community a wireless set so that they could keep up-to-date with the news and government regulations. To this end night prayers came forward to 8.45 p.m. so that the nuns could listen in at 9.00 p.m.. Blackout regulations meant that the last Office had to be said before sunset, Midnight Mass was not permitted at Christmas or any other feast day and once again the Great Clock was stopped in case its chimes should help enemy aircraft navigate.[1] And in 1940 the nuns bought a bigger motor car[2] to replace the Fiat though they still had to be chauffeured.

The Phoney War ended in May 1940 with German forces overrunning Holland, Belgium and France. On May 21st the nuns and their pupils were told to evacuate but there was uncertainty for a few days as to where they would go. A letter from the Prioress to the Bishop of Brentwood[2] said that "the children's parents are agitated and expect us to move. Fourteen children have already gone home. If they leave us now and we do nothing we shall never get these children back and so would lose our school". So the fears of five years before had returned. All turned out well. On May 29th the Prioress wrote[3] to tell the Bishop that the nuns had secured Newnham

Paddox which was about six miles equidistant from Rugby and Coventry near the Warwickshire/Leicestershire border. This was just in time. On May 26th the Dunkirk evacuation had started and, although successful, left air-bases in northern France in enemy hands and made the south-east of England doubly vulnerable, to intensive air-raids in the first instance and then invasion. The area around London would be a likely zone for dropping German paratroopers. New Hall was not a safe place to be for women and children although, when the school had moved away, it was hired by Essex County Council as an emergency hospital for very sick elderly people from Suttons Institution at Hornchurch.[4] The dormitories and infirmaries were used to provide space for 270 hospital beds. The Chapel acted as a store for school and Community furniture. Sister Mary John Daly used to return periodically to see that all was well and to sweep the Chapel.

Newnham Paddox was the home of a Catholic, William Feilding, 10th Earl of Denbigh. His mother was Cecilia Mary Clifford of Chudleigh in Devon[5] whose family's daughters in earlier years had graced the school at Liège, Dean House and New Hall. Further back in time his namesake, William, the 1st Earl of Denbigh, had married a sister of George Villiers, the 1st Duke of Buckingham, a former owner of New Hall. So, in various ways, there were apt historic connections. The house and park were spacious. The grounds had been landscaped by Capability Brown and the large Victorian residence, constructed between 1876 and 1879,[6] would house the Community and the school but was showing signs of age and neglect. The upheaval from New Hall was difficult for those nuns who had never been outside the enclosure or travelled in a motor car. One nun, who had not seen the outside world for decades, is reputed to have asked to travel with her back to the horse![7] At Newnham Paddox, enclosure proved impossible to sustain. The girls were, however, delighted with the grounds and lakes.[8]

Life was as difficult for the school as it was for everyone else in England. Coal was rationed and scarcely any of Newnham Paddox house was heated. However the grounds were full of trees and seven hundred logs were needed for fires every week. Saws and hatchets were distributed and teams of girls carried the logs wherever they were needed with every effort being made to use fallen trees first. Another part of the daily routine was to dig potato trenches and to grow as many vegetables as possible. Meals were inevitably uninspiring with meat cuts being used in as many ways as possible. Uneaten food was re-hashed in whatever ways could be managed and there were "recurrent elderberry and nettle subtleties",[9] the former making a delicious sauce and the latter supplementing vegetable intake. In the circumstances the celebration of the Order's tercentenary was necessarily a quiet affair.

Educationally the priority was to make sure that girls could take their School Certificate examinations. This would have posed difficulties as many of the lay staff had been left behind in Essex. For example in 1940 the French, Games, English, Geography and Junior mistresses at New Hall resigned. The chaos of war-time conditions meant that lay staff stability was no better at Newnham Paddox. Eleven were appointed between September 1940 and January 1944 whose length of stay averaged only eleven months each. English and the Juniors suffered most with a regular annual turnover of teachers.[10] The core of teachers that the nuns could provide was even more important in these fraught circumstances. That the local Anglican vicar agreed to supervise the exams was an unexpected bonus. But there was a bright side. A contemporary prospectus[11] describes the new domestic science department as an addition to the curriculum. It would include a variety of options –cookery, including "plain and fancy" and the preservation of fruits and jams; laundrywork; housecraft, including running a house, simple electrical repairs, accounts, taxes and "sensible buying"; infant care; science, including "soaps and hardness of water", first aid and home nursing; needlework, dressmaking, tailoring and millinery; and churchwork i.e. the making and care of vestments. There is evidence from the pupil accounts of some older teenagers being attracted to the school to learn these skills in self-sufficiency which would have been essential for any prospective housewife in a period of severe shortages that was to last well beyond war-time.

There were a few organisational developments. In 1942 Sister Margaret Helen Terney was appointed Headmistress, the first nun to have this more modern title which replaced that of First Mistress. She had an honours degree in history from Bedford College, London, and had been Mistress of Studies for some years. In 1944 Sister Mary Veronica Boland was given the new title of Housemistress with responsibility for boarding and all out-of-class activities. This worked well and was continued until the school expanded in the 1960s when each house was given its own housemistress.[12]

The school had evacuated to escape the worst effects of the war but found itself close to Coventry which was battered night after night from November 14th 1940 by the Luftwaffe's blitz. The house at Newnham Paddox shook with the blast from explosions and the air was permeated with the smell of the smoke screen that the air raid defences put up to try to obscure the target.[13] On December 22nd 1941 the school suffered its first war casualty when thirteen year old Rosemary Lewis, her parents and brothers were killed in an air-raid on Manchester.[14]

Danger was relative and events were to show that the evacuation from New Hall was propitious. The Battle of Britain in September 1940 saw massive dogfights over Chelmsford and the countryside below was littered with jettisoned German bombs. Other Luftwaffe aircrews involved in the blitz on London also randomly discarded unused bombs en route to the capital if their aircraft were damaged and certainly on the way home if visibility had prevented them unloading their bombs on the intended target.

In Chelmsford Hoffman's, the ballbearings manufacturer, and Marconi, a major research and manufacturing centre for radar and wireless, were prime bombing targets and, from an enemy point of view, conveniently situated within half a mile of each other. In May 1941 seventeen Marconi workers were killed in a raid by a lone bomber. In July 1942 Hoffman's was hit by another lone raider and four workers were killed. October 1942 saw Hoffman's bombed again with four fatalities and this led to the installation of barrage balloons for protection.

Then on March 3rd 1943 there was a heavy raid on Chelmsford. At about 8.15 p.m., just as it started, the German bombers made a concerted attack on New Hall though fortunately most of the bombs fell to the north-west of their target on unoccupied farmland in the villages of Boreham, Broomfield and Little Waltham. Many incendiary bombs, intended to light up the target, fell in fields on the northern side of New Hall – "thanks to the vigilance of staff at New Hall none of the incendiaries were able to cause serious damage".[15] Another major incendiary raid on Chelmsford took place on April 15th but this time the rural areas escaped.

On May 13th 1943 work began on a new USAF aerodrome at Boreham,[16] literally adjacent to New Hall on the eastern side. It was one of ten new airfields in Essex from which bombers would target sites in France and the Low Countries in the lead up to D-Day.[17] The Luftwaffe's intelligence was up-to-date. On the very next day at just before 2.00 a.m. on a bright moonlit night, Chelmsford and Boreham experienced their biggest air-raid yet. Marconi and Hoffman's were targeted once more in an attack which left at least fifty dead and a thousand homeless in Chelmsford. Boreham aerodrome too was bombed with specific intensity and New Hall became, by chance or design, a particular target.

The bombing started with the dropping of a one kilogram incendiary container from which about thirty-four fire bombs scattered in New Hall grounds to light up the scene for the main high explosive bombing run that followed ten minutes later. Most institutions such as factories, hospitals, boarding schools and local government offices had fire watchers on duty all night. The New Hall Hospital staff had proved effective fire-fighters two months earlier but would have had very little time to act on this occasion. The bombs soon rained down as the raiders guided themselves to the target, using the main railway line from Colchester as a navigation aid. The first bombs fell short. One of 250 or 500 kilograms exploded 238 feet west of the west wing making a crater forty-six feet across and twelve feet deep, while another bomb fell the same distance west but seventy-two feet further south. A third large bomb, again either 250 or 500 kilograms, fell a hundred feet to the north side of the centre of the west wing, again leaving a large gaping hole in the earth. A pair of fifty kilogram bombs fell to the south of the building, one about sixteen feet away leaving a crater twenty-three feet by three feet while the other fell eighty feet away leaving a crater twelve feet by four feet. They blew out a lot of windows. So far the bombs were either too short or straddling the building. But then a direct hit was received from one of the largest bombs, a third 250 or 500 kilogram high explosive device, which impacted near the main entrance to the courtyard. An area of the old school containing the two major dormitories was destroyed and twenty old people were trapped in the wreckage. A second high explosive bomb struck the wall of the west wing in the inner courtyard and penetrated a six inch concrete surface before tearing it up for a radius of twenty feet.[18] Blast from this bomb demolished up to fifty feet of the new wing's frontage.

As the Hospital supervisor later explained, the slightly more mobile patients in the upstairs dormitory had been able to get to the shelters when the air-raid sirens sounded. The others in the ground floor dormitory could not be moved and the building collapsed on top of them.[19] One of the nuns described the damage – "beds had fallen from the upstairs dormitories into the Pink Room below. All the Tudor chimneys had fallen down, one of them through the Chapel roof onto Reverend Mother's stall and through the floor … The Great Class and the Little Class were almost in ruins, the line of bay windows had gone and a great deal of damage done to the nuns' cells". The bakehouse, laundry, dairy and priest's room were also destroyed.[20]

Hospital staff and police rushed to the rescue. A massive thunderstorm made their task more difficult.[21] Looking for bodies in the rubble was to take two days. Several old people were dug out alive in the early stages including ninety-two year old Caroline Hamshire and the blind eighty-nine year old Kate Cloake. Both were uninjured.

Seven patients were found dead – eighty-three year old Angelo Clarke from Dagenham, eighty-four year old Sophia Gersen from Gidea Park, fifty-six year old William Holmes from Barking, eighty year old Phillipa Hook-Newman from Romford, eighty-one year old William Mason from Gidea Park, seventy-six year old Frederick Wilson from Dagenham and ninety-two year old Thomas Farrow. Twenty-five patients were taken to hospitals throughout Essex. Four of them died as a result of their injuries – seventy-eight year old Sarah Cooper from Ilford, seventy-three year old William Hill from Walthamstow, eighty-three year old Frederick Middleton from Brentwood and eighty-one year old Mary Poulter from Goodmayes.[22] The nuns' own record of events suggests that the number who died later rose to fifteen.[23]

Boreham airfield was also struck by incendiary containers and other incendiaries and bombs fell in the surrounding area. One large bomb fell in a pea field near the New Hall railway signal box and there was a scattering of bombs in local fields which fortunately did more damage to the fruit, pea, beet and potato crops than to human beings. Perhaps New Hall was not an intended target and was just too close to the airfield to avoid the inevitable inaccuracies from high-level bombing.

On the other hand the number of direct hits and close misses might suggest greater intent, perhaps in the belief that American air force personnel occupied the buildings. Enemy targeting may have been helped by the fact that the huge Elizabethan windows were difficult to blackout effectively.

Whatever the cause, the outcome was that New Hall was now unusable as a hospital. Censorship meant that the news was officially kept from the Essex public until September 10th, two days after Italy had surrendered, a better day for burying bad news. The *Essex Chronicle* reporter detailed the damage sustained over the last four months and somewhat poetically described "the lovely old palace ... given a new glory in the sinister glare". His bulldog spirit was inspired by one small detail − "as I left I saw through a vast gap in a partly demolished wall, a picture of Cardinal Wolsey ... The glass was not even smashed, although all around it was destruction. It bore the inscription 'Be steadfast. Have faith' ". The article concluded with the poignant words of the hospital staff, "We came here for safety ... The irony of it".

On September 14th 1943 the last patients had been transferred elsewhere. At that point official press photographers were allowed on site and pictures of the damage appeared in the *Essex Chronicle* on September 17th. Mr and Mrs Wood, who had installed the nuns' new cooking range just before the war, now moved in, the former taking the title of Bailiff of the Estate.24 They kept an eye on the place. Their ministrations ensured that New Hall did not go entirely to rack and ruin so that reoccupation was feasible in 1946.

In air raids pure chance can determine those who survive and those who are killed. The nuns, teachers and pupils, now at Newnham Paddox, had had luck on their side. They were still in one piece although the chaos of war inevitably had its effect on pupil numbers which fell from sixty-four in 1939, to forty-eight in 1940 and thirty-one in 1941 (at the height of the Blitz) but then picked up a bit to thirty-eight in 1942, and forty-six throughout 1943 and 1944. The havoc of war-time also had its effect on the pupil admission register which became less rich in personal comment on the girls. The necessity of fire-watching at night and the rigours of war-time rationing probably meant that energies were concentrated on greater priorities.

We know that in 1940 some of the girls were evacuated abroad away from war-torn Europe − Joan and Mary Warlow and Diana Ferrier to Canada, Jean and Ann Cowie and Malise Hayden to Bermuda while Priscilla Noble-Matthews went to the USA and Delphine Dowler to South Africa. Four other girls (including three Plowden sisters) are recorded in 1939 as "left owing to war", another, Moira Meyrick, returned to the greater safety of her parents' home in India while Anna Maria Rongaglia's parents took her away at Christmas 1940 after less than a term because Newnham Paddox was too close to the Midlands industrial towns that were being blitzed.

Safety was a relative thing. Britain may have appeared a risky place to live for some but for others, especially Jewish refugees from far worse in Europe, it was a haven. Newnham Paddox gave shelter to Rosemarie Schaffer who had left Vienna when the Nazis invaded Austria in March 1938. She was under the care of the Catholic Committee for Refugees from Germany, came to New Hall in 1939 and joined her parents in Brazil in 1941. Anne Schretter and Ena Eisenbaum stayed for two weeks en route elsewhere, probably the USA, in September 1939. Doris Ehrenstein stayed for two months from February to April 1940. Denise Hohla is described as half-Jewish and half-Catholic and the family name is probably also Viennese. Ann Justus had Jewish and Catholic parents. Johannes Epstein, aged eight, appears to have been a temporary male pupil in the autumn of 1940 and the pupil register records him as an "Austrian refugee; mother had been stoned in the streets of Vienna; December 1940 the whole family went to America". He was paid for at New Hall by a Miss D. Reynolds. The other refugees were welcomed as non-paying guests by the nuns.[25]

The circumstances of the war brought some unusual recruits including brother and sister Nigel (more affectionately known as Sean) and Deirdre Boyd. They arrived just before Christmas 1941, aged nineteen months and three years respectively. Nigel was indubitably the school's youngest ever entrant. They stayed until the school left Warwickshire in 1946. The pupil register notes that they were "put in our charge by their mother who was engaged in war work; Women's Royal Naval Service". People were constantly on the move during the war. The Nuttall-Smith sisters, Benoit and Naomi, were of Danish extraction and stayed for six months in 1942. Their father was in the consular service in the Far East. We do not know what happened to him when the Japanese overran south-east Asia.

In 1945, VE day was celebrated with a large bonfire and bombers flying overhead with all lights flashing. There was a large summer exodus of girls as fathers and brothers were demobilised and families began to return to their homes. In September 1945 there were only twenty-two girls on the books compared with fifty-three at the end of the summer term.[26] When the war ended the Earl of Denbigh gave the nuns a year's notice. They would either have to buy the place or leave Newnham Paddox. They chose the latter. The fact that the Earl demolished the house in 1952[27] suggests that he was in financial difficulty and needed to make economies.

The enforced move was a good time to re-think the traditional structure of the school. The Butler Education Act of 1944 brought to an end the all-in-one elementary school in the state sector and established separate primary and secondary phases with transfer at the age of eleven. The Chapter therefore decided to establish a Junior School at the Goodings near Hungerford in Berkshire leaving the Senior School to return to New Hall[28] and, literally, pick up the pieces in its bomb-damaged premises.

Chapter 26

Back to Base

Goodings, Denford and New Hall 1946-1968

New Hall was now a split site school with a vengeance, the two halves a hundred miles apart. Goodings, in the heart of the Berkshire Downs, had been occupied by the Women's Royal Naval Service during the war. One nun said that "the grounds were a jungle and my scythe came in useful". They had a swimming pool and the Prioress gave the nuns permission to swim – "such an unheard of and undreamt of thing".[1] The house had low ceilings and small rooms and was, in many ways, very suitable for juniors. Sister Magdalen John Earle was appointed its Superior. The foundation of this new house was celebrated at New Hall on August 10th 1947 after which the first Goodings contingent set out by train. They took with them overalls made out of blackout material to protect their habits when the dirty manual work of getting Goodings ready for occupation got underway. In September 1947 there were twenty-two children. The Prioress made frequent visits from New Hall and the Goodings' nuns were driven back to New Hall by Sister Mary Joseph Reynolds for the election of a Prioress in 1948, the first time a nun had driven. By 1949 the pupil numbers had risen to fifty-eight.[2]

On March 8th 1949 Sir Thomas Harrison Hughes' wife Miranda died. Their daughter, Mary, had been at New Hall from 1931 to 1933 and was a relative of one of the nuns. In memory of his wife Sir Thomas gave Denford House to the Community. This larger property was only five miles from Goodings and had 150 acres of land, half of which the nuns were able to let out to tenant farmers. Sir Thomas also conveyed a generous endowment of £25,000 (£543,000 in today's money). Goodings was sold by the Community to Franciscan nuns from Taunton who, to complete an historic circle, had left the Low Countries at the same time as the Canonesses in 1794.

The New Hall Community had paid £15,000 for Goodings in 1946 (£386,100 in today's money), financed by a bank loan about half of which had been paid off by the time it was sold in 1953 for £14,900[3] (only £255,700 in today's money), a significant loss when inflation and the money spent in the intervening period on improvements have been taken into account. As a parting shot the work of Sister Magdalen John was rewarded when in 1952 Goodings was recognised as efficient by the Ministry of Education with the proviso that the nuns should go ahead with the move to more suitable premises at Denford. That was achieved in 1953 and in 1955 efficient status was confirmed.

Denford was a Georgian house in Berkshire, seven miles from Newbury and two from Hungerford. The top class of eleven year olds worked for Common Entrance to schools such as New Hall, Ascot, Woldingham, Heathfield and North Foreland Lodge. Others sat the 11+ for entry to grammar schools in the areas where they lived. Numbers were low to start with but picked up in the mid 1950s. In 1957, when a swimming pool was built, they had reached eighty-eight, in 1960 passed a hundred and in 1966 stood at 140 of whom 115 were boarders.[4] As it was situated near Lambourn, a national centre for racehorse training, one of whose jockeys, Gordon Richards won the Coronation Derby at Epsom, it seemed appropriate in 1954 that riding should be introduced. It was popular from its inception.

From 1962 there was a move to 13+ transfer to the girls' public schools, including New Hall, so the eleven and twelve year olds stayed at Denford. This was an arrangement that would never be comfortable with some of the most able destined to leave at eleven to state and independent grammar schools. It also stretched the capacity of Denford to provide the facilities and specialisms that twelve and thirteen year olds would otherwise have received at a senior school. Although Denford was doing well in numbers the Chapter took the decision to close it in 1967. It was all a question of economics. It was clear that independent boarding schools could not survive with less than 250 pupils and the nuns did not have the personnel or resources to maintain two small schools. Warning signs were seen with the closure of the Jesuits' Beaumont College in Windsor, the Priory School in Haywards Heath and Sacred Heart School in Hove. Moreover at that time the demand for junior boarding education nationally was declining. It was therefore proposed that Denford should be sold and a junior boarding house established at New Hall so that the Juniors and Seniors together would make a viable establishment.[5]

Meanwhile, back at New Hall, the nuns and pupils returning in 1946 after six years away found that the grounds were a wilderness pocked with huge bomb craters while parts of the house and outbuildings were in ruin, much of the frontage shored up with timber baulks and shattered windows boarded over, though repair work had, in fact, been going on since 1943. The process had been started in that year by an immediate sum of £13,323 received from the War Damage Commission (£373,450 in today's money), two-thirds of which was spent by the end of the war.[6] Between 1946 and 1955 a further £87,558 was received from the Commission[7] (£1,770,000 today). However the Commission required the nuns to find 10% of the estimated rebuilding costs so £20,000 of the Community's capital (£500,000 today) was released by the calling in of mortgage loans which the nuns had made from 1901 up to just before the war. Of the fourteen mortgages just three were left intact – to a Miss Muir, the Convent of the Assumption in Ramsgate and New Hall Farm which had had £1,000 injected into it in 1944 (£27,260 today) to get it restarted after four years of unavoidable neglect. The farm lasted as a discrete New Hall business until 1956 when the land was rented out and all the machinery and implements sold.[8] Stocks and shares were, however, left untouched by this post-war reconstruction and continued to bring in about £750 p.a. in dividends[9] (£15,500 today). All the legal work was handled by the convent's solicitors Messrs Blount, Petre and Co., two very familiar surnames that had accounted for thirty-two pupils, one Prioress and several nuns over the last three centuries.

The spirit of schoolchildren had not been entirely lost during the school's enforced exile as one of the water-filled bomb craters had been stocked with roach by some enterprising local schoolboys who enjoyed their coarse fishing.[10] The returning gardeners used another crater by the pump garden for bonfires to consume the vast quantities of undergrowth that they hacked down. On August 15th 1946 on the Feast of the Assumption, the first Mass back in the old building was said rather than sung because the organ was unusable. But, amidst all these difficulties, the school was at last recognised as efficient by the new Ministry of Education and a third House was created, Saint John Fisher.[11]

In their war-damaged building it was a bitter return home. January 1947, the snowiest winter since 1814,[12] produced drifts so deep that they covered the hedges.[13] From January 22nd to March 17th temperatures rarely rose above freezing. On January 29th nearby Writtle measured a temperature of -21°C.[14] Rationing also continued although potatoes were removed from the list in March 1948, bread in July, footwear in November and jam in December. Meat and other food were still on ration and were not taken off until 1953-1954. In such circumstances it was vital to get New Hall gardens and farm functioning again. The cost of education too had gone up. A late 1940s prospectus[15] quotes a pension (still the old term being used) of £140 p.a. (£3,285 today) with an additional five guineas (£122 today) for new pupils to cover use of linen and table silver, a nice contrast to the rationed food that would be eaten off it. The pension was high but so were building costs.

In the spirit of international co-operation that emerged briefly out of World War II, the various houses of the Canonesses of the Holy Sepulchre decided to meet together in Holland at Nijmegen, the first such convention that had ever been held. New Hall, as the sole English house, sent two representatives and two Dutch nuns subsequently visited New Hall for a few weeks.

In 1948 the nuns received a new Constitution. The Prioress would continue to be elected for a renewable fixed term but this was changed to six years from three. Sister Mary Christina O'Donnell, who had been first elected in 1936, continued in office until 1954. The distinction between choir nuns and lay sisters was also abolished. All nuns were now on an equal footing. Up to this point choir nuns had been dedicated to the recitation of Divine Office in the Choir and to the education of the young while the lay sisters, originally women of limited education, undertook domestic and assistant work. Only their oral prayer was in common and the two had also worn different habits, with the lay sisters wearing simpler clothing that could be washed frequently.[16] With mass literacy and education mandatory up to at least fifteen the distinction was no longer necessary. In fact no lay sisters had entered the order since 1938 so the constitutional change was, in effect, a rationalisation of a situation that was naturally coming to pass. From 1948 all nuns had the same habit and timetable. In this respect they were well ahead of the Catholic Church as this distinction within religious orders was not formally abolished world-wide until 1966.

Enclosure, which had been prised open further by the realities of the war, was also being re-examined. In 1954 Pius XII's Apostolic Constitution *Sponsa Christi*, which referred to contemplative and semi-contemplative religious orders, (the Canonesses numbered amongst the latter), reiterated the Church's belief in the total devotion of its priests and religious to God through celibacy and, by natural extension for monastic orders, enclosure. Yet the concept of enclosure as an absolute did not sit easily with religious orders like the Canonesses who were involved in apostolic work. This was probably at the root of Christina Dennett's hesitation in expanding the school back in the 1770s. Those nuns who were teachers were inevitably unenclosed for much of the working week and had to have some knowledge of the world their wards inhabited, even though in their devotional and conventual life outside school hours they would revert to an enclosed separation. However the accession of Pope John Paul XXIII in 1958 meant that redefining enclosure ceased to be a priority. Rome said it was no longer to be pursued. There were other changes in the liturgy too which followed this theme with the High Altar in New Hall Chapel replaced in 1958 by a more open free-standing marble altar.[17] And then , from 1962, the Second Vatican Council dictated events.

As regards the school, repair to war damage took time as it did in much of England. Everywhere money was in short supply. However by 1950 more rooms were ready for use. In 1951 the restored Chapel was opened and the organ played for the first time since 1940. And lacrosse reappeared as a school sport once the large bomb crater in front of the house had been filled. It continued to be known as The Crater Field. In 1952 there were over a hundred pupils for the first time.[18]

A Prospectus from the mid 1950s[19] proudly announces "Recognised by the Ministry of Education". It informs its potential customers that its pupils will be entered for the General Certificate of Education Ordinary and Advanced Level, these two new exams having been introduced in 1951 with certificates awarded for each subject not, as under School Certificate regulations, depending on passes in all subjects where one weak area could deny overall success. Now the list of subjects on the Prospectus had a modern ring – religious knowledge, English Language, English Literature, history, geography, modern languages, Latin, mathematics, science, art, music, needlework, class elocution and drama. Advanced dressmaking classes were available in the Sixth Form and a secretarial course "for those who need to take it". The order of subjects is significant – humanities before science (Linda Marks was the first girl belatedly to attempt a Sixth Form science course at New Hall in 1964-1966) and, as an afterthought, a somewhat grudging acceptance that some future secretaries may not be academically up to it! Parents were also informed that an escort would be provided for their daughters to and from London at the beginning and end of each term provided ten days' notice was given.

A further concession to the modern world came in 1953 when New Hall hired two televisions, one for the Community in the workroom and one for the school in the Hall, to watch the Coronation. In the same year there was a religious vocations exhibition at Olympia which was intended to foster vocations and to break down the barriers between the religious orders and the public. The whole school went in small groups on alternate days.[20] The reality for all religious orders was that if they did not recruit from within their own schools then they would gradually disappear from view.

In 1957, the year that Sister Mary Ignatius Brown became Headmistress, the Campion Wing was added and a swimming pool was opened. Parents were therefore asked to send their girls back to school with really short hair unless it was already in plaits and to discourage them from growing it long at school as there would be daily bathing in the summer term. A hairdresser would visit the school each month "to keep the hair short". The items that girls were required to bring with them were stationery and stamps for a term, a term's supply of soap and toothpaste (but definitely no talcum powder or nail varnish), a Schott wooden descant recorder, a music case, an Osmiroid 65 fountain pen with italic nib medium straight (or left-handed nibs for those of that bent), JACKO skates for roller-skating, a twelve inch ruler, scissors, sellotape, gum, a box of coloured pencils, a small container with needles, cottons, thimble and name-tapes, and a large plastic bag for needlework.

Things were going well. Recovery from war-time dislocation seemed complete. In 1959 the Ministry of Education inspectors concluded that "the school continued to provide a sound education in delightful surroundings". But although rebuilding had been successful the school was tight at the seams.

The intake of girls each year was not a great deal more than in the immediate pre-war years – an average of twenty a year in the three years before the war and an average of twenty-two in the three years after the war which stayed constant for the next ten years up to the end of the 1950s. Nonetheless this still meant that overall numbers had expanded since the last major building programme in 1925 and the move to a 13+ entry in 1962 would require accommodation to be skewed more towards the needs of older teenagers. As the Prioress, Mary Veronica Boland, explained in a letter[21] to the Bishop of Brentwood, New Hall was built for eighty-four girls and currently had 122 on roll.

Extended buildings were planned. New dormitories would enable the old private rooms to be used as study bedrooms for the Sixth Form. These special rooms for those with the cash to pay were, in any case, outmoded by the 1960s. A new building would also contain classrooms and science laboratories. Finance, as ever, would be a major problem as the estimated cost was £55,000 and, at the same time alterations at Denford, including a new Assembly Hall to take its additional eleven and twelve year olds, would add a further £32,000, a total of £87,000 (£1,230,000 today). The Chapter therefore sought the permission of the Bishop to sell their equity investments worth £40,000 (£566,000 today). The convent's mortgage lending business had already virtually ceased in the late 1940s so that left only the income from nuns' dowries as invested capital and that would be retained for convent expenses. Because New Hall Farm had a bank overdraft of £1,500 (£21,240 today) and the school one of £8,500 (£120,360 today) the Prioress informed the Bishop that a mortgage on the property or a loan was also being considered. In the event the latter was the safer route and in July 1962 the Bishop wrote to Rome[22] seeking permission for the nuns to take out a bank loan of £60,000 (£787,000 today) which would be paid off in about fifteen years by raising fees. To back up these financial manoeuvres a buildings appeal was launched in 1963 with Lord Plowden[23] as President, a family name that goes back to the seventeenth century in New Hall's annals, and includes Lady Goring (née Dorothy Plowden) the great eighteenth century benefactress. By 1970 the appeal had raised £53,294[24] (£506,800 today).

In 1962 bulldozers arrived to start work and, in so doing, uncovered the Tudor gatehouse foundations. Work was impeded by another freezing winter. It started to snow on Boxing Day 1962 and sub-zero temperatures continued until March. Rivers froze over and outside games were virtually impossible. Although the new building was opened on November 9th 1963 the original aim, had weather permitted, would

Prioress Reverend Mother Aloysia Magdalen Dolan on her Silver Jubilee in 1934. She was the first moderniser who rescued the school from near closure

Queen Mary's visit June 17th 1938, running late with no time to get out of the car. Back view of the Prioress, Mother Christina O'Donnell

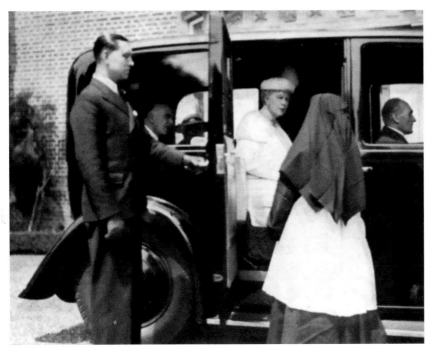

Front of the school showing the magnificent cedars

View of school from avenue including cottage

Bomb damage 1943. South front where the dormitories collapsed killing at least eleven elderly people

Bomb damage 1943. The construction of Boreham airfield next door made New Hall fatally vulnerable

*Happy times at Goodings Preparatory School
immediately after the Second World War*

*Sister Magdalen John Earl, headmistress of
Goodings and Denford, pictured then and now*

Aerial view of Denford, the second site for the Preparatory School, given by Sir Thomas Harrison Hughes

Princess Ann visits the Riding School at New Hall in 1979 and meets an awestruck nun

The assembled School receive a royal wave

Photograph courtesy of John Furze

Farm buildings, pond and east wing before the creation of the Pastoral Centre

Photograph by Annabel Brown

School assembly in the Chapel

Photograph by Annabel Brown

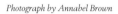

The Octagon, built in 1983

Photograph by Annabel Brown

Walkfares performing arts centre, built in 1992

Under the Cedars – Preparatory School 2004

Aerial view from the front of the School, 2004

surely have been a summer opening ready for the new school year. In 1964 the celebrated film and stage actress, Virginia Maskell (New Hall 1946-1953), came to commemorate the new buildings by performing in a pageant of three acts celebrating New Hall's history. An early 1960s prospectus[25] advertised New Hall for thirteen to eighteen year olds and Denford for those up to thirteen. But this drab document was somehow not in keeping with the New Hall fees of £105 per term (£1,415 today) with extras costing more – instrumental tuition £7 per term (£97 today), Spanish, Italian, German and riding 6 guineas, private elocution 4 guineas and ballet 3 guineas. Dancing was the best bargain at £2.12s.6d. per term(£35 today).

With the decision to close Denford a new junior building, Beaulieu House,[26] was erected where the Pavilion used to be until its demolition in 1955, and was opened for business in September 1967. This development put paid to keeping free-range chickens which had formerly roamed the plot as well as the nuns' practice of feeding tramps, some of whom came as casual labour to pick fruit and peas. With very young children on site this was now considered too risky.[27]

The sale of Denford had gone well. The convent had moved away from Blount, Petre and Co. solicitors in 1959 when Henry Petre died, to the diocesan solicitors Witham Weld and Co., still with a strong historic connection, as fifteen Welds had passed through the school since 1812. The solicitors' professional report on Denford was not optimistic – "we know that the value is £100,000/£120,000 (£1,145,000/£1,374,000 today) but a great deal more is needed and our only chance will be if two keen (and rich!) candidates compete".[28] In the event there were three in the race – the Westminster Bank for a staff college, the Greater London Council for a residential home for "backward children" and the Norland Nursing Training College of Chislehurst. The latter won a bidding game with a price of £142,500 (£1,631,625 today).[29]

The school virtually doubled in size overnight with 162 new pupils coming to New Hall in 1967 of whom seventy-seven were from Denford, either coming to continue their junior education or transferring to the Senior School, a vast increase on the average of thirty-seven new pupils in each of the previous four years. This was all part of the new Prioresss' plan. Sister Mary Christopher O'Connor had just been elected and wanted to make New Hall more financially viable. To meet this explosion in numbers Owen and Southwell were added as Houses, to make five in all, and the academic structure of the senior school changed to Departments based on subject rooms where the pupils went to the teacher. Small tutor groups were also introduced.[30]

Alongside all this educational activity significant changes were taking place in the Catholic Church. In 1962 Pope John Paul XXIII summoned the Second Vatican

Council to Rome with his visionary words, "I want to throw open the windows of the Church so that we can see out and the people can see in". After his death in 1963 the Council was continued by Pope Paul VI until the completion of its deliberations in 1965. The principal consequences of the Council are now well-known, notably the introduction of vernacular languages to replace the Latin Mass and the audible celebration of Mass by the priest facing the people. One of the last decrees in 1965, on the Adaptation and Renewal of Religious Life, *Perfectae Caritatis*,[31] was to have an impact on the lives of the Canonesses. Semi-contemplative nuns, such as the Canonesses, who were dedicated to apostolic work in education, were encouraged to forsake cloistered enclosure. Their habit was to be simple and modest and was to be suitable to the circumstances and needs of their work. The manner of living, praying and working was to be adapted to "the modern physical and psychological circumstances of the members". All nuns were to be given the opportunity for education and training to degree level, if appropriate, after the novitiate and not sent directly into apostolic work. Constitutions were to be re-written and obsolete laws were to go.

Prioress Mary Christopher O'Connor shepherded the nuns through the changes that were required. The nuns' headdress was made simpler with the all-enveloping wimple disappearing. The ceremonial choir cloak was discarded. Novices wore black veils, instead of white, like professed nuns so as not to be conspicuous. Ceremonial was simplified to obtain quiet and repose. Grace at meals was in English. The Prioress was no longer addressed as Reverend Mother but as Mother or Mother Prioress. The Community timetable changed to less arduous hours starting at 7.00 a.m. with Lauds, then three other major religious offices during the day and ending at 9.15 p.m. with Compline[32] compared with the previous regimen of a 4.30 a.m. start with Meditation, night prayers at 8.00 p.m. and up to eight other major religious offices in between.[33] Going back to roots, an Augustinian chaplain was appointed in 1964 though he was replaced very soon by diocesan priests.[34] In 1969 the nuns' plainchant was sung in the vernacular. In 1972 further changes were made to the nuns' day to fit more naturally with school activities and in 1975 the Retro-Choir disappeared and the nuns' stalls moved in front of the High Altar.[35] That some of these changes were quite delayed signifies the difficulty that some of the Community had in coming to terms with the new order of things.

The demands of a modern twentieth century state and a reforming Pope had converged. New Hall was now a thriving school with increasing numbers. The main thrust of its curriculum was firmly locked into the pattern which served all schools, state or independent, religious or secular, and the nuns, well before the requirements of the Second Vatican Council, had made sure that their members were appropriately educated and trained. But modern education was much more specialist in its approach and expensive in terms of equipment, buildings and salaries and the recruitment of nuns with appropriate skills could not keep pace with needs. Increasingly lay staff were appointed.

The liturgy and religious observances that were central to the life of the school were also changing. These changes received a mixed reception in the Catholic Church generally and the older nuns, who had been used to a particular form of life and worship, also found them difficult.

With the Junior and Senior schools now united on the same site, education had become big business. Roles were reversing. New Hall was now a school with a convent attached.

Chapter 27

Modern Times

New Hall 1968-2001

Under the inspirational leadership of the Prioress, Sister Mary Christopher O'Connor (1966-1978), the school continued to move forward rapidly. While the nuns were adjusting to the implications of the Second Vatican Council and numbers in the convent were reducing, the number of girls in the school was leaping ahead. In net terms, when leavers are subtracted from new pupils, the increase had been at a rate of about four per annum from 1945-65 but rocketed to fifty in each year from 1966 to 1969.[1] A quarter of this expanded intake was from schools abroad and just under a quarter were non-Catholics, with little overlap between the two groups. These increased numbers inevitably continued to shift the teaching staff balance towards a large lay majority while adding a fascinating diversity to the school student population. This would have delighted the Prioress with her passion for ecumenism and going out to meet the world. It was significant that, in her office, she had a large map of the world over which she frequently pored.[2] But she not only had the vision. She could also get the best out of people. She gave staff delegated responsibility and let them get on with it while giving full support, only requiring that she be kept informed. She could also "combine holiness with a sense of fun" and was a "spontaneous and a gifted mimic".[3] One of her most important appointments was that of Sister Mary Francis Wood as Headmistress (1963-1986) who, as a small girl, had presented the posy to Queen Mary way back in 1938. Mary Francis was another visionary leader who introduced day girls and got her teeth into the necessities of marketing and publicity. Through her ecumenical enthusiasm which she shared with the Prioress and an outward going personality, the new Headmistress put the school on the local map and ensured that it was represented in the Chelmsford area in educational and pastoral forums. With these two at their different helms there was an explosion of purposeful activity.

By 1970 New Hall had 355 pupils (treble the number in 1966) with three streams of entry, sixty-eight in the Sixth Form and a new Language Laboratory.[4] In that same year new study bedrooms and a Sixth Form wing were completed and the latter was opened with a Hallowe'en Ball. The Sacred Heart dormitory was turned into a conference room and music rooms, and the staff room and library were relocated. When Denford transferred to New Hall in 1967 their ponies came with them to form a flourishing Riding School.[5] The indoor Riding School was built in 1970-1971 which gave the opportunity to invite disabled children to visit, the start of a long association.

In 1972 the Junior Section in Beaulieu was closed[6] and New Hall reverted to an 11-18 school. After a ten year experiment it had proved impractical to continue with a 13+ entrance system. The state grammar schools and independent day schools were attractive prospects for eleven year olds and New Hall needed to be in the market at that stage. Once started at an 11-18 school parents were unlikely to transfer their children again two years later. Furthermore the large increase in Senior School numbers needed accommodation and teaching space. But the loss of the Junior School meant that all pupils would have to be recruited from outside with no natural progression from within.

In 1973 the *New Hall Chronicle*[7] was resurrected after an absence of thirty-five years. It observed that since the end of World War II "the world, society and the Church have undergone rapid and sweeping changes, leaving the older generation confused and creating much tension and insecurity in the young", but the latter were not so preoccupied that they could not manage the challenge of the Duke of Edinburgh Award that was introduced that year.

The 1973 diary of Sister Mary Joseph Reynolds,[8] the first nun to drive a car back in 1948, gives us some further insights into the tensions that times of rapid change could bring for older nuns. At its simplest level motorway driving was a chore as " the lorry drivers do not like us keeping to the middle lane"! Nor did new religious interpretations convince her. In January "Father Michael preached a spontaneous sermon to tell us that angels and devils are hardly more than figurative conceptions of the Oriental mind. I was furious. May every angel of every choir help me to worship ... and may Mary overcome every devil on earth". Father Michael was not having a happy time. In February he "preached before Mass and was ticked off by Sister Mary Francis Wood for the omission in his sermon of the vital Presence of God at Mass since he over-emphasised God's presence in people. He was grateful for the criticism". So Father Michael was a diplomat as well! He would have needed to be. Angels were to cause him trouble twice more that year.

The school gave Sister Mary Joseph great pleasure, even if all these extra girls could be noisy. In January "the children's 'Hallo! Ma'ams' are altogether delightful and the staff's amicability most consoling". In February "the school has a very nice set of children ... The Fifth are being given new privileges to prepare them for being Sixth Formers. They may put out their lights at ten and go out at weekend in home clothes. They seemed delighted". And then in March, "so many activities going on in the school that it is hard to keep pace with it all". She also kept a watchful eye on moral proprieties. Towards the end of January "I went to Chelmsford and bought books. One of the books, *The Card* by Arnold Bennett is not, according to Miss Mercer, the right sort for our children so I may change them for *Sense and Sensibility* ... Saw a number of Fishes shopping, one with her boy friend Colin (all above board)". Old Fishes' marriages and children were normally good news but in February there was an ounce of regret at one engagement – "another 'might be nun' otherwise occupied".

She seems to have missed the greater quiet and repose that the convent used to have before the school grew so large and lay teachers arrived in droves. In January she complained of the "vile racket from the television next door". At Easter, despite their amicability, she welcomed the "escape from the staff who come to tea in the Refectory". On the other hand some staff showed considerable subtlety. In June "I had that wonderfully cultured Italian teacher ... who blossomed like a rose over whatever I said. She is pleased that her former impression of nuns has changed since her contact with us". The mechanised world of the twentieth century particularly disturbed her tranquillity. In September, "such traffic in the night, with a south wind ... battering it against the front of the house and the south cells. It was like being below Niagara Falls. The roar washed down on us until a train's clatter topped the sound of the lorries". The Niagara Falls was also an in-house euphemism for a flushing toilet so this comment may have had extra meaning!

And the world outside was even more complex to understand as she recorded her ever-increasing list of catastrophes culled from reading the *Daily Telegraph* – Ireland, Vietnam, Andy Warhol, the Soviet Union, the trade unions, homosexuality, Communist China, the value of the pound, Hell's Angels, muggers, the pill, drugs, the BBC and Watergate. In February she felt that "England is fast becoming a complacent Sodom and Gomorrah" and in March concluded that "reading the paper two days running is really most depressing". In May she began to doubt President Nixon's honesty over the Watergate break-in but added "I don't know exactly what 'bugging' means but I will find out". By July she clearly had done so – "at last I have understood the Watergate scandal".

A running theme throughout the year was the effect of inflation and industrial militancy on the Heath Government. Politically the nuns' position appears not to have changed since 1931 when they first voted. In January, "Mr Heath is having a horrible and lonely time in trying to keep prices and wages down. All out battle with the trade unions and their puppets in the Labour Party". In February the BBC's claim to be impartial was judged to be "communistic and atheistic". In July "if the Labour Party get in our schools will be suppressed ... the rude derogatory abuse of the [Labour] opposition blind the half-blind public so that they only see the snags ... The Socialist Party is not free like the Conservatives".

The fuel crisis, with the quadrupling of oil prices after the 1973 Arab-Israeli War and the cut by Arab states in oil sold to Britain for giving diplomatic support to Israel, also had its effects. On February 12th there was "a short electricity cut in the afternoon and a long one in the evening during Prep". In March "a sense for economy is percolating through the house. I must not take so much bath water". In late November the diary notes, "oil shortage ... no one is to take more than two half-baths a week. No windows are to be left open for more than ten minutes and then the radiators must be turned off ... We are not to drive round unnecessarily". Six days later "we had run out of oil and the boilers were off ... The laundry is piled up with unwashed garments ... Petrol ration books are now being issued". Fortunately fresh oil supplies arrived the next day but only just enough to keep going as suppliers tried to juggle all their customers. Yet another week on and "our House has had oil delivered to it in the nick of time". The probability is that most of the girls regarded it all as a big game as they usually do if lessons might be disrupted.

The dreaded traffic, which so disturbed Sister Mary Joseph, was to have a much more visible impact on New Hall's grounds. They had already been cut in two by the railway line in 1843. In 1969 a new by-pass road had been proposed as the old two-way London road was inadequate. Compulsory purchase meant that the school lost the section of the avenue to the south of the level crossing. The nuns were appropriately compensated by the Ministry of Transport including a specific sum to rebuild the gardener's cottage which had been just on the south side of the crossing. The Ministry also bought a strip of land on the school side of the railway line from a local farmer which provided a new entrance from White Hart Lane.[9] This is still the way into the school on a half-mile west-east private road parallel to the north of the railway swinging north along the remaining half of the avenue to the school with an exit to the east. All the new roads were opened in 1973 when the internal one-way system for traffic was also introduced.

In 1974[10] the Sixth Form passed a hundred for the first time, there were two Cambridge successes and a new tutorial system started which brought all girls into a personal relationship with a member of staff over and above the resident house team. It helped integrate the pastoral and academic sides of school work, the resident and non-resident staff and nuns and lay staff.

In 1977 absolute responsibility for the management of the school was relinquished by the nuns. A group of Administrative Trustees was set up to act in the quasi-capacity of a Board of Governors and included representatives of parents and staff, as well as nominees with legal, financial and administrative experience. It first met on July 3rd 1977 under the chairmanship of Father Patrick Barry, Headmaster of Ampleforth. This did not alter the spiritual and legal position of the Chapter but was a sensible recognition by them that the big business that education had now become required a wider range of advisory experience. The Bursar, a more modern title for the Procuratrix, also ceased to be a Community office and passed into lay hands. The 1978 prospectus,[11] in colour for the first time, described a school of 500, split into 370 boarders and 130 day pupils. In these more child-centred times the brochure was full of photographs of happy and active pupils, rather than pictures of the nuns that had been the custom in earlier times. On the staff list there were only thirteen nuns and thirty-eight lay staff, of whom six were men and they were all Heads of Department!

In 1978 New Hall's Voluntary Service Association reorganised its activities into six action groups – the Playgroup to provide a break for problem families; the Deaf and Dumb Group with girls learning sign language; the Blind Group which, because of the number of charities already supporting the blind, was soon changed to Help the Aged; Across which continued the existing work of taking pilgrimages to Lourdes; and Riding for the Disabled which had been an independent activity since 1970. Each group was staffed by sixth formers and parents. The Riding for the Disabled group, which worked with children from the Drummond Spastic Centre at Kelvedon, received a visit from Princess Anne in 1979. In 1987 the Voluntary Association received a special award from NatWest as it also did in 2005, with the Nationwide Building Society's Award for Voluntary Endeavour. All aspects of this voluntary work were fundamental to the ecumenical vision of the convent and school which had become such a central part of its mission since the mid 1960s.

The standard of horsemanship for the able-bodied was also very high. In 1976 New Hall received the British Horse Society's approval, a tribute to the work of Sister Bernadette Stokes, who had been the inspiration. She had certainly caught the eye of the national press – "the Nun wears jodhpurs by permission of the Pope" proclaimed the *Daily Express* on May 3rd 1971, giving publicity to one of the less expected outcomes of the Second Vatican Council. Sister Bernadette left in 1978 so Lieutenant Colonel Wesley was appointed as riding master and the school became more competitively outward looking, so much so that in 1979 New Hall won the Inter-Schools Championship at Hickstead. As a result the school authorities made £7,000 available for the purchase of new horses and ponies (£21,770 today) and the Riding School turned into a business providing six, ten or twelve month courses, depending on the rider's age and ability, with learners receiving all their tuition and accommodation free plus the use of school facilities. These learners were, in effect, working "apprentices" who put in $7\frac{1}{2}$ hour days with three days off a fortnight and five weeks holiday a year. One or two male pupils were included in their number. Local applicants were preferred as they did not need bed and board. The Riding School personnel would therefore gain a qualification and, at the same time, teach over 150 girls in the main school who had chosen riding as an option. Extra income would be earned by teaching outside clients at the weekends.[12] However, the Riding School's forty stables, floodlit indoor arena, extensive grazing and two cross-country courses proved to be costly. Lieutenant-Colonel Wesley's declining health caused his retirement in 1989 so, at that point, the Riding School was closed and its business started afresh under different ownership at East Hanningfield.

Some of the reforms of Margaret Thatcher's Conservative Government (1979-1990) caused heart-searching, none more so than the 1980 Assisted Places Scheme whereby able children who satisfied certain academic criteria would have their places subsidised by the state at independent schools. New Hall was reluctant to participate. As the official voice of New Hall said in the 1980 *New Hall Chronicle*, "the philosophy of New Hall is based on the comprehensive principle, meeting not only or even primarily, academic competition but always balancing this with the boarding needs. We felt that the scheme of its nature was divisive ... It would not help those with parents overseas or who are likely to be mobile, those with difficult home circumstances, the handicapped or those unsuited to the sometimes very large co-educational school". However, from 1996 the School did utilise the scheme in a small way with a maximum of fifty pupils in the Preparatory and Senior Schools benefitting. The Labour government phased out the scheme from 1997.

Finance continued to be a problem. The nuns had paid for post-war repairs and extensions with loans and by selling off investments and calling in mortgages. Since then part of fee income had been earmarked each year for capital projects as there had been no endowments to provide an income stream, save that for Denford in 1949. There were debts to be paid and fees had risen sharply in recent years although some of this was to keep pace with double figure inflation. In 1980 two more major expenses loomed – the need to extend the gymnasium to provide adequate facilities for the increasing number of girls and the need to link up with mains drainage which was one mile distant. This also involved the demolition of the water tower, a familiar landmark and eyesore.

1980 was the 500th anniversary of the founding of the Canonesses of the Holy Sepulchre at Kinroy. Cardinal Basil Hume came for the Speech Day celebrations as guest of honour. He paid tribute to the nuns. "Whatever the future holds for us we ought to be clear that our forefathers have handed on to us something extremely precious. Those who have gone before us have done great work for God in our schools". Four years later he was to return to New Hall with Robert Runcie, Archbishop of Canterbury, John Habgood, Archbishop of York and leaders of other churches represented on the British Council of Churches, for the New Hall Consultation,[13] an ecumenical initiative in keeping with the Community's desire to share experiences with other Christians.

In 1982 the BBC Open University team featured New Hall in its Planning and Purpose in the Curriculum unit as an example of good convent education. The producer was struck by the "caring community". The bigger the school became (it was now 499) the more difficult this was to sustain so the tutor support system was restructured again reducing groups to fifteen pupils. 1982 also saw three more changes – fencing started as a school sport; two mini-computers were introduced - "the only two obedient morons to be found on the premises" one wit observed; and the nuns simplified their habit a stage further – "no more are nuns recognisable by eyes, nose and mouth but also by ears and hair colour", commented one student journalist.

In 1983 disease raised its ugly head again. "Mystery bug hits School" proclaimed the *Essex Chronicle* headline on March 4th. "Doctors believe a mystery illness that forced New Hall School ... to close two weeks ago may strike again ... 130 girls and staff fell victim to a 'flu type bug which caused a severe rash". The paper reported that, although the school opened again that week, after an extended half-term, "eighty girls failed to return ... Many are still unpleasantly poorly." Doctors around the country, treating the girls at their homes, said "they have never seen anything like it before". Because the illness was confined solely to members of the school, and was not passed on to anyone else when the girls returned home, doctors concluded that it was "a chemical not a virus". In fact it turned out to be Haverhill Fever, named after the place in Massachusetts where it first occurred in 1926, otherwise known as rat-bite fever, which is not contagious between human beings but is caught by exposure to rat-bite or rat urine. The headache, nausea, fever, red skin eruptions and, sometimes, temporary blindness that follow were, as the paper reported, very unpleasant but not life-threatening. The immediate cause of suspicion was the fresh unpasteurised milk supply from New Hall Farm which was stopped by Government order, as that had been the cause back in 1926 in the USA when milk had been adulterated by rat urine. New Hall Farm was eventually exonerated with its milk supplies passing every stringent Ministry test. The cause was never officially established but was probably attributable to the recent installation of new water pipes at New Hall to link up with mains drainage which disturbed the tranquillity and bladders of the local rat population. Henceforth, however, New Hall Farm sold all its milk to the Milk Marketing Board and the school purchased pasteurised milk from normal commercial sources.[14]

In October 1986 New Hall found a new way to further its spiritual quest and support the Bishop's search for accommodation for retreats when the Diocesan Pastoral

Centre opened. Sister Mary Francis Wood had made the initial financial arrangements with money raised by a diocesan-wide appeal for £180,000[15] (£325,000 in today's values) to supplement the contributions from the Community and the Diocese. Sister Mary Rose Henderson was the Centre's first Director from 1987 to 1993 since when it has had a team directorate of Sisters Angela Morris, Diana Impey and Mary Stephen Grindon-Welch. The Barn, as it is better known, a former cattle fodder store, has been a powerful force for ecumenical good, enabling Christians of various denominations, and the spiritually curious of none, to explore their faiths and spirituality with input from some of New Hall's most experienced nuns as well as a variety of outside sources. In providing these opportunities the nuns have been able to exemplify one of the fundamental Augustinian tenets, hospitality. The first Anglican women priests held a retreat at the Pastoral Centre on the eve of their ordination, and since 1990 the caring professions in the National Health Service and Social Services have been coming for mid-week courses in this wonderfully tranquil atmosphere.[16]

In 1990, as though to compensate for the loss of the Riding School in the previous year, a building to house the Faculty for Performing Arts was opened, and was called Walkfares thus resurrecting the name of one of the ancient manors adjacent to that of New Hall. A tree planting scheme was also inaugurated to enhance the area between Walkfares and the new housing developments to the north. The new building was opened by Sam Wanamaker, Hollywood film director and inspiration behind the reconstruction of Shakespeare's Globe Theatre in Southwark. The second phase of Walkfares' development was opened by the Catholic peer, Lord Longford, in 1993.

As a delightful intermission between these events the Guides were revitalised in 1991 after nearly seventy years absence and BBC Radio 4's *Any Questions* visited New Hall in 1992 to commemorate the 350th anniversary of the school's foundation when a giant birthday cake with 350 balloons and candles was produced.[17]

At the 1993 Speech Day Headmistress Sister Margaret Mary Horton said:

> "Old Fishes ask 'Has everything changed?' Yes, to the physical layout, numbers, mix of day and boarding, ecumenical development, the full collaboration of the Community with lay colleagues, attention to academic standards, the extension of the curriculum. Thirty years ago we built the original Campion Wing and have since added the Octagon, the Campion extension and Walkfares as large self-contained areas, not to mention conversions and refurbishments, as well as complete renewal of heating and drainage systems and catering facilities – all from fee income of which 10% is reserved".

But, she added:

"Not everything has changed — we have always been counter-culture; we build our communities on values that are not in the mainstream of contemporary society. From the seventeenth century... there has been a spirit that has had to fight against the odds, against the trends in society. It has involved being ... acceptable to, indeed respected by, the society of the time and yet promoting values which are less and less acceptable to that same society".

These were stirring words. The "loathsome League tables" and the need to "satisfy Social Services Inspectors", the lot of every boarding establishment, were just two of the modern millstones round the neck that she abhorred. But the more cut-throat educational market of the late twentieth century was one of those social trends that could not be escaped. How to combine competition and spirituality was a real challenge especially in a world of declining church attendance and growing materialism.

In late 1993 the 350th anniversary of the English House at Liège was jointly celebrated at Chelmsford Cathedral by the Catholic Bishop of Brentwood, Thomas McMahon, and the Anglican Bishop of Chelmsford, John Waine, a sign of ecumenical friendship. In the summer a Thanksgiving Mass was celebrated at New Hall by Cardinal Basil Hume.

In 1994 the new co-educational Preparatory School opened with forty-eight pupils. Numbers rocketed to 200 within two years, giving a natural progression for many girls through into New Hall Senior School and, from 2006, for boys too. Boys' boarding facilities were also provided from 2003 for eight to eleven year olds. This came at a needy time as intake in the Senior School was dropping in the mid 1990s. In the twenty years up to 1994 intake in all year groups averaged just under 120 a year.[18] In the second half of the 1990s it was only ninety-five. There had also been a reversal in the balance of boarders and day pupils. In the mid 1970s three-quarters of girls were boarders, in the mid 1980s about two-thirds, a half in 1993 and just one-third in 1997. With a constant number of girls this would have brought a marked drop in income and therefore was even more serious with a smaller intake (partly a reflection of a general demographic dip) which by 1995 had translated into a Senior School of 403, ninety-six less than in 1987.

With fewer British girls wanting to board, the nature of the boarding houses changed. In the 1970s and 1980s about 33% of boarders were from overseas schools. In the 1990s the figure averaged 60% rising to 80% in 1998. This was not just a New Hall phenomenon. Boarding education is still a prized asset for girls from other countries but is less sought after by British families. The range of countries from which New

Hall boarders come has also become much more diverse in the last ten to twenty years. Traditionally the Catholic countries of Europe, especially Spain, and Catholic ex-pats had provided most of the intake of boarders from overseas schools. The huge changes in international politics and the world economy since 1990 mean that New Hall now welcomes students from mainland China, Hong Kong and Japan; from Tanzania, Ghana, Uganda, Nigeria and Zambia; from Mexico and the USA; from Australia and New Zealand; and from Croatia, Russia and Poland.

In 1997 Sister Anne-Marie Brister became Headmistress. She was a most capable Cambridge historian and an excellent teacher who took a year out, working in British Leyland at Cowley after graduating and qualifying as a teacher, to get a feel for some of the issues in the outside world. Her tenure of office started sadly with the loss of Sixth Form cancer victim Jane Anderson. In 1998 a new swimming pool was opened in her memory, funded by an appeal to parents. Over four years Sister Anne-Marie took the school forward academically to reach standards that had not been seen before. She saw the school through its joyful 200th anniversary celebrations in 1999 with another grand ecumenical service at Chelmsford Cathedral where the address was given by the Anglican Bishop of Bradwell, Laurie Green. It was also significant, as evidence of New Hall's continuity, that Clare Petre, the latest of a long line of thirty-one Petre girls stretching back to 1715, should be finishing her school career in such a momentous year. A further joyous celebration came in 2001 when the nuns' CD, *Eternal Light*, shot to number two in the UK classical charts, with the proceeds going to support sister convents in the Congo, Brazil and particularly Rwanda, where the convent was destroyed and six sisters killed in the 1994 Rwandan massacre. This was the first time that the nuns' singing had been heard outside the convent chapel. Sadly, within five years, it would not be heard even there.

As the new millennium opened there was a question not only as to whether Sister Anne-Marie would be the last nun to hold the position of Headmistress, but also whether the number of nuns was falling so fast that the Community's future at New Hall might be in doubt.

Chapter 28

The Closing of a Chapter

Underlying all the changes that had occurred in the Church and education since the 1960s, religious orders in general and the Canonesses in particular were not attracting new vocations. Only three nuns had been professed at New Hall in the twenty year period 1987-2006 and ten in the period 1967-1986, compared with nineteen in the period 1947-1966.[1] But this was a common European and North American phenomenon and had also extended to low recruitment for the priesthood. By 2004 the number of nuns in women's religious orders in North America had declined by one half.[2] Europe's figures would at least have been similar.

It was not just a question of a slowing down of recruitment but also, from the 1960s, of nuns leaving their orders in increasing numbers to fulfil their vocation outside their religious communities. This was an unintended result of the Second Vatican Council's decision to involve women more in church life. It is in stark contrast to the "unreformed" Church in the post-war decades prior to the Council when the number of women entering religious orders rose significantly.[3] The subsequent general decline is reflected in the experience of the Canonesses. Only one nun left the order up to 1959 but seven left between 1960 and 1975.[4] In general young women with a sense of vocation began to find other avenues of fulfilment — as lay teachers (which attracted many teaching religious away from their orders), in the public sector generally or in the international aid organisations, while still being able to live out their faith.

In 2001 the Headmistress, Sister Anne-Marie Brister, left New Hall to go back to her first love, class teaching, in a Catholic Voluntary School in the south of England. Mrs Katherine Jeffrey, New Hall's first lay Headmistress (or Principal as the title soon became) was subsequently appointed, an Oxford graduate in PPE with further degrees in Catholic theology and educational management. Under her "inspirational leadership"[5] the school has continued to blossom as seen in its 2004 Inspection Report.

In 2005 the Governors and senior management team decided that boys will be admitted from 2006 to ensure that numbers, now reaching 750 in the Preparatory and Senior Schools, remain buoyant and the finances strong while, at the same time, enabling families to have all their children educated at the same school, coeducationally from the age of three to eleven and in the Sixth Form, and in single-sex classes from eleven to sixteen. So New Hall will no longer have the tag of the oldest Catholic girls' school in England although, as the Bishop of Brentwood, Thomas McMahon, said at Exhibition Day in 2005, it will be the Diocese's only Catholic independent school for senior boys.

This move to co-education may seem like an almost inevitable progression following on from others in the 1980s and 1990s which have seen an increased intake from overseas, then an increase in day girls as boarding became less fashionable and finally an increase in non-Catholics as the school's decision to follow a more ecumenical route coincided with a sharp decline in the Catholic birth-rate. Yet this capacity to adapt has been the exception rather than the norm. Since the 1950s three-quarters of Catholic independent schools nationally have closed. Given that context New Hall deserves great credit for thinking ahead and bucking the trend, and this was recognised by the Institute of Directors in 2005 who gave Katherine Jeffrey the East of England Businesswoman of the Year award, the first time it had ever gone to a not-for-profit business.

With the nuns no longer leading the school or involved in significant numbers in teaching, they decided to vacate New Hall in May 2005 and move to Colchester, leaving the whole premises to be used by the school. In more than one sense a Chapter at New Hall had closed. A new Catholic charity, New Hall School Trust, took ownership of the New Hall premises from August 1st 2005. In 2006 a boys' boarding house, Priory House, will open in converted premises within the former convent area, one of the most historic and beautiful parts of the campus.

Any institution that has been in existence a long time will have had its ups and downs. Some are imposed from outside. The school, both at Liège and New Hall was periodically threatened and, at times, seriously affected by war, twice causing migration, one permanent, to England in 1794, and the other temporary, to the Midlands in 1940 and was once, in the 1690s, near starvation, although these crises seem to have strengthened its resolve.

For the first 125 years, however, although the convent was secure the school barely got going. From the very start it seems unclear just how central the school was supposed to be in the mission of the early nuns, as it certainly remained very small in numbers, even in peace-time, and was sometimes non-existent. Although the school did eventually develop as a major activity in the mid 1770s and quickly got over the turbulence of the migration to England in 1794, it seemed to drift along at a gentle pace from the 1820s with many places unfilled and then did not respond to the changing public view of girls' needs in education in the second half of the century. Aggravated by internal friction, it declined rapidly just before World War I to a critical point when it nearly closed. Even the period of recovery after the war was marred by a closure panic in 1935. There were further signs of slowness of response. It took a very long time to send nuns to become formally qualified as teachers, to enter girls for public examinations and to gain recognition by the Ministry of Education as an efficient school. When recognition did come girls' advanced science education was slow to appear on the scene, albeit that the dislocation of war did not help. Yet there are periods of determination and fixed purpose, most notably under Prioress Christina Dennett in the 1770s to move the school to centre stage, Prioress Aloysia Dolan in the 1920s to start the modernisation process which was continued by Prioress Mary Veronica Boland, and the influential combination of Prioress Mary Christopher O'Connor and Headmistress Mary Francis Wood for two decades from 1966, when the school was urged forward with powerful energy and vision and grew rapidly in size. Despite some downturns, it continued to adapt to the constantly changing market pressures of the 1980s and 1990s.

For its first 300 years this was very much a family school. Old Catholic families sent generation after generation of girls to the school, whether in Liège or in England, a number of them to become nuns. That these families were so often intermarried meant that there was a web of sisters, aunts and cousins attending the school at any one time, forming the branches of a large and complex family tree. These relationships emerge frequently through the pages of this book and some nuns today say that it was this family loyalty that got the school back on its feet after World War II. That was its great strength but the school could not rely on it in the second half of the twentieth century when a decline in the birth-rate and in the economic position of the old landed families meant that New Hall would need to look to a broader market. This market has never really stayed stable as, on the one hand the British increasingly favoured day schooling or, at most, weekly boarding, while a modern era of relatively cheap air transport and electronic communication has meant a growing interest in Africa, Asia and South America for English education.

But that is the world looking at the convent from the outside in. It is also important that we look at the world of the nuns from the inside out. Since 1642 they have been concerned with the immortality of the soul, with this life lived in accordance with the scriptures and the Church's teaching as a preparation for eternity. All the other requirements of education that might be necessary would be as nothing if they eclipsed this central purpose. The nuns were also part of a hierarchical Catholic Church which for most of the first half of the twentieth century had not yet fully emerged from the defensive mind-set of the nineteenth century when the Church was legal but still, in many eyes, suspect. In England virtually up to the time of the Second Vatican Council it showed a fortress mentality[6] led by an episcopacy that had typically not been educated at British universities but in Rome and in their public actions were seen by some to be concerned primarily with the welfare of their own Catholic institutions, fearful that state intervention in the nation's social life would lead to practices inimical to Catholic principles. Ecumenism was not yet on the map. Even the affable, cricket-loving Cardinal Hinsley was reprimanded by Rome in 1940 for publicly saying the Lord's Prayer with the Anglican Bishop of Chichester.[7] These tensions were reflected in life in the Brentwood Diocese during the episcopacies of Bishop Arthur Doubleday (1920-1951)[8] and Bishop George Beck (1951-1955)[9] as described in the Diocese's official history. That is the context in which the nuns were living and working. It should be no surprise that modernisation, however desirable, was a more complicated process for those working within what was felt to be a cautious framework where "the principle that it was always safer to obey"[10] was the guiding tenet and one not conducive to initiative. Yet when the Second Vatican Council opened the door to change, the nuns did respond and ecumenism became one of their fundamental inspirations.

Over its history New Hall seems to have had Catholicism in the brickwork. Henry VIII had been named Defender of the Faith by the Pope, even though he then seriously blotted his copy-book. Mary Tudor represented the pinnacle of Catholic opposition to Protestant uniformity. Sir Thomas Wharton was imprisoned for celebrating the Old Faith. The future Charles I set out from New Hall to try to marry the Catholic Spanish Infanta. The 1st Duchess of Buckingham, as a staunch Catholic, lost control of her children when she was widowed. Charles II, who converted to Catholicism on his death-bed, and the Catholic James II both visited. By contrast the two most furious Protestant owners of New Hall did not stay long. Oliver Cromwell soon moved out and the 2nd Baron Waltham, who tried to get into Parliament on a virulently anti-Catholic ticket, died without heirs with his estate ironically finding its way into the hands of his Catholic brother-in-law, John Luttrell-Olmius, the last owner of New Hall before the nuns, who smoothed the path for their takeover. It is as though the spirit of Mary Tudor was determined that the Mass she prized above all else should, despite some interruptions, continue to be celebrated in her beloved New Hall.

In 1550 Jane Dormer described the New Hall of Mary Tudor as "the only harbour for honourable young women given any way to piety and devotion. It was a true school of virtuous demeanour". In the succeeding centuries society may have changed hugely but the underlying beliefs and principles of religious faith remain as a bedrock. In these days of obligatory mission statements, Jane Dormer's description stands as a model of concision and a most apposite description of New Hall under the Canonesses of the Holy Sepulchre.

Appendix A

Prioresses of the Canonesses of the Holy Sepulchre

Mother Margaret de L'Escaille	1642-1652
Susan Hawley, Mother Mary of the Conception	1652-1698
Helena Dolman, Mother Marina Helena	1698-1720
Catherine de Rouveroit, Mother Susan	1720-1739
Mary Percy, Mother Christina	1739-1749
Jane Withenbury, Mother Xaveria	1749-1770
Mary Dennett, Mother Christina	1770-1781
Bridget Westby, Mother Austin	1781-1786
Bridget Clough, Mother Aloysia	1786-1816
Elizabeth Gerard, Mother Regis	1816-1843
Ann Clifford, Mother Aloysia Austin	1843-1844
Anna Maria Blount, Mother Teresa Joseph	1844-1869
Caroline Corney, Mother Alphonsa	1869-1873
Julia Mary Butler, Mother Aloysia Austin	1873-1912
Cecilia Kendal, Mother Joseph Sales	1912-1918
Mary Agnes Dolan, Mother Aloysia Magdalen	1918-1936
Edith O'Donnell, Mother Christina	1936-1954
Margaret Frances Boland, Mother Veronica	1954-1966
Mary Bridget O'Connor, Mother Christopher	1966-1978
Jennifer Elizabeth Roskell, Mother Magdalene	1978-1990
Mary Angela Foley, Mother Gabriel	1990-2002
Teresa Lenahan, Sister	2002-

Headmistresses/Principals of New Hall School

At Liège and then in England it can be assumed that the Prioress was also in charge of the school. At some unknown stage a First Mistress became a quasi-Headmistress in the school under the Prioress. The term Headmistress was first used in 1942 and the term Principal from 2005.

Sister Margaret Helen Terney	1942-1957
Sister Mary Ignatius Brown	1957-1963
Sister Mary Francis Wood	1963-1986
Sister Margaret Mary Horton	1986-1997
Sister Ann-Marie Brister	1997-2001
Katherine Jeffrey	2001-

Appendix B

Inflation and the value of the pound

"Inflation: the Value of the Pound 1750-2002", the House of Commons Research Paper by Grahame Allen, calculates the historic value of the pound in modern money for every year from 1750. Thus £1 in 2002 was worth £136.29 in 1750, and so on (see Table 13). I have used Allen's paper as the authoritative base for this book. For values before 1750 (see Table 12) I have used an adjusted version of "Comparing the Purchasing Power of Money in Great Britain from 1264 to Any Other Year Including the Present" by Lawrence H. Officer (see Economic History Services, 2001 on http://www.eh.net/hmit/ppowerbp/). His calculations are very close to Allen's from 1922 to the present day. But in the period 1750-1922 he is on average about 13.5% below Allen's values, about 15% if one looks at just the 1750-1780 period and precisely 15.24% if one chooses 1750 where the House of Commons paper begins. I have therefore added 15.24% to Officer's calculations before 1750 to bring them into line.

Allen makes four sensible caveats – calculations do not include any allowance for movements in exchange rates; any statistical comparison cannot take account of the fact that products being purchased were markedly different between eras (e.g. cars are vital in the modern era, candles were vital in the eighteenth century); within and between eras, the quality of goods will vary affecting value for money; and any overall inflation figure disguises that fact that some prices are going up much higher than the average rate (e.g property in the last fifty years) and others down (e.g. electronic goods in the last thirty years) so that the value of goods relative to each other will not necessarily be the same at different periods

When one looks at Tables 12 and 13, one can see that the forty-fold price inflation since 1939 has not always been the experience of those running the convent. Between 1750 and 1938 prices rose only threefold. Indeed there was a twenty year period of price deflation between the two world wars and the value of the pound held very steady from about 1854 to 1913. On the other hand although the pound appears to be worth much the same in 1643 and 1754 there are significant ups and downs in between as war and peace and bad or good harvests had their effect.

Table 12:

Values of the £ before 1750; "Comparing the Purchasing Power of Money in Great Britain from 1264 to Any Other Year Including the Present" adjusted upwards by 15.24%

1516 £421.24	**1658** £112.31	**1676** £128.58	**1694** £123.47	**1712** £125.95	**1731** £148.18
1622 £138.73	**1659** £103.65	**1677** £122.66	**1695** £106.47	**1713** £117.43	**1732** £150.08
1642 £130.26	**1660** £106.08	**1678** £120.56	**1696** £105.72	**1714** £130.46	**1733** £142.69
1643 £131.20	**1661** £111.97	**1679** £127.89	**1697** £100.05	**1715** £125.80	**1734** £134.66
1644 £136.65	**1662** £94.35	**1680** £124.51	**1698** £100.02	**1716** £127.26	**1735** £131.21
1645 £126.41	**1663** £107.48	**1681** £125.95	**1699** £108.76	**1717** £131.18	**1736** £135.82
1646 £127.51	**1664** £110.43	**1682** £128.18	**1700** £128.19	**1718** £138.36	**1737** £138.21
1647 £109.12	**1665** £117.79	**1683** £131.51	**1701** £138.09	**1719** £129.50	**1738** £142.21
1648 £94.23	**1666** £109.27	**1684** £121.74	**1702** £143.55	**1720** £130.46	**1739** £126.35
1649 £88.38	**1667** £125.75	**1685** £131.66	**1703** £133.90	**1721** £135.96	**1740** £112.99
1650 £86.48	**1668** £120.52	**1686** £130.57	**1704** £139.81	**1722** £133.83	**1741** £125.90
1651 £103.06	**1669** £126.84	**1687** £145.49	**1705** £148.31	**1723** £137.84	**1742** £142.29
1652 £111.97	**1670** £125.75	**1688** £150.24	**1706** £147.35	**1724** £131.47	**1743** £155.75
1653 £125.31	**1671** £129.79	**1689** £137.60	**1707** £137.70	**1725** £120.99	**1744** £153.28
1654 £133.62	**1672** £132.17	**1690** £143.50	**1708** £114.19	**1726** £125.97	**1745** £139.50
1655 £136.64	**1673** £113.96	**1691** £132.01	**1709** £112.43	**1727** £112.62	**1746** £137.90
1656 £129.79	**1674** £107.43	**1692** £118.34	**1710** £112.81	**1728** £109.56	**1747** £140.13
1657 £118.56	**1675** £123.50	**1693** £106.37	**1711** £109.17	**1729** £127.99	**1748** £132.81
				1730 £137.77	**1749** £135.84

Table 13:

Values of the £ from 1750, House of Commons Library Research Paper 03/82, "Inflation: the Value of the Pound 1750-2002".

1750	£136.29	1772	£93.93	1794	£81.78	1816	£59.92	1838	£68.15	1860	£74.74
1751	£139.02	1773	£93.93	1795	£73.95	1817	£52.86	1839	£63.77	1861	£73.17
1752	£133.67	1774	£92.68	1796	£69.51	1818	£52.66	1840	£62.62	1862	£74.74
1753	£136.29	1775	£99.30	1797	£77.23	1819	£53.88	1841	£63.77	1863	£77.23
1754	£131.15	1776	£100.74	1798	£78.99	1820	£59.41	1842	£69.51	1864	£78.10
1755	£139.02	1777	£100.74	1799	£70.21	1821	£67.49	1843	£78.10	1865	£77.23
1756	£133.67	1778	£97.90	1800	£51.49	1822	£78.10	1844	£78.10	1866	£73.17
1757	£110.33	1779	£106.94	1801	£46.03	1823	£73.17	1845	£74.74	1867	£68.82
1758	£110.33	1780	£110.33	1802	£59.92	1824	£67.49	1846	£71.66	1868	£69.51
1759	£119.84	1781	£105.32	1803	£63.19	1825	£57.45	1847	£63.77	1869	£73.17
1760	£124.13	1782	£103.75	1804	£61.51	1826	£60.97	1848	£73.17	1870	£73.17
1761	£131.15	1783	£92.68	1805	£53.06	1827	£64.96	1849	£78.10	1871	£72.41
1762	£126.38	1784	£91.46	1806	£55.17	1828	£66.84	1850	£82.75	1872	£69.51
1763	£121.95	1785	£96.54	1807	£56.51	1829	£67.49	1851	£85.81	1873	£66.84
1764	£112.11	1786	£96.54	1808	£54.30	1830	£70.21	1852	£85.81	1874	£69.51
1765	£108.61	1787	£96.54	1809	£49.65	1831	£63.77	1853	£78.10	1875	£70.93
1766	£106.94	1788	£92.68	1810	£48.27	1832	£66.82	1854	£68.15	1876	£70.93
1767	£102.22	1789	£93.33	1811	£49.65	1833	£73.17	1855	£66.20	1877	£71.66
1768	£103.75	1790	£92.68	1812	£43.72	1834	£79.90	1856	£66.20	1878	£73.17
1769	£112.11	1791	£92.68	1813	£42.64	1835	£78.10	1857	£69.51	1879	£76.38
1770	£112.11	1792	£91.46	1814	£48.95	1836	£70.21	1858	£76.38	1880	£73.95
1771	£103.75	1793	£89.12	1815	£54.73	1837	£68.82	1859	£77.23	1881	£74.74

continued over

Table 13:

continued

1882 £73.95	**1902** £75.55	**1922** £34.93	**1942** £28.96	**1962** £13.12	**1982** £2.17
1883 £74.74	**1903** £74.74	**1923** £37.17	**1943** £28.03	**1963** £12.87	**1983** £2.07
1884 £76.38	**1904** £74.74	**1924** £37.37	**1944** £27.26	**1964** £12.46	**1984** £1.98
1885 £78.99	**1905** £74.74	**1925** £37.37	**1945** £26.53	**1965** £11.90	**1985** £1.86
1886 £79.90	**1906** £74.74	**1926** £37.57	**1946** £25.74	**1966** £11.45	**1986** £1.80
1887 £80.83	**1907** £73.95	**1927** £38.62	**1947** £24.05	**1967** £11.16	**1987** £1.73
1888 £79.90	**1908** £73.95	**1928** £38.62	**1948** £22.35	**1968** £10.66	**1988** £1.65
1889 £78.99	**1909** £73.17	**1929** £39.05	**1949** £21.72	**1969** £10.12	**1989** £1.53
1890 £78.99	**1910** £72.41	**1930** £40.18	**1950** £21.06	**1970** £9.51	**1990** £1.40
1891 £78.10	**1911** £72.41	**1931** £41.87	**1951** £19.31	**1971** £8.69	**1991** £1.32
1892 £78.10	**1912** £70.21	**1932** £42.91	**1952** £17.69	**1972** £8.11	**1992** £1.27
1893 £78.99	**1913** £70.93	**1933** £43.99	**1953** £17.16	**1973** £7.43	**1993** £1.25
1894 £79.90	**1914** £70.93	**1934** £43.99	**1954** £16.83	**1974** £6.41	**1994** £1.22
1895 £80.83	**1915** £63.19	**1935** £43.72	**1955** £16.12	**1975** £5.16	**1995** £1.18
1896 £81.78	**1916** £53.47	**1936** £43.44	**1956** £15.34	**1976** £4.42	**1996** £1.15
1897 £79.90	**1917** £42.64	**1937** £41.87	**1957** £14.82	**1977** £3.82	**1997** £1.12
1898 £79.90	**1918** £34.93	**1938** £41.38	**1958** £14.36	**1978** £3.53	**1998** £1.08
1899 £78.99	**1919** £31.74	**1939** £40.18	**1959** £14.30	**1979** £3.11	**1999** £1.07
1900 £75.55	**1920** £27.47	**1940** £34.41	**1960** £14.16	**1980** £2.64	**2000** £1.03
1901 £75.55	**1921** £30.09	**1941** £31.03	**1961** £13.68	**1981** £2.36	**2001** £1.02
					2002 £1.00

Notes on sources

Chapter 1: An Order out of Chaos; The Nuns and New Hall to 1516

1. William of Tyre *Historia rerum in partibus transmarinis gestarum* on www.fordham. edu/halsall/source/tyre-cde.html#godfrey
2. Anon, *History of the New Hall Community of the Canonesses of the Holy Sepulchre*, p2
3. http://87.1911encyclopedia.org/S/SE/SEPULCHRE_CANONS_REGULAR_OF _THE_HOLY.htm
4. M. Powicke, *The Thirteenth Century 1087-1216*, p80
5. A.L. Poole, *Domesday Book to Magna Carta*, p189
6. Anon, *op.cit.*, p6
7. Anon, *op.cit.*, p.7
8. Sister Mary Stephen, "The Changing Face of New Hall; the Honour of Beaulieu" *in Boreham: History, Tales and Memories of an Essex Village*
9. "New Hall, Boreham 1062-1799", *Essex Review*, Vol XVII, April 1908, pp57-66; July 1908 pp121-132, extracts in Essex Record Office T/P 341/1
10. S. Thurley, *The Royal Palaces of Tudor England; Architecture and Court Life 1460-1547*, p44
11. D. Andrews, *New Hall ... an historic building in perspective*, lecture 2000
12. P. Morant, *The History and Antiquities of the County of Essex, Volume 2, 1763-8*, p14

Chapter 2; Of Palaces and Kings; New Hall 1516-1530

1. S. Thurley, *The Royal Palaces of Tudor England; Architecture and Court Life 1460-1547*, p1
2. ibid p44
3. ibid p45
4. ibid p49
5. ibid p58
6. D. Andrews, *New Hall ... an historic building in perspective*, lecture 2000
7. A. Weir, *Children of England; the Heirs of King Henry VIII 1547-1558*, p19
8. S. Thurley, *op.cit.*, p83
9. ibid pp203-204 and Anon, *History of the New Hall Community of the Canonesses of the Holy Sepulchre*, p142

10. S. Thurley, *op.cit.*, pp197-199

11. ibid p164

12. ibid p171

13. ibid p70

14. ibid p114

15. ibid p150

16. ibid p152

17. ibid p133

18. ibid p70

19. Sister Mary Stephen, "The Changing Face of New Hall; the Honour of Beaulieu" in *Boreham: History, Tales and Memories of an Essex Village*

20. Calendar of State Papers Domestic, Elizabeth vol xi Addend. Feb 12th 1561 quoted in Anon, *History of the New Hall Community of the Canonesses of the Holy Sepulchre* p xii

21. D. Andrews, *op.cit.*

22. *Archive Records of the Community History in the 20th century: an anonymous memoir of the years since 1900*, New Hall Archive

23. *Travels of Cosmo the Third, Grand Duke of Tuscany, through England during the reign of Charles II* 1669, London; 1821, p466-471

24. D. Andrews, *op.cit.*

25. J.J. Scarisbrick, *Henry VIII*, p149

26. ibid p192

27. Retha M. Warnicke, *The Rise and Fall of Anne Boleyn: Family Politics at the Court of Henry VIII*, p64

28. David Starkey, *The Queens of Henry VIII*, p298

Chapter 3; The Great Escape; New Hall 1530-1553

1. Anon, *History of the New Hall Community of the Canonesses of the Holy Sepulchre*, p134

2. H. Prescott, *Mary Tudor; the Spanish Tudor*, p57 for this quotation and pp56-58 for the whole episode

3. G.R. Elton, *England under the Tudors*, p202

4. A. Weir, *Children of England: The Heirs of King Henry VIII 1547-1558*, p98: Weir deals with the attempted escape in detail pp98-115 as does H. Prescott, *op.cit.*, pp165-181

5. A. Weir, *op.cit.*, p103

6. D. Andrews, *New Hall ... an historic building in perspective*, lecture 2000

7. A. Weir, *op.cit.*, p105

8. ibid p112

9. ibid p115

10. ibid p122; Weir deals at length with the reactions to the attempted escape as does H. Prescott, *op.cit,* pp182-208

11. A. Weir, *op.cit.*, p127

12. A. Plowden, *Lady Jane Grey, Nine Days Queen*, p82

13. H. Prescott, *op.cit.*, p225

14. A. Weir, *op.cit,* p186

Chapter 4; A House fit for a Queen; New Hall 1553-1622

1. *Calendar of State Papers Domestic, Elizabeth vol xi Addend. Feb 12th 1561* quoted in Anon *History of the New Hall Community of the Canonesses of the Holy Sepulchre* p xii

2. G.R. Elton, *England under the Tudors*, pp275-276

3. Letter from Nicholas Jekyll to William Holman, February 23rd 1725, Essex Record Office D/Y 1/1/111/105

4. This episode is dealt with in Anon, *op.cit,* pp136-137 and "The Breaking of the Storm", R.C. Foley, *Essex Recusant* Vol 7 No 1 1961

5. "Queen Elizabeth's Progresses through Essex", *Essex Journal*, Vol 1 No 1, January 1966

6. P. Ryan, "Woodham Walter Hall – its site and setting" in *Essex Archaeology and History* 30 1999, pp178-195

7. N. Williams, *Elizabeth I, Queen of England*, pp163-169

8. I. Dunlop, *Places and Progress of Elizabeth I*, p35

9. D. Andrews, *New Hall ... an historic building in perspective*, provides information of the architectural details of the house and of Sussex's will.

10. ibid

11. ibid

12. Z. Dovey, *An Elizabethan Progess; The Queen's Journey into East Anglia 1578*

13. E. Jenkins, *Elizabeth and Leicester*, p218

14. ibid pp280-281

15. ibid p288

16. ibid p304

17. ibid p313

18. ibid p319

19. F. Emmison, "Historic Essex Houses in Elizabethan Wills", *Essex Journal*, Summer 1992 Vol 27 No 2 pp35-37

Chapter 5; An English Country Garden; New Hall 1622-1660

1. A. Stewart, *The Cradle King, A Life of James VI and I*, p271

2. ibid pp281-282

3. Sister Margaret Helen, "A Dragon's Tale: Of Who Comes and Who Goes" in *Boreham: History, Tales and Memories of an Essex Village*

4. For the extraordinary story of the ride to Spain see P. Grigg, *King Charles I*, pp77-8; R. Lockyer *Buckingham: The Life and Political Career of George Villiers, 1st Duke of Buckingham 1592-1628* pp134-165; and A. Stewart, *op.cit.*, pp315-329

5. M. Allan, *The Tradescants; their plants, gardens and museum 1570-1662*, p28

6. ibid p67

7. ibid pp97-99

8. D. Andrews, *New Hall ... an historic building in perspective*, lecture 2000

9. Anon, *History of the New Hall Community of the Canonesses of the Holy Sepulchre*, p139

10. Sister Mary Stephen, "The Changing Face of New Hall; the Honour of Beaulieu" in *Boreham: History, Tales and Memories of an Essex Village*

11. M. Allan, *op.cit.*, pp108-110

12. ibid p118

13. D. Dymond, *Captain John Mason and the Duke of Buckingham*, p13

14. ibid p15

15. ibid pp16-17

16. ibid p17

17. A. Fraser, *King Charles II*, p20

18. Anon, *op.cit.*, p139 and "New Hall, Boreham 1062-1799", *Essex Review*, Vol XVII, April 1908, pp57-66; July 1908 pp121-132, extracts in Essex Record Office T/P 341/1

Chapter 6; The Nuns' Story; Liège 1642-1657

1. A.C.F. Beales, *Education under Penalty*, pp72-73

2. ibid pp28-48 for a detailed analysis of the educational penalties

3. Lord John Petre, "The Penal Laws and the Petre Family", *Essex Journal*, Spring 1994 Vol 29 pp7-13

4. J. Walter, *Understanding Popular Violence in the English Revolution: The Colchester Plunderers*, pp201-234 for an analysis of the anti-Catholic nature of agitation in north Essex and south Suffolk.

5. Anon, *History of the New Hall Community of the Canonesses of the Holy Sepulchre*, p15

6. ibid p87

7. ibid pp15-34 deals with the early days and also gives considerable biographical detail of the early nuns

Chapter 7; Nuns' business; Liège 1642-1670

1. This 640 page account book in New Hall Archives was originally divided into seven sections, each with a different heading, receipts for money, pensions for novices, portions for canonesses, income from rents etc.. These are started at intervals throughout the book. As the years went on the initial subdivisions proved unsatisfactory and the order of the accounts became a little confused.

2. J. McNamara, *Sisters in Arms: Catholic Nuns through two millennia*, pp533-535

3. Anon, *History of the New Hall Community of the Canonesses of the Holy Sepulchre*, p19

4. The Book of Benefactors has also been collated in print in *Records of the English Canonesses of the Holy Sepulchre at Liège, now at New Hall 1652-1793*; the records for 1662-1669 are on pp31-37

5. Book of Benefactors, *op.cit.*, pp178-179

Chapter 8; Moncks at New Hall; New Hall 1660-1713

1. "New Hall, Boreham 1062-1799", *Essex Review*, Vol XVII, April 1908, pp57-66; July 1908 pp121-132, extracts in Essex Record Office T/P 341/1

2. D. Burcher, "New Hall through the Eyes of 17th and 18th century visitors" in *More about Boreham: History, Tales and Memories of an Essex Village*

3. M. Ashley, *General Monck* pp212-213

4. ibid p243

5. *Travels of Cosmo the Third, Grand Duke of Tuscany, through England during the reign of Charles II 1669*; London; 1821 pp466-471

6. M. Ashley, *op.cit.*, p54

Chapter 9; War and Peace; Liège 1670-1712

1. Anon, *History of the New Hall Community of the Canonesses of the Holy Sepulchre*, p41

2. The Book of Benefactors in *Records of the English Canonesses of the Holy Sepulchre at Liège, now at New Hall 1652-1793*, pp31-63.

3. Anon, *op.cit.*, p39

4. Recorded anonymously in the inside cover of the Accounts book 1642-1770.

5. The Boarders' Accounts in *Records of the English Canonesses of the Holy Sepulchre at Liège, now at New Hall 1652-1793* pp180-203.

6. Anon, *op.cit.*, p37

Chapter 10; Lords and Ladies; Liège 1713-1777

1. The Book of Benefactors in *Records of the English Canonesses of the Holy Sepulchre at Liège, now at New Hall 1652-1793*, pp63-88.

2. http://lancingvillage.co.uk/Lanchist1.htm

3. The Boarders' Accounts, *op.cit.*, p196

4. www.stirnet.com/HTML/genie/british/gg/goring2.htm

5. Catholic Encyclopaedia 1913 on www.newadvent.org/cathen/12167b.htm

6. Anon, *History of the New Hall Community of the Canonesses of the Holy Sepulchre.*, Appendix C, p6

7. Anon, *op.cit.*, p43

8. The Book of Benefactors, *op.cit.*, pp65-67

9. The Boarders' Accounts in *Records of the English Canonesses of the Holy Sepulchre at Liège, now at New Hall 1652-1793* pp209-216

10. R.G.E. Wood "Catherine Petre" in the *Oxford Dictionary of National Biography*, www.oxforddnb.com

11. The Book of Benefactors, *op.cit.*, pp68-72

12. ibid pp66-88

13. ibid p71

14. O. Baldwin and T. Wilson, "Anastasia Robinson" in *Oxford Dictionary of National Biography*, www.oxforddnb.com
15. Anon, *op.cit.*, p45
16. The Book of Benefactors, *op.cit.*, p72 and footnote
17. J. Bossy, *The English Catholic Community 1570-1850*, p54
18. Lord John Petre, "The Penal Laws and the Petre Family", *Essex Journal*, Spring 1994 Vol 29, pp7-13
19. The Boarders' Accounts, *op.cit.*, pp203-247
20. R. Hoffman, *Princes of Ireland, Planters of Maryland; A Carroll Saga 1750-1782*, p103
21. Anon, *op.cit.*, Appendix C, p5
22. ibid Appendix C, pp4-6
23. ibid p53 and pp56-58
24. M.D.R. Leys, *Catholics in England 1559-1829*, pp165-166
25. G. Avery, *The Best Type of Girl: a history of girls' independent schools*, p182
26. Anon, *op.cit.*, p57
27. ibid p49

Chapter 11; The school of virtuous demeanour; Ladies' Education in the 1770s

1. Genesis 2, 18
2. Genesis 3, 16
3. A. Fraser, *The Weaker Vessel: woman's lot in seventeenth century England*, p87
4. R. Baird, *Mistress of the House: Great Ladies and Grand Houses 1670-1830*, pp15-16
5. Proverbs 12,4
6. Margaret Cavendish, *Philosophical and Physical Opinions* (1655) on http://www.pinn.net/~sunshine/march99/cavndsh.html
7. A. Fraser *op.cit.*, pp176-177
8. 1790s poster, New Hall Archives.
9. See Chapter 3 and A. Weir, *Children of England: The Heirs of King Henry VIII 1547-1558*, p103
10. Anon, *History of the New Hall Community of the Canonesses of the Holy Sepulchre*, p81
11. A. Vickery, *The Gentleman's Daughter*, p.202
12. M. Mullett, *Catholics in England and Ireland 1558-1829*, p.144
13. ibid p.144
14. R. Porter, *English Society in the Eighteenth Century*, p23
15. R. Baird, *op.cit.*, p21
16. ibid pp132-154
17. A. Fraser, *op.cit,* pp157-158
18. F. Bengsten, "Ladies Boarding Schools in Essex 1791-1861: Two Case Studies – Billericay and Maldon", *Essex Archaeology and History* 32 (2001) pp222-227

Chapter 12; The Young Ladies of Liège 1770-1794

1　Volume 1 of the pupil register runs from 1770-1807; Volume 2 from 1807-1837; Volume 3 from 1837- 1946. They are to be found in New Hall Archives

2　B. Dolan, *Ladies of the Grand Tour*, p.92

3　M. Leys, *Catholics in England 1559-1829*, p159

Chapter 13; Revolution; Liège 1789-1794

1.　From the nuns' accounts the Liège florin seems to have depreciated to a level of ten to the pound sterling compared with about fifteen in earlier years.

2.　This account of the revolution in Liège is largely taken from Anon, *History of the New Hall Community of the Canonesses of the Holy Sepulchre*, pp85-95

3.　J. Thompson, *The French Revolution*, p8

4.　ibid p430

Chapter 14; Grudging Acceptance; Catholic Relief 1778-1791

1.　A. Fraser, *King Charles II*, pp454-455

2.　R. Porter, *English Society in the Eighteenth Century*, pp178-179

3.　J. Bossy, *The English Catholic Community 1570-1850* pp100-103 gives details of the location of the major Catholic families

4.　M. Leys, *Catholics in England 1559-1829*, p119

5.　http://home.it.net.au/~barleys/stafford.htm

6.　J. Bossy *op.cit.*, p104

7.　E.R. Norman, *Church and Society in Modern Britain 1700-1850*, p125

8.　E. Worrall, "Watching Lord Petre II": *Essex Recusant* Vol 7 No 2 1965

9.　E. Worrall, "The Congregation of Witham Place Chapel, 1766-1800"; *Essex Recusant*, Vol.4 No. 1 1962

10.　L. Colley: *Britons, Forging the Nation 1707-1837*, p329

11.　M. Leys, *op.cit.*, p120

12.　Letter of February 24th 1791 from John Needham to Catherine Chichester, a nun 1790-1791, before her premature death, New Hall Archives

13.　R. Porter, *op.cit.*, p171

14.　M. Leys, *op.cit.*, pp130-131

15.　The work of the Catholic Committee before and after the Relief Acts is well-covered in P. Kennedy, *The Catholic Church in England and Wales 1500-2000* Chapter 7

16.　L. Colley, *op.cit.*, p23

Chapter 15; Migration; Liège to England 1794

1.　An account of the flight to England was written by Mother Joseph Smith (Procuratrix at the time) and revised some twenty years later by Mother Aloysia Austin Clifford, herself one of the party. Father John Laurenson of the Jesuits' Liège Academy also left an account of the simultaneous migration of the Academy to Stonyhurst. Extracts from both these accounts are to be found in Anon, *History of the New Hall Community of the Canonesses of the Holy Sepulchre*, pp95-110

2. Account of Father John Laurenson quoted in Anon *op.cit.*, p97
3. Volume 1 of the pupil register 1770-1807, New Hall Archive
4. Anon *op.cit.*, p102
5. This detail about the oak chests is mentioned in the 1992 350th anniversary Flower Festival brochure
6. Anon *op.cit.*, p108
7. ibid p131

Chapter 16; Neither here nor there; Holme Hall and Dean House 1794-1798

1. Anon, *History of the New Hall Community of the Canonesses of the Holy Sepulchre*, pp115-119 describes life at Holme Hall
2. M. Bence-Jones, *The Catholic Families*, p114
3. ibid p183
4. Anon *op.cit.*, pp120-121 describes life at Dean House
5. Henrietta Goldie on June 18th; see pupil register Vol. 1 1770-1807, New Hall Archives
6. Mother Agatha (Catherine Stourton) quoted in Anon, *op.cit*, p122
7. *Days of Yore* handwritten by Henrietta Goldie, New Hall Archives
8. Anon, *op.cit.*, p143
9. P. Ziegler, *King William IV*, p75
10. Anon, *op.cit.*, p123

Chapter 17; Coming Home; New Hall 1713-1802

1. Sister Margaret Helen, "A Dragon's Tale: Of Who Comes and Who Goes" in *Boreham: History, Tales and Memories of an Essex Village*
2. www.hoaresbank.co.uk
3. www.irs.princeton.edu/krueger/04_28_2005.htm
4. Conversation with John Furze of New Hall Farm
5. D. Burcher, "New Hall through the Eyes of 17th and 18th century visitors" in *More about Boreham: History, Tales and Memories of an Essex Village*
6. House of Commons Journal Vol 9 www.british-history.ac.uk
7. D. Andrews, *New Hall ... an historic building in perspective*, lecture 2000
8. http://archiver.rootsweb.com/th/read/PORTUGAL/1999-02/0919918406
9. The Political World www.oup.co.uk/pdf/0-14-924693-9pdf
10. www.angeltowns.com/town/peerage/peersw1.htm
11. Election poster in *Essex Elections and the Great Reform Bill* published by Essex Record Office; original to be found at Essex Record Office D/DU/65/86
12. D. Andrews, *op.cit.*

13. E. Burgess, "The Olmius Family" in *More About Boreham: History, Tales and Memories of an Essex Village*, 1996

14. www.luttrellstown.ie/present-history.htm

15. Anon, "The Waltham Mausoleum" in *More About Boreham: History, Tales and Memories of an Essex Village*

16. Fragment of the original McEvoy letter in the New Hall Archives

17. Anon, *History of the New Hall Community of the Canonesses of the Holy Sepulchre*, pp124-127 and p143 for an account of the move to New Hall and some of the early work done on adapting the premises.

18. ibid p128

19. ibid p143

Chapter 18; La Crème de la Crème; New Hall Families 1799-1829

1. All calculations have been made from an analysis of the pupil register Vol 1 1770-1807 and Vol, 2 1807-1837, New Hall Archives

2. Catholic Directory 1803, New Hall Archives

3. Catholic Directory 1795, New Hall Archives

4. E.S Worrall, "A Funeral Monument in Gosfield Churchyard": *Essex Recusant* Vol 6 No 3

5. M. Leys, *Catholics in England* 1559-1829, p88

6. ibid p90

7. ibid pp187-188

8. ibid p61

9. ibid pp204-205

10. ibid p198

11. ibid p115

12. Catholic Directory 1877, New Hall Archives

13. M. Leys, *op.cit.*, p103

14. ibid p128

15. ibid p161

16. M.D. Petre, *The Ninth Lord Petre*, p305

17. Catholic Directory 1877, New Hall Archives

18. Anon, *History of the New Hall Community of the Canonesses of the Holy Sepulchre*, p177

19. ibid pp160-162

20. Essex Record Office T/B 175/32

21. Sister Antony Magdalene, (aka Frances Russell 1894-1898), *Memoirs; Recollections of a Nonagenarian 1880-1970*, New Hall Archives

22. Anon, *op,cit.*, p175

Chapter 19; A Genteel British School; the Young Ladies 1799-1829

1. See pupil register Vol 1 1770-1807 and Vol 2 1807-1837, New Hall Archive
2. J. Flanders, *The Victorian House: Domestic Life from Childbirth to Deathbed*, p303
3. Letter from John Talbot, September 10th 1835, New Hall Archives
4. J. Flanders, *op.cit.*, p52
5. Essex Record Office T/B 165/85 Nuns' Medicine Book 1803-1868
6. J. Flanders, *op.cit.*, p45
7. ibid p46
8. *Regulations for the Kitchen 1835-1895*, New Hall Archives
9. J.R. Smith, *The Speckled Monster*, p12
10. ibid p56
11. ibid p50
12. Letter of February 22nd 1798 R.J. Gandolfi to Maria, New Hall Archives
13. Letter of March 17th 1798 R.J. Gandolfi to Maria, New Hall Archives
14. Letter of April 27th 1799 R.J. Gandolfi to Maria, New Hall Archives
15. Original trust deed in New Hall Archives

Chapter 20; Financial Ups and Downs; New Hall 1830-1859

1. E.R. Norman, *Church and Society in Modern Britain 1700-1850*, pp464-466
2. Essex Record Office Q/CR 3/2/10
3. Balance of Accounts 1820-1915 Ledger, New Hall Archives
4. Extracts from the Diary of Clarissa Bramston (née Trant), New Hall Archives
5. M. Bence-Jones, *The Catholic Families*, p178
6. J. S. Cotton, rev. Jason Thompson "Frances Elaine Burton" in the *Oxford Dictionary of National Biography*, www.oxforddnb.com
7. M. Bence-Jones, *op.cit.*, p242
8. www.teara.govt.nz/1966/C/CliffordSirCharlesBt/CliffordSirCharlesBt/en
9. 1850s prospectus, New Hall Archives
10. Anon, *History of the New Hall Community of the Canonesses of the Holy Sepulchre*, p209
11. White's Directory 1848 p338, copy in New Hall Archives
12. Rev. W.J.T. Smith "Education and Boreham" in *Boreham; History, Tales and memories of an Essex Village*
13. P. Kennedy, *The Catholic Church in England and Wales 1500-2000*, p203
14. Anon, *op.cit.*, p186
15. Essex Record Office T/B 165/45
16. Anon, *op.cit*, p178
17. Letter of March 7th 1906 from Father Heery to T.W. Hunter, Brentwood Diocesan Archives
18. Anon, "When Boreham had a railway station" in *More about Boreham: History, Tales and Memories of an Essex Village*

19. D.I. Gordon, *A Regional History of the Railways of Great Britain; Volume 5 – Eastern Counties*, Chapter 2 "Central Essex", pp37-56

20. J. Booker, *Essex and the Industrial Revolution*, pp153-154

21. ibid p152

22. Anon, *op.cit.*, p175

23. *Chelmsford Chronicle*, December 3rd 1841

24. H. Grieve, *The Sleepers and the Shadow, Chelmsford: a town, its people and its past: Volume 2 From Market Town to Chartered Borough 1608-1688*, p320

25. Balance of Accounts 1820-1915 Ledger, New Hall Archives, for end of year balances

26. Essex Record Office T/B 165/45; the Record Office suggests that the date is 1860-1880 but the number of pupils declared on the form matches with the 1860 figure as worked out from the pupil register Vol. 3 1837-1946, New Hall Archives.

27. Balance of Accounts 1820-1915 Ledger

28. Essex Record Office T/B 165/33

29. Anon, *op.cit.*, p185

30. Balance of Accounts 1820-1915 Ledger

Chapter 21; A Steady Ship in a Moving Sea; New Hall 1860-1889

1. Catholic Encyclopaedia on www.newadvent.org/cathen/05789c.htm

2. All the evidence on pupils has come from the pupil register Volume 3 1837-1946, New Hall Archives.

3. Anon, *History of the New Hall Community of the Canonesses of the Holy Sepulchre*, pp189-190

4. S. Fletcher, *Feminists and Bureaucrats; a study in the development of girls' education in the 19th century* p3

5. ibid p23

6. ibid p42

7. ibid p103

8. ibid p60

9. ibid p173

10. Anon, *op.cit.*, p208

11. S. Fletcher, *op.cit.*, pp108-109

12. ibid p100

13. www.gdst.net/gdst.asp

14. S. Fletcher, *op.cit.*, p171

15. ibid p101

16. ibid p110

17. ibid p176

18. Anon, *op.cit.*, pp202-203 and Sister Mary Peter, *Archive Records of Community History, Part 1 1900-1946*, New Hall Archives

Chapter 22; Decline; New Hall 1890-1914

1. Catholic Encyclopaedia 1913 on www.newadvent.org/cathen/
2. Sister Antony Magdalene, (aka Frances Russell 1894-1898), *Memoirs; Recollections of a Nonagenarian 1880-1970*, New Hall Archives
3. Notes made in 1899 by Father Sidney Smith, Brentwood Diocesan Archive
4. Sister Antony Magdalene, *op.cit.*
5. ibid
6. Sister Mary Peter, *Archive Records of Community History, Part 1 1900-1946*, New Hall Archives
7. All details concerning pupils come from the pupil register Vol 3 1837-1946, New Hall Archives
8. A. Tuckwell, *That Honourable and Gentlemanlike House, a history of King Edward VI Grammar School, Chelmsford*, pp65-66
9. Anon, *History of the New Hall Community of the Canonesses of the Holy Sepulchre*, pp203-204
10. Sister Antony Magdalene, *op.cit.*
11. Essex Record Office T/B 165/32
12. *Memories of Margot Jackson*, New Hall Archives
13. Sister Antony Magdalene *op.cit.*
14. ibid.
15. Anon, *op.cit.*, p143
16. *Memories of Margot Jackson*
17. ibid
18. ibid
19. Sister Mary Peter, *op.cit.*
20. ibid.
21. Anon, *op.cit.*, p212
22. Quoted in the *New Hall Chronicle*, April 1927, New Hall Archives
23. Conversation with Sister Mary Magdalene Roskell

Chapter 23; The Great War; New Hall 1914-1918

1. Diary of Sister Ann Frances Trappes-Lomax, in New Hall Archives is the source for all diary references in this chapter
2. www.worcestershireregiment.com/wr.php?main=inc/bat_7
3. Sister Antony Magdalene, (aka Frances Russell 1894-1898), *Memoirs; Recollections of a Nonagenarian 1880-1970*, New Hall Archives
4. Sister Mary Peter, *Archive Records of Community History, Part 1 1900-1946*, New Hall, Archives
5. Sister Antony Magdalene, *op.cit.*
6. www.worcestershireregiment.com/wr.php?main=inc/bat_7

7. Sister Antony Magdalene, *op.cit.*

8. ibid

9. Sister Mary Peter, *op.cit.*

10. ibid.

11. Winifred Matthews, *Memoirs of New Hall 1925-1927*, New Hall Archives

12. Pupil register Volume 3 1837-1946 for all details concerning pupils, New Hall Archives

13. Sister Antony Magdalene, *op.cit.*

14. Prospectus, probably from 1915 or 1918, New Hall Archives

15. *New Hall Chronicle* October 1936, obituary of Reverend Mother Aloysia Magdalen Dolan, New Hall Archives

16. Sister Antony Magdalene, *op.cit.*

Chapter 24; Modernisation; New Hall 1919-1939

1. *Fishes Pool*, copies from Easter 1919 in New Hall Archives

2. Sister Mary Peter, *Archive Records of Community History, Part 1 1900-1946*, New Hall Archives

3. D. Carradine, *The Decline and Fall of the British Aristocracy*, p82

4. M. Bence-Jones, *The Catholic Families*, pp269-271

5. ibid p283

6. D. Carradine, *op.cit.*, pp472-487

7. S. Curtis and M. Boultwood, *The History of English Education since 1800*, p303

8. Sister Mary Peter, *op.cit.*

9. 1920 Prospectus, New Hall Archives

10. Separate sheet summarising uniform changes, New Hall Archives

11. Winifred Matthews, *Memoirs of New Hall 1925-1927*, New Hall Archives

12. Winifred Matthews, *op.cit.* and also School Extension Building Ledger 1922, New Hall Archives

13. *Fishes Pool*, 1924, New Hall Archives

14. Pupil register Volume 3 1837-1946, New Hall Archives

15. *New Hall Chronicle*, July 1926, New Hall Archives

16. Sister Mary Peter, *op.cit.*

17. Separate sheet summarising uniform changes, New Hall Archives

18. Winifred Matthews, *op.cit.*

19. Sister Mary Peter, *op.cit.*

20. *New Hall Chronicle*, October 1926

21. Sister Antony Magdalene, (aka Frances Russell 1894-1898), *Memoirs; Recollections of a Nonagenarian 1880-1970*, New Hall Archives

22. Sister Mary Peter, *op.cit.*

23. Winifred Matthews, *op.cit.*

24. A/C Pensioners 1777-1959, Servants 1785-1845, Staff 1760-1952, New Hall Archives

25. Prospectus of mid 1920s, New Hall Archives

26. *Fishes Pool* 1921-1924 as indicated

27. *New Hall Chronicle* as dated in the text

28. Winifred Matthews, *op.cit.*

29. Sister Mary Peter, *op.cit.*

30. *New Hall Chronicle*, October 1932

31. Sister Mary O'Connor as quoted in Sister Mary Peter, *op.cit.*

32. *New Hall Chronicle*, October 1932

33. Sister Antony Magdalene, *op.cit.*

34. ibid

35. *New Hall Chronicle*, October 1934

36. 1935 Prospectus, New Hall Archives

37. Pupil register, Volume 3 1837-1946

38. Letter from Mary Veronica to the Bishop of Brentwood, March 8th 1936, Brentwood Diocesan Archives

39. Sister Mary Peter, *op.cit.*

40. ibid

41. *Essex Chronicle*, June 24th 1938

42. Taped interview with Eileen Lodge

43. A/C Pensioners 1777-1959, Servants 1785-1845, Staff 1760-1952, New Hall Archives

44. Insurance 1907-1948 Ledger, New Hall Archives

45. Sister Mary Peter, *op.cit.*

46. Pupil register, Volume 3 1837-1946

Chapter 25; Evacuation; New Hall and Newnham Paddox 1939-1946

1 Sister Mary Peter, *Archive Records of Community History, Part 1 1900-1946*, New Hall Archives

2 Letter of May 27th 1940 from Mary Christina, Prioress, to the Bishop of Brentwood, Brentwood Diocesan Archives

3 Letter of May 29th 1940 from Mary Christina, Prioress, to the Bishop of Brentwood, Brentwood Diocesan Archives

4 A. Begent, *Chelmsford at War*, p5

5 www.thepeerage.com/p2286.htm

6 www.newnhampaddox.com/gardens_history_5.htm

7 Conversation with John Furze of New Hall Farm

8 Sister Antony Magdalene, (aka Frances Russell 1894-1898), *Memoirs; Recollections of a Nonagenarian 1880-1970*, New Hall Archives

9 ibid

10 Staff details in A/C Pensioners 1777-1959, Servants 1785-1845, Staff 1760-1952, New Hall Archives

11 Newnham Paddox Prospectus, New Hall Archives

12 Sister Mary Peter, *op.cit.*

13 ibid

14 Pupil register, Volume 3 1837-1946, New Hall Archives

15 A. Begent, *Chelmsford at War*, p26

16 ibid p31

17 B. Jones, "War-Time Airfield" in *Boreham: History, Tales and Memories of an Essex Village*

18 A. Begent, *op.cit.*, p42

19 *Essex Chronicle*, September 10th 1943

20 Sister Antony Magdalene, *op.cit*

21 *Essex Chronicle*, September 10th 1943.

22 A. Begent, *op.cit.*, p42

23 Sister Mary Peter, *op.cit.*

24 ibid.

25 Details of evacuated pupils and refugees come from the pupil register Volume 3 1837-1946 and the ledger A/C Pensioners 1777-1959, Servants 1785-1845, Staff 1760-1952, both in New Hall Archives

26 Pupil register, Volume 3 1837-1946

27 Sister Mary Peter, *op.cit.* and M. Bence-Jones, *The Catholic Families*, p311

28. Sister Mary Peter, *op.cit.*

Chapter 26; Back to Base; Goodings, Denford and New Hall 1946-1968

1. Sister Antony Magdalene, (aka Frances Russell 1894-1898), *Memoirs; Recollections of a Nonagenarian 1880-1970*, New Hall Archives

2. Sister Mary Peter, *Archive Records of Community History, Part 2 1946-1967*, New Hall Archives

3. Capital a/c 1943-59 Messrs Blount Petre and Co (Capital Cash Account), New Hall Archives and C Ledger, otherwise unlabelled, New Hall Archives

4. Report by Messrs Chilton, Chartered Surveyors, February 3rd 1966, New Hall Archives

5. Sister Mary Peter, *op.cit.*

6. Capital a/c 1943-59 *op.cit.*

7. C 1946 "House" Ledger, New Hall Archives

8. 1956 auction schedule, New Hall Archives

9. Investment C ledger 1944-50, New Hall Archives

10. A. Begent, *Chelmsford at War*, p42

11. Sister Mary Peter, *op.cit.*

12. www.metoffice.com/education/secondary/students/winter.html

13. Sister Mary Peter, *op.cit.*

14. www.personal.dundee.ac.uk/~taharley/1947_weather.htm

15. Late 1940s prospectus, New Hall Archives

16. Sister Mary Peter, *op.cit.*

17. ibid

18. ibid

19. Mid 1950s Prospectus, New Hall Archives

20. Sister Mary Peter, *op.cit.*

21. Letter May 30th 1962, Mary Veronica to the Bishop of Brentwood, Brentwood Diocesan Archives

22. Letter July 2nd 1962, the Bishop of Brentwood to His Eminence in Rome, Brentwood Diocesan Archives

23. Letter February 12th 1965, Mary Veronica to the Bishop of Brentwood, Brentwood Diocesan Archives

24. New Hall Development Fund III Convent Ref No X41106A, New Hall Archives.

25. Early 1960s Prospectus, New Hall Archives

26. Sister Mary Peter, *op.cit.*

27. Conversation with John Furze of New Hall Farm

28. Letter April 19th 1966 from Brendan Garry, Denford Sale File, New Hall Archives

29. Letter from Witham Weld and Co., Denford Sale File, New Hall Archives

30. Sister Mary Peter, *op.cit.*

31. www.ewtn.com/library/COUNCILS/v2relig.htm

32. Sister Mary Peter, *op.cit.*

33. ibid

34. ibid

35. Sister Antony Magdalene, *op.cit.*

Chapter 27; Modern Times; New Hall 1968-2001

1. An unlabelled book in New Hall Archives lists pupils who came and left each year from 1951-1982.

2. Conversation with Sister Pauline Crowther

3. *Daily Telegraph* obituary, December 3rd 2003

4. 1968 Prospectus, New Hall Archives

5. Sister Mary Peter, addendum to *Archive Records of Community History, Part 2 1946-1967,* New Hall Archives

6. ibid.

7. *New Hall Chronicle* 1972, New Hall Archives

8. *Diary of Mary Joseph Reynolds*, New Hall Archives

9. Sister Mary Peter, *op.cit.*

10. Information from here onwards is from the *New Hall Chronicle* as per the date in the text
11. 1978 Brochure, New Hall Archives
12. Extract from an article in *Riding Magazine* October 1982 by Carol Foster quoted in *New Hall Chronicle* 1983, New Hall Archives
13. S.M. Foster, *A History of the Diocese of Brentwood, 1917-1992*, p146
14. Conversation with John Furze of New Hall Farm
15. S.M. Foster, *op.cit.*, pp160-161
16. Conversation with Sister Angela Morris
17. *Essex Chronicle*, October 9th 1992
18. All the figures in this and the next paragraphs are worked out from the Admission Registers 1976-1989 and 1989-1998, New Hall Archives

Chapter 28: The Closing of a Chapter

1. Sister Mary Peter, *Archive Records of Community History, Part 2 1946-1967*, New Hall Archives
2. http://www.msnbc.msn.com/id/746329/
3. http://gunston.doit.gmu.edu/liannacc/ERel/S2-Archives/REC04/Berman_Ianaccone_Ragusa%20-%20Catholic%20Fertility.pdf
4. Sister Mary Peter, *op.cit.*
5. 2004 Inspection Report on www.newhallschool.co.uk/home/senior/isi-inspection
6. K. Aspden, *Fortress Church, the English Roman Catholic Bishops and Politics 1900-1963*, deals thoroughly with all these issues
7. P. Kennedy, *The Catholic Church in England and Wales 1500-2000*, p261
8. S.M. Foster, *A History of the Diocese of Brentwood 1917-1992*, p91
9. ibid p104
10. ibid p89

Bibliography

Primary Sources

The New Hall Archive enables the patient historian to track every pupil since the school opened in 1642. The labyrinthine accounts book 1642-1770 does not run chronologically throughout but, once it has been informally indexed, the early sporadic pupils can be identified amongst much fascinating business and financial information. There are then three much more approachable specific pupil registers in book form, the first from 1770-1807, the second from 1807-1837 and the third from 1837-1946. All three can be supplemented by the account books which record fees paid. From 1946 conventional registers take over, though they are less informative about individual pupils.

On the financial side the most useful volumes are the Balance of Accounts ledgers after 1770 which provide essential summaries of the annual financial position of the convent and the school and these are supplemented by several score contributory volumes which deal by subject with disbursements, pensions, rents, garden, farm etc.. Another very useful volume contains financial records of the pensioners 1777-1959, servants 1785-1845 and staff 1760-1952. Some of the records have been codified in printed volumes, notably the *Records of the English Canonesses of the Holy Sepulchre at Liège, now at New Hall 1652-1793*, published by Sint-Kruis (Brugge) 1997 which has a transcript of the boarders' accounts and book of benefactions in the Liège period. The fascinating *Regulations for the Kitchen 1835-1895* are also a good read and show that hunger was not a problem at nineteenth century New Hall, a pleasant contrast to earlier privations in Liège.

Letters are very useful and the nuns have several from the eighteenth and nineteenth century which have been illustrative of life at the time, especially the correspondence of Mr Gandolfi in the 1790s and the exciting fragment of Michael McEvoy's letter in 1798 confirming the purchase of New Hall. The Brentwood Diocesan Archive has copies of some more recent letters that have helped in understanding the crisis points of the 1930s when there was some question about the future of the school. The Denford and Goodings files in the New Hall Archive also contain very useful correspondence and, together with one of the solicitor's account books, have enabled the immediate post-1945 period of the school's history to be better understood.

First-hand accounts have been extremely valuable. On the one hand there are the visitors to New Hall before 1799 such as John Evelyn, the Grand Duke of Tuscany, Thomas Baskerville and the Earl of Oxford and, after the nuns took up residence, Clarissa Bramston in the 1830s. Then there is the view from within, with pride of place going to Mother Joseph Smith's epic account of the migration in 1794 and Henrietta Goldie's detailed description of life at Dean House 1797-1798. Unfortunately most of the nineteenth century is barren ground until its very close when we have the memories of Pearl Bourke 1894-1898, the anonymous 1899 history, and then, just before the First World War, the memories of Margot Jackson and Dorothy Smyth-Piggott. The diary of Sister Ann Frances Trappes-Lomax provides a very human insight into the way that the war affected the convent. One of the first lay teachers, Winifred Matthews 1925-1927 provides a different perspective from outside the convent. The nuns became aware of the need to create their own record in the twentieth century to supplement the 1899 history so Sister Mary Peter Davies compiled her *Archive Records of Community History, Part 1 1900-1946* and *Part 2 1946-1967* and Sister Antony Magdalene Russell her *Memoirs; Recollections of a Nonagenarian 1880-1970*, both invaluable and systematic, the latter showing occasional indiscretions that delight the historian. The 1973 diary of Sister Mary Joseph Reynolds shows how one nun, brought up in the enclosed tradition, tried to cope with the turbulent religious and educational change of the 1960s and 1970s. Last but not least, we have the *Fishes Pool* magazine that ran from 1918 to 1924 followed by the *New Hall Chronicle* which disappeared when the school was evacuated in 1940 and reappeared in 1973. To supplement these there are all the people I have been able to talk to about modern day New Hall whose names are in the introduction to this book.

The archive contains some old prospectuses from the 1790s, 1850, the First World War period, 1920, the mid 1920s, 1935, the early 1940s , the late 1940s, the mid 1950s, the early 1960s and 1968. It also contains many photographs, some of which have been used in this book, although their source has not been specifically acknowledged. The Catholic Directories have also been a useful source to get an idea of what was happening in the Catholic world of education around New Hall as have other directories such as White's 1848 Directory for Chelmsford.

Newspapers are extremely useful and we are lucky to have the local newspapers available on microfiche in the Essex Record Office and the Local Studies section of Chelmsford County Library, though one needs to have clues from other sources to know where to look, otherwise the needle in the proverbial haystack would prove an easier challenge. The Essex Record Office also contains microfiche of many of the Community's records from which the Medicine Book and advice given by the nuns' lawyers in the face of nineteenth century tax demands have proved to be particularly interesting.

Secondary Sources

Two on-line references have been very useful, namely the Catholic Encyclopaedia of 1913 on some of the great Catholic families that supported the school at Liège and New Hall and the new Oxford Dictionary of National Biography.

In addition I have consulted the following books and articles:

Allan, M   *The Tradescants: their plants, gardens and museum 1570-1662*, Michael Joseph, 1964

Allen, G   *Inflation: the Value of the Pound 1750-2002*, House of Commons Library Research Paper 03/82

Andrews, D   *New Hall ... an historic building in perspective*, lecture 2000, printed copy in New Hall Library

Anon   *History of the New Hall Community of the Canonesses of the Holy Sepulchre*, Manresa Press, 1899

Anon   *Travels of Cosmo the Third, Grand Duke of Tuscany, through England during the reign of Charles II 1669*, London, 1821

Anon   "When Boreham had a railway station" in *More about Boreham: History, Tales and Memories of an Essex Village*, Boreham Histories Project, 1996

Anon   "The Waltham Mausoleum" in *More about Boreham: History, Tales and Memories of an Essex Village*, Boreham Histories Project, 1996

Ashley, M   *General Monck*, Jonathan Cape, 1977

Aspden, K   *Fortress Church, the English Roman Catholic Bishops and Politics 1900-1963*, Gracewing, 2002

Avery, G   *The Best Type of Girl: a history of girls' independent schools*, Andre Deutsch, 1991

Baird, R   *Mistress of the House: Great Ladies and Grand Houses 1670-1830*, Phoenix, 2004

Beales, A.C.F   *Education under Penalty: English Catholic Education from the Reformation to the Fall of James II, 1547-1689*, London, 1963

Begent, A.J   *Chelmsford at War*, Ian Henry Publications, 1999

Bence-Jones, M   *The Catholic Families*, Constable, 1992

Bengsten, F   "Ladies Boarding Schools in Essex 1791-1861: Two Case Studies – Billericay and Maldon", *Essex Archaeology and History* 32, 2001

Booker, J   *Essex and the Industrial Revolution*, Essex County Council, 1974

Borer, M.C   *Willingly to School: a History of Women's Education*, Lutterworth Press, 1976

Bossy, J   *The English Catholic Community 1570-1850*, Darton, Longman and Todd, 1975

Burcher, D   "New Hall through the eyes of 17th and 18th century visitors" in *More About Boreham, History, Tales and Memories of an Essex Village*, Boreham Histories Project, 1996

Burgess, E   "The Olmius Family" in *More about Boreham: History, Tales and Memories of an Essex Village*, Boreham Histories Project, 1996

Carradine, D   *The Decline and Fall of the British Aristocracy*, Picador, 1990

Colley, L   *Briton: Forging the Nation 1707-1837*, Yala Nota Bene, Yale University Press, 1992

Curtis, S and Boultwood, M   *An Introductory History of English Education since 1800*, University Tutorial Press, 1964

Davidoff, L & Hall, C   *Family Fortunes: men and women of the English middle class 1780-1850*, Hutchinson, 1987

Dolan, B   *Ladies of the Grand Tour*, Flamingo, 2002

Dovey, Z   *An Elizabethan Progress, The Queen's Journey into East Anglia 1578*, Sutton Publishing, 1996

Dunlop, I   *Places and Progress of Elizabeth I*, Jonathan Cape, 1962

Dymond, D   *Captain John Mason and the Duke of Buckingham*, Portsmouth Paper No. 17, Portsmouth City Council, 1972

Elton, G.R   *England under the Tudors*, London Methuen, 1960

Emmison, F   "Historic Essex Houses in Elizabethan Wills", *Essex Journal*, Summer 1992 Vol 27 No 2

Flanders, J   *The Victorian House: Domestic Life from Childbirth to Deathbed*, HarperCollins, 2003

Fletcher, S   *Feminists and Bureaucrats: a study in the development of girls' education in the 19th century*, Cambridge University Press, 1980

Foley, R.C   "The Breaking of the Storm", *Essex Recusant* Vol 7 No 1 1961

Foster, S.M   *A History of the Diocese of Brentwood 1917-1992*, The Diocese of Brentwood, 1994

Fraser, A   *King Charles II*, Arrow, 1997

Fraser, A   *The Weaker Vessel: woman's lot in seventeenth century England*, Phoenix Press, 1984

Gaunt, G   "Queen Elizabeth's Progresses through Essex", *Essex Journal*, Vol 1 No 1, January 1966

Gordon, D.I   *A Regional History of the Railways of Great Britain, Volume 5 – Eastern Counties*, David and Charles, 1968

Gregg, P   *King Charles I*, Phoenix Press, 1981

Grieve, H   *The Sleepers and the Shadows; Chelmsford, a town, its people and its past; Volume 2; From Market Town to Chartered Borough 1608-1888*, Essex Record Office, 1994

Harthorn, M.J   "Education and Essex women abroad", *Essex Recusant* Vol 7 No 1, April 1965

Hoffman, R   *Princes of Ireland, Planters of Maryland; A Carroll Saga 1750-1782*, University of North Carolina Press, 2000

Jenkins, E   *Elizabeth and Leicester*, Panther, 1972

Jones, B   "War-time airfield" in *Boreham: History, Tales and Memories of an Essex Village*, Boreham Histories Project, 1988

Kennedy, P   *The Catholic Church in England and Wales 1500-2000*, PBK Publishing, 2001

Leys, M.D.R   *Catholics in England 1559-1829*, Longman, 1961

Lockyer, R   *Buckingham: The Life and Political Career of George Villiers, 1st Duke of Buckingham 1592-1628*, Longman, 1981

McNamara, J.   *Sisters in Arms, Catholic Nuns through two millennia*, Harvard University Press, 1998

Margaret Helen,   "A Dragon's Tale: Of Who Comes and Goes" in *Boreham: History,*
Sister   *Tales and Memories of an Essex Village*, Boreham Histories Project, 1988

Mary Stephen,   "The Changing Face of New Hall; the Honour of Beaulieu" in
Sister   *Boreham: History, Tales and Memories of an Essex Village*, Boreham Histories Project, 1988

Morant, Philip   *The History and Antiquities of the County of Essex, Volume 2*, 1768

Mullett, M.A   *Catholics in England and Ireland 1558-1829*, MacMillan, 1998

Norman, E.R   *Church and Society in England 1779-1970*, Clarendon Press Oxford, 1976

O'Donoghue, G,   "Consumer Price Inflation since 1750", *Economic Trends 604*,
Goulding, G   March 2004, Office of National Statistics
& Allen, G

Officer, L   "Comparing the Purchasing Power of Money in Great Britain from 1264 to Any Other Year Including the Present", *Economic History Services*, 2001, on http://eh.net/hmit/ppowerbp/

O' Leary, J.G   "A Royal Recusant in Essex", *Essex Recusant* Vol 5 No 3, December 1963.

Parsons, G   "Victorian Roman Catholicism: Emancipation, Expansion and Achievement" in *Religion in Victorian Britain: 1 Traditions*, Manchester University Press, 1988

Petre,   "The Penal Laws and the Petre Family", *Essex Journal*, Spring 1994
Lord John   Vol 29

Petre, M.D   *The Ninth Lord Petre*, London Society for Promoting Christian Knowledge, 1928

Plowden, A   *Lady Jane Grey, Nine Days Queen*, Sutton Publishing, 2004

Poole, A.L   *From Domesday Book to Magna Carta 1087-1216*, Oxford, 1951

Porter, R   *English Society in the Eighteenth Century*, Penguin, 1982

Prescott, H.F.M   *Mary Tudor, The Spanish Tudor*, Phoenix, 2003

Roach, J   *Public Examinations in England and Wales 1850-1900*, Cambridge University Press, 1971.

Ross, P.L   *The John Tradescants, Gardeners to the Rose and Lily Queen*, Peter Owen, 1984

Rowley, N   *Essex Elections and the Great Reform Bill*, Essex Record Office Publication No. 68, 1976

Ryan, P   "Woodham Walter Hall – its site and setting" in *Essex Archaeology and History* 30 1999,

Scarisbrick, J.J   *Henry VIII*, Yale University Press New Haven and London, 1997

Shanahan, D   "A letter from New Hall in 1624", *Essex Recusant* Vol 16 No 3, December 1974.

Smith, J.R   *The Speckled Monster; Smallpox in England 1670-1970*, Essex Record Office, 1987

Smith W.J.T   "Education and Boreham" in *Boreham; History, Tales and memories of an Essex Village*, Boreham Histories Project, 1988

Starkey, D   *The Queens of Henry VIII*, Chatto and Windus, 2003

Stewart, A   *The Cradle King, a Life of James VI and I*, Pimlico 2004

Thompson, J.   *The French Revolution*, Blackwell, 1943

Thurley, S   *The Royal Palaces of Tudor England; Architecture and Court Life 1460-1547*, Yale University Press, 1993

Tuckwell, A   *That Honourable and Gentlemanlike House: a history of King Edward VI Grammar School, Chelmsford, 1551-2001*, The Printing Place, 2000

Vickery, A   *The Gentleman's Daughter: women's lives in Georgian England*, Yale University Press, 2003

Vincent. W.A.L   *The Grammar Schools: their continuing tradition 1660-1714*, John Murray, 1969

Walter, J   *Understanding Popular Violence in the English Revolution: The Colchester Plunderers*, Past and Present Publications, Cambridge University Press, 1999

Warnicke, R.M   *The Rise and Fall of Anne Boleyn: Family Politics at the court of Henry VIII*, Cambridge University Press, 1989

Watson, J.S   *The Reign of George III* 1760-1820, Oxford, 1960

Weir, A   *The Six Wives of Henry VIII*, Pimlico, 1992

Weir, A   *Children of England: The Heirs of King Henry VIII 1547-1558*, Pimlico, 1997

Williams, B   *The Whig Supremacy 1714-1760*, Oxford, 1962

Williams, N   *Elizabeth I, Queen of England*, Sphere, 1971

Worrall, E.S   "Number of Essex Papists in 1780", *Essex Recusant* Vol 3 No 1, 1961

Worrall, E.S   "The Congregation of Witham Place Chapel 1766-1800", *Essex Recusant* Vol 4 No 1, 1962

Worrall, E.S   "Essex Families and the Canonesses Regular of the Holy Sepulchre", *Essex Recusant* Vol 4 No 2, 1962

Worrall, E.S   "18th century Jesuit Priests in Essex IV", *Essex Recusant* Vol 5 No 2, December 1963

Worrall, E.S   "The Essex Register of Oaths subscribed under the Catholic Relief Act 1778", *Essex Recusant* Vol 6 No 1, 1964

Worrall, E.S   "A Funeral Monument in Gosfield Churchyard", *Essex Recusant*, Vol 6 No 3, 1964

Ziegler, P   *William IV*, Harper and Row, 1973

Finally Philippa Gregory's historical novel, *Earthly Joys*, is a wonderfully imaginative reconstruction of Tradescant's time at New Hall and his relationship with the 1st Duke of Buckingham. It is not to be missed but not to be taken too literally!

Index